Ancient Egyptian Literature

VOLUME III: THE LATE PERIOD

Published under the auspices of
The Gustave E. von Grunebaum Center
for Near Eastern Studies
University of California, Los Angeles

Ancient Egyptian Literature
A Book of Readings

by
Miriam Lichtheim

VOLUME III: THE LATE PERIOD

UNIVERSITY OF CALIFORNIA PRESS
Berkeley   Los Angeles   London

UNIVERSITY OF CALIFORNIA PRESS
BERKELEY AND LOS ANGELES, CALIFORNIA
UNIVERSITY OF CALIFORNIA PRESS, LTD.
LONDON, ENGLAND

Library of Congress Cataloging in Publication Data

Lichtheim, Miriam, 1914–   comp.
  Ancient Egyptian literature.

  Includes bibliographical references.
  CONTENTS: v. 1. The Old and Middle Kingdoms.—
v. 2. The new kingdom.—v. 3. The late period.
  1. Egyptian literature—Translations into
English. 2. English literature—Translation from
Egyptian. I. Title.
PJ943.L5   893'.1   75-189225

PRINTED IN THE UNITED STATES OF AMERICA

1 2 3 4 5 6 7 8 9

Preface

This is the concluding volume of my translations of ancient Egyptian texts. It spans the last millennium of Pharaonic civilization, from the tenth century B.C. to the first century A.D., a millennium of profound changes in Egypt and in the entire ancient Near East.

As in the preceding volumes, the selection of texts includes monumental inscriptions and works written on papyrus. The arrangement is both chronological and topical. The biographical inscriptions range from the tenth century B.C. to the first century B.C., thus descending through all phases of Late Period history. The royal inscriptions illuminate some of the high points of war and peace.

The hymns to the gods mirror the timelessness and quietude of the temple cult maintained throughout wars and foreign domination. And the selection of Demotic literary texts, all dating from the Greco-Roman period, presents ancient Egyptian imaginative and reflective thought in its final phase.

I am very grateful to my colleague Professor Klaus Baer for having read the greater part of the manuscript before it went to press and for having suggested a good number of corrections and other improvements.

M. L.

Santa Monica, California
September 30, 1978

Contents

Chronology of the Late Period

Thirtieth Dynasty	378-341
Nectanebo I (Nekht-nebef)	378-360
Nectanebo II (Nekht-hor-heb)	349-341
Second Persian Domination	341-332
Artaxerxes III (Ochos)	341-338
Darius III (Codoman)	335-330
Alexander the Great	332-323
Ptolemaic Period	323-30
Ptolemy I Soter	323-282
Ptolemy V Epiphanes	205-180
Ptolemy XII Neos Dionysos	80-51
Cleopatra VII Philopator	51-30
Roman Period	30 B.C.-324 A.D.

Note: Only kings mentioned in the texts and comments of this volume are listed here. Note also that some of the dates are conjectural.

Abbreviations and Symbols

AEO	A. H. Gardiner. *Ancient Egyptian Onomastica*. 3 vols. Oxford, 1947.
ANET	*Ancient Near Eastern Texts Relating to the Old Testament*, ed. J. B. Pritchard. Princeton, 1950; 3d ed., 1969.
APAW	*Abhandlungen der Preussischen Akademie der Wissenschaften*.
ASAE	*Annales du Service des Antiquités de l'Égypte*.
BAR	J. H. Breasted. *Ancient Records of Egypt*. 5 vols. Chicago, 1906–1907. Reprint, 1962.
Berlin Festschrift	*Festschrift zum 150 jährigen Bestehen des Berliner Ägyptischen Museums*. Staatliche Museen zu Berlin. Mitteilungen aus der ägyptischen Sammlung, 8. Berlin, 1974.
BIFAO	*Bulletin de l'Institut Français d'Archéologie Orientale du Caire*.
Bonnet, *RÄRG*	H. Bonnet. *Reallexikon der ägyptischen Religionsgeschichte*. Berlin, 1952.
Borchardt, *Statuen*	L. Borchardt. *Statuen und Statuetten von Königen und Privatleuten im Museum von Kairo*. Vol. II. Catalogue général . . . du Musée du Caire. Berlin, 1925.
Bresciani, *Letteratura*	E. Bresciani, *Letteratura e poesia dell' antico Egitto*. Turin, 1969.
Brugsch, *Thesaurus*	H. K. Brugsch. *Thesaurus Inscriptionum Aegyptiacarum*. 6 parts. Leipzig, 1883–1891. Reprint, 1968.
Brunner-Traut, *Märchen*	E. Brunner-Traut. *Altägyptische Märchen*. Dusseldorf and Cologne, 1963. 2d ed., 1965.
CdÉ	*Chronique d'Égypte*.
Černý, *Copt. Dic.*	J. Černý. *Coptic Etymological Dictionary*. Cambridge, 1976.
CRAIBL	*Comptes rendus de l'Académie des Inscriptions et Belles-lettres*.
Erichsen, *Lesestücke*	W. Erichsen. *Demotische Lesestücke*. Leipzig, 1937.
Esna	S. Sauneron. *Esna*. 5 vols. Cairo, 1959–1963.

Glossar	W. Erichsen. *Demotisches Glossar.* Copenhagen, 1954.
Harris,	J. R. Harris. *Lexicographical Studies in Ancient Egyptian*
Minerals	*Minerals.* Akademie der Wissenschaften, Berlin. Institut für Orientforschung. Veröffentlichung, 54. Berlin, 1961.
JAOS	*Journal of the American Oriental Society.*
JARCE	*Journal of the American Research Center in Egypt.*
JEA	*Journal of Egyptian Archaeology.*
JNES	*Journal of Near Eastern Studies.*
Kees,	H. Kees. *Die Hohenpriester des Amun von Karnak von*
Priester	*Herihor bis zum Ende der Äthiopenzeit.* Probleme der Ägyptologie, 4. Leiden, 1964.
Kees,	H. Kees. *Das Priestertum im ägyptischen Staat.* Probleme.
Priestertum	der Ägyptologie, 1. Leiden, 1953. *Nachträge,* 1958.
Kitchen,	K. A. Kitchen. *Ramesside Inscriptions, Historical and*
Inscriptions	*Biographical.* Oxford, 1968–.
Kitchen,	K. A. Kitchen. *The Third Intermediate Period in Egypt.*
Third	Warminster, 1973.
Intermediate	
Leclant,	J. Leclant. *Recherches sur les monuments thébains de la*
Recherches	*XXVe dynastie dite éthiopienne.* Institut Français d'Archéologie Orientale du Caire. Bibliothèque d'étude, 36. Cairo, 1965.
Lefebvre,	G. Lefebvre. *Romans et contes égyptiens de l'époque*
Romans	*pharaonique.* Paris, 1949.
Legrain,	G. Legrain. *Statues et statuettes de rois et de particuliers.*
Statues	Vol. III. Catalogue général... du Musée du Caire. Cairo, 1914.
Mariette,	A. Mariette. *Monuments divers recueillis en Égypte et*
Mon. div.	*en Nubie.* Paris, 1872–1889.
MDIK	*Mitteilungen des deutschen archäologischen Instituts, Abteilung Kairo.*
Mélanges	*Orient Ancien.* Institut Français d'Archéologie Orientale du Caire. Mémoires, 66. Cairo, 1934–1961.
Maspero I	
MIO	Akademie der Wissenschaften, Berlin. *Mitteilungen des Instituts für Orientforschung.*
Miscellanea	*Miscellanea Gregoriana: Raccolta di scritti pubblicati nel*
Gregoriana	*i centenario dalla fondazione del Pont. Museo Egizio.* Rome, 1941.
Montet,	P. Montet. *Géographie de l'Égypte ancienne.* 2 vols. Paris,
Géographie	1957–1961.
MPON	*Mitteilungen aus der Papyrussammlung der österreichischen Nationalbibliothek (Papyrus Erzherzog Rainer).*

Müller, *Liebespoesie*	W. M. Müller. *Die Liebespoesie der alten Ägypter.* Leipzig, 1899.
Mythus	W. Spiegelberg. *Der ägyptische Mythus vom Sonnenauge (Der Papyrus der Tierfabeln "Kufi")* nach dem Leidener Demotischen Papyrus I 384. Strassburg, 1917.
NGWG	*Nachrichten von der Gesellschaft der Wissenschaften zu Göttingen.*
OLZ	*Orientalistische Literaturzeitung.*
OMRO	Leiden. Rijksmuseum van Oudheden. *Oudheidkundige mededeelingen.*
Otto Gedenkschrift	*Fragen an die altägyptische Literatur; Studien zum Gedenken an Eberhard Otto.* Wiesbaden, 1977.
Otto, *Inschriften*	E. Otto. *Die biographischen Inschriften der ägyptischen Spätzeit.* Probleme der Ägyptologie, 2. Leiden, 1954.
Pierret, *Recueil*	P. Pierret. *Recueil d'inscriptions inédites du Musée Égyptien du Louvre.* 2 vols. Paris, 1874–1878.
P. Krall	E. Bresciani. *Der Kampf um den Panzer des Inaros (Papyrus Krall).* MPON, n.s. 8. Vienna, 1964.
PM	*Topographical Bibliography of Ancient Egyptian Hieroglyphic Texts, Reliefs, and Paintings,* by B. Porter and R. L. B. Moss. 7 vols. Oxford, 1927–1951. 2d ed., 1960–
RB	*Revue Biblique.*
RdÉ	*Revue d'Égyptologie.*
Roeder, *Götterwelt*	G. Roeder. *Die ägyptische Götterwelt.* Die ägyptische Religion in Texten und Bildern, 1. Zurich 1959.
RT	*Recueil de travaux relatifs à la philologie et à l'archéologie égyptiennes et assyriennes.*
Sachau Festschrift	*Festschrift Eduard Sachau,* ed. G. Weil. Berlin, 1915.
SAK	*Studien zur altägyptischen Kultur.*
Schott, *Liebeslieder*	S. Schott. *Altägyptische Liebeslieder, mit Märchen und Liebesgeschichten.* Zurich, 1950.
Studi Rosellini	*Studi in memoria di Ippolito Rosellini.* 2 vols. Pisa, 1949–1955.
Untersuchungen	*Untersuchungen zur Geschichte und Altertumskunde Ägyptens.*
Urk. II	*Urkunden des ägyptischen Altertums, Abteilung II: Hieroglyphische Urkunden der griechisch-römischen Zeit,* ed. K. Sethe. Leipzig, 1904.
Urk. III	*Urkunden des ägyptischen Altertums, Abteilung III: Urkunden der älteren Äthiopenkönige,* ed. H. Schäfer. Leipzig, 1905.

Urk. VIII   *Urkunden des ägyptischen Altertums, Abteilung VIII:*
                 Thebanische Tempelinschriften aus griechisch-römischer
                 Zeit, ed. K. Sethe and O. Firchow. Berlin, 1957.
Vercoutter,   J. Vercoutter. *Textes biographiques du Sérapéum de Mem-*
  Textes   *phis.* Bibliothèque de l'École des Hautes Études, IVe
  biogr.   section, 316. Paris, 1962.
Volten,   A. Volten. *Demotische Traumdeutung.* Analecta Aegyp-
  Traum-   tiaca, 3. Copenhagen, 1942.
  deutung
Wb.   *Wörterbuch der ägyptischen Sprache,* ed. A. Erman and
                 H. Grapow. 7 vols. Leipzig, 1926–1963.
Westendorf,   W. Westendorf. *Koptisches Handwörterbuch.* Heidel-
  Kopt. Hw.   berg, 1965–1977.
ZÄS   *Zeitschrift für ägyptische Sprache und Altertumskunde.*

Half brackets⌐ ¬are used instead of question marks to signify
doubt.

Square brackets [ ] enclose restorations.

Angle brackets ⟨ ⟩ enclose words omitted by the scribe.

Parentheses ( ) enclose additions in the English translation.

A row of three dots . . . indicates the omission in the English translation of one or two words. A row of six dots . . . . . . indicates a longer omission.

A row of three dashes – – – indicates a short lacuna in the text.

A row of six dashes – – – – – – indicates a lengthy lacuna.

Introduction

The Uses of the Past

The last millennium of Pharaonic civilization, the time from the end of the New Kingdom to Egypt's conversion to Christianity, is a complex period consisting of several distinct phases. In the past this long and eventful stretch of history has often been summarily treated as a phase of decline, in keeping with the tendency in much past and recent historiography of interpreting ancient civilizations in terms of "rise and decline." Now the Late Period is being studied perceptively, and there is also a more refined understanding of the currents that transformed the civilizations of the ancient Near East into the Christian nations of the Byzantine world.

In political terms, the Late Period was a time of retreat. Egypt lost its imperial position, withdrew to its natural borders, became subject to repeated foreign invasions, and ultimately lost its independence. Moreover, for much of the Post-Imperial Epoch (to use the term proposed by K. A. Kitchen in his comprehensive study of the *Third Intermediate Period*) Egypt was troubled by internal divisions resulting from the weakness of the ruling dynasties. The invasion of Egypt by the egyptianized kings of Nubia restored the royal power of a single dynasty over most of the country. But this Nubian dynasty, the Twenty-fifth, soon fell victim to the Assyrian invasions of Egypt which culminated in the sack of Thebes in 663 B.C.

From 656 to 525 B.C. Egypt was once more united under its own kings, the Twenty-sixth Dynasty, natives of the Delta city of Sais. Saite rule brought a marked revival of political strength, prosperity, and cultural flowering. It was also the time in which many Greeks settled in Egypt and became a significant element in the population. The Persian conquest of 525 ushered in a long period of Persian domination. When independence was regained in 404, Egypt enjoyed a final flowering under the native kings of the Twenty-eighth, Twenty-ninth, and Thirtieth dynasties. In 341 Persia reconquered Egypt, but this second Persian dominion was brief, ending with Alexander the Great's entry into Egypt in 332.

Alexander was greeted as liberator. But the subsequent Macedonian kingship subjected Egypt to a foreign rule far more severe in its effects than Persian dominion had been. Although the Ptolemies

3

assumed Pharaonic ceremonial, their Greek culture and the imposi-
tion of a Greek administration turned the Egyptians into second-class
citizens. As individuals, Egyptians and Greeks consorted with and
influenced each other, and by the second century the two peoples had
drawn closer together. But the Macedonian king could not be the
spokesman for Egypt's national culture. Thus, under the weight of
the imposed Hellenism and bereft of its own leadership, Egyptian
civilization became muted and subdued. It continued to endure and it
even absorbed with surprising elasticity elements of Greek culture in
art and literature.

All the while both the Greek and the Egyptian ways of life were
transformed by the changes in man's outlook which operated throughout the Hellenistic world. If this changing outlook is to be summed up
in a single phrase, it may be called the quest for salvation. It was an
age of spiritual distress and of groping for new answers. And when
excessively exploitative Roman rule had drained Egypt's wealth and
enslaved its people, the time was ripe for the Egyptians to embrace
with fervor the new gospel of Christ. Then the Egyptians destroyed
with their own hands the civilization that they had built and cherished
for three thousand years. The Egyptian turned Christian is a new
man. With him begins a new chapter in the history of Egypt and the
history of man.

The hieroglyphic inscriptions of the Late Period continue the
principal genres of the earlier eras: private autobiographies, royal
accounts of victories and royal decrees, and hymns to the gods. All
these monumental inscriptions were composed in the classical literary
language which we call Middle Egyptian. Perfected in the time of the
Middle Kingdom, Middle Egyptian had subsequently achieved the
status of a classical, normative language. It had become obligatory for
all monumental inscriptions, though here and there these inscriptions
were infiltrated by forms and phrases taken from the vernacular of
the New Kingdom, the so-called Late-Egyptian.

The scribes of the Late Period handled this classical language,
which was now very far removed from their own vernacular, with
varying degrees of skill. Studying it as a heritage to be cherished and
used, they not only employed its grammar and vocabulary, but also
drew from the vast store of works kept in libraries old formulations
and phrases to be woven into new patterns. Thus, the monumental
inscriptions of the Late Period are characterized by an eclectic use of
the classical tongue (using the term "eclectic" without any disparaging
connotation). The forms of the language are those of the Middle
Kingdom; the expressions, when not freshly coined, are drawn from
both Middle and New Kingdom stores. Now and then some Pyramid

Texts of the Old Kingdom were copied. But by and large the Middle and New Kingdoms, rather than the Old Kingdom, furnished the models.

The same eclecticism, combined with fresh inspiration, characterizes the art of the Late Period. The statues, inscriptions, and tomb reliefs of, for example, Montemhet exhibit the whole range of this eclecticism along with new artistic inspiration, the latter dominating in the powerful modeling of his portrait sculpture.

Another use to which the past was put in the Late Period was to compose inscriptions with propagandistic purposes in the disguise of works of the past. Such pseudepigrapha are the *Bentresh Stela* and the *Famine Stela*. The *Bentresh Stela* purports to be a decree of Ramses II but is in fact a work of either the Persian or the Ptolemaic period. It is a tale of wondrous healing performed by the Theban god Khons-the-Provider, and it is a piece of propaganda on behalf of this god. The *Famine Stela* claims to be a decree of King Djoser of the Third Dynasty, whereas it is a work of Ptolemaic times, probably composed by the priesthood of the temple of Khnum at Elephantine, and designed to buttress the Khnum temple's claim to revenues obtained from the region of Elephantine and from Lower Nubia.

Yet another example of the desire to use the prestige of the past for the benefit of the present is the so-called "Memphite Theology," inscribed on the *Shabaka Stone*. In this work King Shabaka of the Twenty-fifth Dynasty alleges to have copied an early work which he had found in worm-eaten condition. The claim, along with the strongly archaizing language of the text, misled generations of Egyptologists into assigning the composition to the Old Kingdom. A recent article by F. Junge (*MDIK*, 29 [1973], 195–204) makes it appear certain that it is a work of the Twenty-fifth Dynasty. Readers of this anthology should in their minds transfer this text from Volume I of *Ancient Egyptian Literature* into the context of the pseudepigrapha of the present volume.

The *autobiographical inscriptions* of the Late Period reveal a mentality and a piety that are traditional and yet subtly different from the attitudes of the past. There is less optimism and more concern. It is no longer assumed that righteous living guarantees a successful life. Success and happiness are now thought to depend entirely on the grace of the gods. The individual can achieve nothing without their help; but the will of the gods is inscrutable. Yet life was not prized any less. Piety itself demanded that life should be enjoyed. Thus, enjoyment of life is a basic theme of the autobiographies. And the exhortation to value life remains central to the moral code of the *Instructions*.

The one real calamity was a premature death. Three biographical inscriptions—the tomb inscription of *Thothrekh son of Petosiris*, the stela of *Isenkhebe*, and the stela of *Taimhotep*—have as their main theme a lament over an early death. The introduction of such a lament into the autobiography seems to be an innovation of the Late Period. The lament over death had been a regular feature of the burial ceremony, and its formulas had been inscribed in the tombs in scenes showing the funeral. But to make the autobiography the carrier of a lament over an early death meant changing its whole character, for its purpose had always been to record a successful life. Thus, when a lament over a premature death became the main content, the original purpose of the autobiography was canceled. In this changed form the autobiography had become an epitaph and had come to resemble the Greek epitaphs of the Hellenistic period.

Greek epitaphs had also undergone an evolution. They began in classical Greece as brief statements of "Here lies." In Greco-Roman times they grew into elaborate poetic reflections about life and death, some pious and hopeful, others frankly skeptical, and they incorporated increasing amounts of biographical narrative. It may therefore be suggested that the subgroup of Egyptian biographical inscriptions, the kind that lamented an early death, had become akin to the Greek epitaph in its Hellenistic form, a form in which sorrow over death was combined with biographical detail. Thus, an Egyptian and a Greek literary genre, each of which had started from a different premise, had converged. Add to this the fact that there came into existence a mixed Greco-Egyptian population. If we then encounter in Greco-Roman Egypt Greek epitaphs that reflect attitudes akin to those of the Egyptians, and often also invoke Egyptian gods, the underlying factors would seem to be a combination of spontaneous convergence and mutual influence. In any case, the Greek epitaphs from Egypt bear witness to the Hellenistic amalgam of creeds and customs which Alexander's empire brought into being.

Here are two Greek epitaphs from Egypt, the first of Ptolemaic, the second of Roman date (W. Peek, *Griechische Grabgedichte, griechisch und deutsch* [Berlin, 1960], nos. 155 and 426)

> I. *A happy old man*
> Wanderer, my name's Menelaos, Doros my father's,
> Sailor was I and a happy old man when I died.
> My children's loving hands entombed me, I thanked
> Helios, grateful for the sweet gift.
> Stranger, recite to me now the appropriate saying,
> "Joy to the dead in the earth," double the wish for you.

II. *An unfortunate young woman*
    Who died here? — Herois. — How and when? —
    Heavy-wombed
    In pained labor she set down her burden,
    Mother was she for a moment, the child perished also.
    What was the luckless one's age? — Two times nine
    Years of flowering youth had Herois. Light may
    The earth be on her, may Osiris bestow cooling water.

The Nubian kings of the Twenty-fifth Dynasty, and the Saite kings of the Twenty-sixth, were men of marked energy and enterprise. Among their surviving inscriptions, the great *Victory Stela of King Piye* occupies the foremost place, owing to its outstanding qualities of factualness and vividness. It combines an unusually detailed account of the campaign with an equally unusual portrayal of the thoughts and feelings of Piye and his adversaries. It is also noteworthy that the scribe who wrote it handled the classical language in such a way as to convey spontaneity and vigor. This account of a victorious campaign fills to the limit the scope of Egyptian historiography, which had always meant royal accounts of royal deeds. Only in the end, when the king was a foreigner, could the priest Manetho, inspired by Greek professional historiography, undertake to write, in Greek, a history of Egypt.

Under the Ptolemaic administration the temples of Egypt continued to have a privileged status, and the Ptolemies assumed the Pharaonic duty of building and rebuilding the sanctuaries. It is an irony of history that the best preserved temples of ancient Egypt are those that were built in Greco-Roman times: the temples of Philae, Kom Ombo, Edfu, Dendera, and Esna. Their numerous religious inscriptions acquaint us in detail with the elaborate daily ritual and with the lengthy ceremonies of the great festivals. This is the context of the many hymns to the gods. They are frequently difficult to understand, for the priestly tendency to hermeticism here attained full scope. The *Hymns to Hathor* have poetic merit. As to the difficult *Great Hymn to Khnum,* with its curious physiology of the human body, I included it here largely in order to direct the reader to S. Sauneron's magisterial volumes on the Esna temple and its festivals.

The cult of Osiris entailed hymns of a particular kind: lamentations over the death of the god, chanted by priestesses representing the goddesses Isis and Nephthys. Such lamentations probably existed in the early periods also, but the texts of this type which have been preserved all date from the Late Period. The *Lamentations of Isis and Nephthys* included here were appended to a copy of the *Book of the*

Dead and thus adapted to the use of an individual person, an adaptation made possible by the practice of associating every dead person with Osiris.

All the texts written in the classical language utilize the three styles which I discussed briefly in the previous volumes: prose, poetry, and an intermediate form which I called "orational style." The orational style is characterized by metrically formed lines phrased as direct speech, or, in the case of royal encomia cast in either the first or the third persons. This prose-poetry differs from prose in that the sentences have a regular rhythmic pattern, and differs from poetry in that it lacks the specifically poetic devices, such as strophes. This theory of three styles is tentative, for the principles of Egyptian metrics are not really known. A discussion of the problems of Egyptian metrics may be found in my article, "Have the Principles of Egyptian Metrics Been Discovered?" (*JARCE*, 9 [1971/72], 103–110).

Demotic literature.—"Demotic" is the term (borrowed from Herodotus II,36) which designates the cursive writing developed from Late-Hieratic and, along with it, the language written in that script. Demotic writing was first used in the middle of the seventh century, under the Saite Dynasty. The Demotic language was the vernacular of the period. It was employed in the composition of belles lettres and for nonliterary texts of daily life, such as contracts, lawsuits, and tax receipts. It goes without saying that all the works written in the vernacular have more vitality and color than the texts composed in the classical language. In relation to New Kingdom belles lettres—the *Tales, Love Poems, School Texts,* and *Instructions*—Demotic belles lettres show both continuity and change. No Demotic love poems have come to light, nor was the genre "school texts" continued. But *Tales* and *Instructions* flourished abundantly.

In the *Tales* the principal innovations are greater length and complexity, the use of motifs derived from Greek literature, and the appearance of animal fables. These aspects are pointed out in the prefaces that introduce the translations. Here I should like to stress that Prince *Setne Khamwas*, the hero of the two tales named for him, was a passionate antiquarian. The historical prince Khamwas, the fourth son of Ramses II, had been high priest of Ptah at Memphis and administrator of all the Memphite sanctuaries. In that capacity he had examined decayed tombs, restored the names of their owners, and renewed their funerary cults. Posterity had transmitted his renown, and the Demotic tales that were spun around his memory depicted him and his fictional adversary Prince Naneferkaptah as very learned scribes and magicians devoted to the study of ancient monuments and writings. The antiquarian passion attributed to these princes is yet another indication of the strong sense of the past which is so notable a feature of Late Period culture. Modern scholars have tended to interpret this harking back to the past as a symptom of decay. In my view it was a source of strength which helped the Egyptians to maintain their native culture in the face of Hellenism during six centuries of Greco-Roman domination.

The Demotic *Instructions* depart from their prototypes in several respects. The earlier Instructions had portrayed human characters and situations by drawing vignettes of life. Their word portraits were build up through sequences of interconnected sentences composed in the orational style. The Demotic Instructions consist of single self-contained sentences written in plain prose, with each sentence occupying one line on the page. Thus each sentence is grammatically complete, and its independence is graphically underlined by the equation of a sentence with a line on the page. Several consecutive sentences may, but need not, deal with the same topic. Hence an Instruction can be very miscellaneous in its overall character, as is the case in the *Instruction of Ankhsheshonq*.

The *Instruction of Papyrus Insinger* has more coherence and structure. The individual sentences are grouped into chapters by means of chapter headings and conclusions; and each chapter is more or less devoted to one topic. Yet nearly all sentences are self-contained and independent of one another. This method of composition results in transpositions, variations, omissions, and other changes and errors in the transmission of the text. *Papyrus Insinger* abounds in all these and thereby greatly impedes the understanding. The morality of the *Instruction of Ankhsheshonq* is utilitarian, sometimes humorous, and occasionally cynical, while that of *Papyrus Insinger* is serious and pious.

Papyrus Insinger was written in the first century A.D. It is one of several copies of a long morality text. Whatever the original date of the composition may have been, in its surviving copies this Instruction is the latest of the Egyptian Instructions and one that makes a fitting ending to ancient Egyptian literature. Its ethics is one of endurance rather than of action. The virtue that it places above all others is moderation, a sense of the right measure. Wisdom lies in self-control and in a pious acceptance of what the gods may send. Inscrutable and unpredictable, the divine will manifests itself through Fate and Fortune.

The emphasis on the concept of fortune evokes Hellenistic popular thought. The notion of the reversal of fortune had been current in Egyptian thought at least since the New Kingdom; but the emphasis that *Papyrus Insinger* places on fate and fortune as the arbiters of life is unprecedented and suggests the effect of Hellenistic thinking. Greeks and Egyptians alike were participating in, and being transformed by, the currents of Hellenistic universalism, syncretism, and pessimism which were undermining all the polytheistic cultures of the Mediterranean world and paving the way for the new gospel of the kingdom of heaven.

PART ONE

Texts in the Classical Language

I. Biographical Inscriptions

The dignitaries who administered Thebes and the Thebaid during the Post-Imperial epoch, under a rapid succession of kings and under the changeless governance of Amun of Thebes, are represented here by *Djedkhonsefankh, Nebneteru, Harwa*, and *Montemhet*, all four members of the clergy of Amun. The first two served kings of the Twenty-second Dynasty, while the last two held office under the Twenty-fifth (Nubian) Dynasty.

With the Twenty-sixth Dynasty, which hailed from Sais, the center of power was once again in the north. The restoring activities of the Saite Dynasty are illustrated by the biography of *Peftuaneith*, who records his work of rebuilding at Abydos. The destruction of the Saite Dynasty through the Persian conquest of Egypt is reflected in the biography of *Udjahorresne*, who alludes guardedly to the calamity of the Persian conquest and dwells at some length on his successful efforts to restore normal life through collaboration with the Persian conquerors after they had settled down to rule.

The career of *Somtutefnakht* spans three eras: the final years of Egyptian independence under the Thirtieth Dynasty, the brief second Persian domination, and the destruction of the Persian empire by Alexander the Great. *Petosiris*, the high priest of Thoth at Hermopolis Magna, looks back on long years of service to his town in the last decades of the fourth century, when Persian dominion ended and Macedonian rule was installed. The biography of *Wennofer*, inscribed on a coffin, is wholly devoted to the praise of a life enjoyed.

The sorrow over premature death is the theme of the biographical inscription of *Thothrekh son of Petosiris* and of the biographical stelae of *Isenkhebe* and *Taimhotep*.

STATUE INSCRIPTION OF DJEDKHONSEFANKH

From the Temple of Luxor

Cairo Museum 559

The near-independence of the Thebaid in the time of the Twenty-first Dynasty was terminated by Sheshonq I, the founder of the Twenty-second Dynasty. He brought the Theban region back under royal control by means of two related measures: appointing sons of the royal house to the leading priestly positions at Thebes, notably the positions of "First Prophet" and "Second Prophet" of Amun, and having members of the royal family marry into the established Theban families. The career of

13

Djedkhonsefankh illustrates this policy; and his autobiography typifies the biographical style of the period.

Djedkhonsefankh (Djed-khons-ef-ankh) came from a Theban family of long lineage and he married the daughter of Iuput, second son of Sheshonq I and high priest of Amun. Thus, when Osorkon I succeeded his father Sheshonq I, Djedkhonsefankh, the husband of his niece, was a favored courtier; and eventually he was made "Fourth Prophet" of Amun of Thebes. After the death of Osorkon I, Djedkhonsefankh continued to serve the royal house as well as Thebes and its god Amun.

His autobiography is inscribed on a block statue of dark granite, 1.02 m high. He is seated with legs drawn up under the chin and wrapped in a long garment in the posture called block, or cube statue, a posture common in statuary since the New Kingdom and especially favored in the Late Period. The text in thirteen horizontal lines covers the front and sides of the body, and there are six text columns on the back plinth. In addition, eight short text columns, now more than half destroyed, are inscribed on the feet. These tell that the statue was dedicated by his eldest son.

Just as the statue is carved with skill, so the text is composed with deliberation and with a striving for effect by means of uncommon words and phrases. The basic translations of Janssen and Otto can, I believe, be improved in a number of places, especially through the recognition that, except for the text on the plinth, Djedkhonsefankh's speech is cast in the orational style. The speech consists of couplets formed through parallelism of content, that is to say, the second sentence of each couplet enlarges upon the theme of the first sentence through amplification or contrast.

Publication: G. Daressy, *RT*, 16 (1894), 56−60.   Borchardt, *Statuen*, II, 105−108 and pl. 94.   J. M. A. Janssen in *Studi Rosellini*, II, 119−129 (best text and translation).

Translation: Otto, *Inschriften*, pp. 132−134 (abridged).

Comments: H. Kees, *ZÄS*, 74 (1938), 82; *idem, Priestertum*, pp. 206 ff. Kitchen, *Third Intermediate*, pp. 219, 289, 308.

(1) The one honored by Amun, great favorite of the lord of Thebes; the Fourth Prophet of Amen-Re, King of Gods, the herald and follower of Amen-Re, King of Gods; the chief incense-bearer before Amun; the one who performs the robing and prepares his holy chapel; the monthly priest of the House of Amun of the third phyle; the second prophet of Mut, mistress of heaven, the prophet of Khons of Benent;[1] the chief scribe of the temple of Khons; the priest who goes in front of him whose throne endures, Amen-Re, King of Gods; the prophet of Amun, Conqueror-of-foreign-lands; the prophet of Amun, the living protection; the guardian of the chest of the House of Amun of the second phyle; the Eyes of the King in Ipet-sut, the Tongue of the King in Upper Egypt; who begs jubilees for his lord the King from the gods of this land; the fan-bearer to the right of the King, who strides freely in the palace; the true intimate of Horus, his beloved, Djedkhonsefankh, son of the prophet of Amen-Re, King of

Gods, who saw the sacred Horus of the palace, Nespernebu; (3) born
of the sistrum player of Amen-Re, Nesmut; he says:

Hail to you who will come after,
Who will be in future times!
I shall make you call me blessed,
For my destiny was great.
Khnum fashioned me as one effective,
An adviser of excellent counsel.
He made my character superior to others,
He steered my tongue to excellence.
I kept my mouth clean of harming him who harmed me,
My patience turned my foes into my friends.
I ruled my mouth, was skilled in answer,
Yet did not acquiesce in evil-doing.

The people (5) reckoned me as openhanded,
For I despised the piling up of riches.
I caused them all to greet me for my excellence,
Hand-kissing to my *ka* and saying of me:
"The progeny of his father,
His mother's godly offspring!"
No one reviled my parents on account of me,
They were much honored owing to ⟨my⟩ worth.
They found me helpful while they were on earth,
And I supply them in the desert vale.[2]
I did not let my servants call me "our master,"
I made myself the image of their father.

The Good God praised me, *Sekhem-kheperre-sotpenre*,[3]
His heirs[4] praised (7) me again, still more than he.
As each one reigned he was content with me,
For they perceived my worth among the folk.
The country's nobles strove to copy me,
Because my favor with the king was great.
I strayed[5] not from his majesty at the palace,
He did not exclude me from his falcon-ship.
His drink was sweet, I ate with him,
I sipped wine together with him.
The god esteemed me for attending him agreeably,
I was advanced[6] in keeping with my worth.
Thus was I foremost in the heart of Horus,
As he is great among mankind.

When I reached Thebes in (my) old age,[7]
(9) I did what was favored in Ipet-sut.
Appointed king's speaker at its[8] head,
I did not give praise to him who flattered me.
I prevented expenses beyond the king's orders,
I protected the goods of its poor.
I put respect of its lord before them,
I restrained the arms of its robbers.
I was constant in sending reports to the king,
In cases of relieving hardships.[9]
He gave assent to what I said,
He favored me above his courtiers.
My goodness was a sheltering refuge,
A fundament that would not ever tilt.

If I kept (11) my mouth clean of doing harm,
He increased their members among the attendants.[10]
If I [walked] on the water of my lord,[11]
He protected them more than the chest in the tomb.
If I safeguarded his majesty's orders to me,
They were promoted in the palace.
If I raised a son above the rank of his father,
Their requests were fulfilled as they wished.
If I scattered my wealth on everybody,
They thought ⟨me⟩ the equal of Hu.[12]
If I hated slander, loved assent,
A voice was raised for them to guard them from evil.
I was thus a god for them,
They knew my action when he[13] bestowed favors.
When they succeeded me in the king's service,
Their rank was through me in accord with my wish.

May I see the children of their children,
While I remain on earth!
May my body be young in their descendants,
While I am here thereafter!
I shall not vanish for I know:
God acts for him whose heart is true!

On the back plinth

(1) The one honored by Khons, great favorite of the lord of Benent; the fourth prophet of Amen-Re, King of Gods, Djedkhonsefankh, justified; son of the priest of Amen-Re, King of Gods, and intimate of Horus in his palace, Nespernebu, justified; he says: When I was in

charge of the loaves, my lord Amun enriched me. (3) I was constant in lending grain to the Thebans, in nourishing the poor of my town. I did not rage at him who could not pay. I did not press him so as to seize his belongings. I did not make him sell his goods to another, so as to repay the debt (5) he had made. I sated (him) by buying his goods and paying two or three times their worth. One cannot equal what I did in any respect. I did not quarrel with him who had robbed me, for I knew one does not get rich by theft. God does what he wishes!

NOTES

1. Name of the Khons temple at Karnak.

2. Lit., "My supplies (or, "surpluses") are for them," etc., i.e., he provided mortuary offerings for his parents.

3. Throne name of King Osorkon I.

4. The heirs of Osorkon I were the ephemeral Sheshonq II and his brother Takelot I, either in this order of succession (so Kitchen, *Third Intermediate*, pp. 309–310) or in the reverse order (see K. Baer, *JNES*, 32 [1973], 6–7).

5. Neither Janssen's "Seine Majestät entfernte mich nicht," nor Otto's "Ich trat seiner Majestät . . . nicht zu nahe," is correct. As *Wb.* 5,328–9 indicates, the principal meaning of *tši* is "leave, depart from," and that is the sense required here.

6. Janssen interpreted the flesh sign (hieroglyph F51) in *tši* and, in the same line, in *spr* as having the value *f*, as it often has in the Late Period. If so, the seated man determinative must stand for *wi*, and *spr* must be given an unattested causative sense. He thus obtained "er erhöhte mich," and "er liess mich Theben erreichen." The more plausible solution (and the one inherent in Otto's translation though Otto did not explain it) is to give to the sign F51 the value *w* (see H. W. Fairman, *ASAE*, 43 [1943], 266 f.), and to take *tsw.i* as passive *sdm.f* and *sprw.i* as active *sdm.f*. Hieroglyph F51 also has the value *i*, as for example in the Serapeum stela SIM 4110, line 2 (see Vercoutter, *Textes biogr.*, p. 49 and p. 51, note D), but that does not suit here.

7. The arrival in Thebes refers to his return to Thebes in his old age, where he continued to serve the king.

8. The feminine suffix here and in the following sentences refers to Thebes.

9. Or, "in cases of resolving difficulties." The same expression occurs on the Berlin statue of *Harwa*, see p. 27 with note 12.

10. This series of six sentences, each beginning with the particle *in*, is crucial for the understanding of the whole text. Janssen took the sentences to mean that Djedkhonsefankh was proclaiming that his loyal services to the king had been of benefit to the courtiers, while Otto thought the common people were the beneficiaries. It seems to me that Djedkhonsefankh is not referring to the courtiers or to the people at large but rather to the members of his own family. His kinsmen were the ones who were helped by his favored position. Seen in this light, the concluding sentences of line 13, in which he invokes *his* descendants, become meaningful, whereas to hail the future generations of courtiers

in general would make little sense. On the particle *in* with conditional sense see now J Osing, *SAK*, 1 (1974), 268–273.

11. To "walk on (or, be on) someone's water" means to be loyal and devoted.

12. "Hu" would here be not the divine utterance but rather the personification of food.

13. The king.

STATUE INSCRIPTION OF NEBNETERU

From Karnak

Cairo Museum 42225

A handsome block statue of grey granite, 1.10 m high. The cartouches of King Osorkon II are inscribed on Nebneteru's shoulders. In addition, his right shoulder bears the inscription "First Prophet of Amun, Harsiese." In this way Nebneteru pays homage to the chief pontiff of Thebes. Incised on the front of the body are the standing figures of Amun, Re, Ptah, and Osiris, with each god addressing a blessing to Nebneteru.

Below the scene is the beginning of the biographical inscription. The texts are distributed over the surfaces in the following order. On the front is an introductory autobiographical statement in the first person, which ends with an appeal to the priests of the temple. On the right side is a list of titles and epithets cast in the third person followed by a prayer on behalf of Nebneteru, such as might be spoken by his son. On the left side is the principal autobiographical inscription, ending in another appeal to the priests to safeguard and supply his statue. On the back plinth is a summary of his offices and titles. On the base two vertical and two horizontal lines repeat the titles of Nebneteru and add those of his son Hor, who dedicated the statue of his father.

Like Djedkhonsefankh before him, Nebneteru belonged to a leading Theban family whose members held important positions in the Theban priesthood and at court, and were related to the ruling dynasty through marriages with princesses of the royal house. Nebneteru's principal courtly office was that of "royal secretary," an office which entailed extensive administrative duties.

Of special interest in his autobiography is Nebneteru's expression of satisfaction with his exceptionally long life, and his emphatic exhortation to the reader to enjoy life, to eschew worries, and to shun the thought of death.

Publication: Legrain, *Statues*, III, 58–62 and pl. 32.

Partial text, translation, and study: H. Kees, *ZÄS*, 74 (1938), 73–87, and *idem, ZÄS*, 88 (1962/3), 24–26.

Translation: Otto, *Inschriften*, pp. 136–139.

Comments: Legrain, *RT*, 30 (1908), 73–74, 160, and 165 f.   Kees, *Priestertum*, pp. 223 ff., and *idem, Priester*, p. 108.   Kitchen, *Third Intermediate*, pp. 211–213.

On the front of the body in eight columns

(1) The prince, count, royal seal-bearer, prophet of Amun in Ipet-sut, royal secretary,[1] Nebneteru, son of the mayor, vizier, mouth of Nekhen, Neseramun, born of Muthetepti, says:

I was one unique and excellent,
Great in his town,
Much esteemed in the temple.
Amun appointed me door-opener of heaven,[2]
So that I saw his form (3) in lightland.
He introduced me to the palace in private,
So that I saw Horus in his image.[3]
I sought what was useful for my town in my time,
My concern[4] was for the house of god.
He gave me rewards in blessings,
He requited (me) as he wished.

He provided me with a son to take office,
On my entering the land of my permanence.
(5) I saw his worth as he circled the shrine,
As one honored by the King in the palace,
The prophet of Amun, fan-bearer at the King's right,
Royal secretary of the Lord of the Two Lands, Hor.
I saw my sons as great priests,
Son after son who issued from me.
I attained the age of ninety-six,
Being healthy, without illness.
If one desires (7) the length of my life,
One must praise god for another in my name.[5]

O priests, divine fathers of Amun!
You shall be on earth without want
Through the favor of Amun,
If you give water to my statue,
For whose worship ⟨my⟩ *ba* rises early!
For the *ka* of the priest and royal secretary, Tery,[6]
Every day unendingly.

On the right side in thirteen horizontal lines

(1) Long live the prince, count royal seal-bearer,
Prophet who opens the doors of heaven in Ipet-sut;
Chief seer who contents the heart of Re-Atum in Thebes,

Who enters the palace in private;
The eyes of the King throughout the land,
Who comes praised from the palace;
A mouth skilled in confidential speech,
Provider of Upper Egypt in his time;
Whose coming is awaited in the palace,
Whose wisdom has advanced his *ka*;
The royal (3) secretary for Upper Egypt, Nebneteru,
Son of the prince, count, royal seal-bearer,
Prophet of Amun in Ipet-sut,
Mayor, vizier, mouth of Nekhen,
Guide of the whole land, *setem*-priest,
Leader of all kilts, prophet of Maat, Neseramun;
Son of the prophet and door-opener of heaven in Ipet-sut,
First prophet of Mont, Lord of Thebes,
Intimate of the King in the palace,
Fan-bearer at the King's right,
Royal secretary of (5) Pharaoh, Nebneteru.[7]

May your city-god act for you,
Amen-Re, Lord of Thrones-of-the-Two-Lands,
Sole god, truly benign, whose glory endures,
Lord of all in heaven, on earth,
The lightlander who rises in lightland,
By whom everyone lives,
Exalted of form, lord of joy,
Presiding over Thrones-of-the-Two-Lands!

And Re-Harakhti, the radiant,
Whose serpent shines,
Who is bright in (7) the eyes of all;
And great Ptah, South-of-his-Wall,
Lord of Memphis, Lord of Maat,
Who created all there is;
And Osiris, Lord of eternity,
Ruler of everlastingness:

May they love you as you come in peace,
May they renew your *ka* in the sanctuary.
May your seat be spacious as when you were on earth,[8]
May all the living love you.
May you inhale myrrh and sweet ointment,
And receive (9) the cleansing of the Two Lords.[9]
May the two jars give you their content,
May you receive the loaf in the hall.

May your *ba* be brought to the altar daily,
May the arm be bent at your tomb.
May the water of the revered be given you
From the hands of the servants of god.
May all kinds of food be poured out
In the sanctuary by the great priests.
(11) May your limbs be fashioned anew,
May your body be blessed afresh,
In reward for your having entered before god,
And having seen Amun in the hall of columns.
You have opened the doors of the portal of lightland,
You have brought sunlight from the eastern mountain.[10]
You have entered pure with words of cleansing,
You have made great your monthly cleansing.
Your hand was sound, your tongue exact,
(13) Your mouth shut against speaking falsely.
Your tongue was guarded − − − . . . ,[11]
Your speech was free of evil.
All good things shall be given you,
An offering befitting one like you.

On the left side in thirteen horizontal lines

(1) Long live the prince, count, royal seal-bearer,
Prophet, door-opener of heaven in Ipet-sut,
Who enters into the secret of the portal of this land,
Palace councillor who guides the land with his counsel,
Great dignitary in Upper Egypt,
Royal secretary of Upper Egypt, Nebneteru, justified;
Son of the mayor, vizier, mouth of Nekhen,
Prophet of Maat, Neseramun, justified; he says:

I lived on earth as intimate of the God,[12]
As eyes of the King in Ipet-sut,
One who gave direction in all work (3) to the ignorant,
Who guided the craftsmen by the rule.
Who knew his speech when speaking in the palace,
Who removed the wrong in every matter,
Who contented all the gods with their purifications.
I addressed the people in a manner they liked,
I judged everyone according to his nature,
I gave attention to what he wished.
I spent my lifetime in heart's delight,
Without worry, without illness.
I made my days festive with wine and myrrh,

I banished languor (5) from my heart.[13]
I knew it is dark in the desert vale,[14]
It is not foolish to do the heart's wish.

The prophet of Amun, the royal secretary, Tery, he says:
Happy is he[15] who spends his life
In following his heart with the blessings of Amun![16]
He granted my office of door-opener of heaven,
He appointed me intimate of the palace.
Having surpassed the lifespan of any man (7) in my time,
I reached the desert vale with his blessings.
How the land mourned when I passed away,
My kin not differing from the people![17]
Do not fret because the like will happen,[18]
It is sad to live with head on knee![19]
Do not be tightfisted with what you own,
Do not act empty-handed with (9) your wealth!
Do not sit in the hall of heart's concern,[20]
Foretelling the morrow before it has come!
Do not deny[21] the eye its water,
Lest it come unawares!
Do not sleep with the disk in the east,
Do not thirst at the side of beer![22]
The west seeks to hide[23] (11) from him who follows his heart,
The heart is a god,
The stomach is its shrine,
It rejoices when the limbs are festive!

O priests, divine fathers of Amun,
Who enter the heaven upon earth,
Very pure at the monthly feast,
Who bring the Eye at the two strides of the moon:[24]
Do not remove my statue from its place,
Beware of Amun's reproach!
(13) Perform the royal offering for my *ka* every day,
With every leftover from Amun,
Bread, beer, wine, and oil
From the table of the Lord of Thebes,
For the *ka* of this excellent noble!

On the back plinth in four columns

(1) The prince, count, royal seal-bearer,
Prophet of Amun in Thebes,
Supervisor of the prophets of all the gods,

Special one to the King,
Intimate of the King,
Favorite in the palace,
Whom the King gave riches and praises
Because of the greatness of his knowledge.
A great one in his office,
Outstanding in his rank,
Who removed the wrong in every matter.
Chief seer[25] (3) who contents the heart of Re-Atum in Thebes,
Chief of works on all monuments of the house of Amun,
Royal secretary for Upper Egypt, Nebneteru, justified;
Son of the prince, count, royal seal-bearer,
Prophet of Amun in Ipet-sut,
Mayor, vizier, overseer of the companions of the palace,
Setem-priest, leader of all kilt-wearers,
Judge, mouth of Nekhen, intimate of Horus in the palace,
Prophet of Maat, Neseramun, justified,
Born of Muthetepti.

NOTES

1. Lit., "King's scribe of letters" (or, "documents"). This is Nebneteru's principal courtly office.

2. Nebneteru's particular function as a priest of Amun of Ipet-sut (Karnak) was to open the doors of the sanctuary during the daily ritual. "Heaven" and "lightland" (horizon) are words for the temple.

3. Just as Nebneteru could approach the god in his shrine, so also did he have access to the king at the palace, the king as Horus being the earthly image of Amun.

4. The verb $ḥ3m$, "to catch fish," here has a metaphorical sense which is not quite clear. As to the spelling with feminine t and four strokes, Kees read it as the collective $ḥ3m.t$ and rendered "so dass es gesammelt ist." I propose to take the fourth stroke as the suffix of the first person. As to the meaning, I see it in the light of the expression $ḥ3m-ib$, which occurs in line 9 of the left-side inscription, where the context suggests "worry," "anxiety," or "concern." Hence I render "my concern," but some doubt remains.

5. So following Kees, but the writing of ky, "another," is odd, and the sense is not clear.

6. Nickname of Nebneteru.

7. In addition to giving his father's name and offices, Nebneteru records the ranks and titles of his grandfather Nebneteru after whom he was named.

8. To have a "spacious seat" means "to be at ease."

9. It seems that $km.k$ stands for $gm.k$. The "Two Lords" are Horus and Seth.

10. I.e., the morning sun enters the temple when the doors are opened.

11. The missing sign obscures the meaning.

12. Lit., "one who enters upon the god"; the "god" here is the king.

13. *Wrd-ib* is "lassitude" in the sense of "languor" and "passivity," and *fk3.n.i wrd.i n ib.i* must convey the idea of overcoming the heart's lassitude. This sense is obtained from the root *fk3*, "uproot, expel," not from *fk3*, "reward, bribe." Kees's rendering, "Ich gewährte meinem Herzen Aufschub," does not suit.

14. This is the only remark about the land of the dead: it is dark there. All other alleged references to the gloom of the afterlife, which Kees had read into lines 8–10 in his rendering in ZÄS, 74 (1938), 79, were due to mistranslations which Kees subsequently corrected in ZÄS, 88 (1962/3), 24–26.

15. *W3d wy* appears to be an idiom for "happy is," or, "blessed is." In *Ancient Egyptian Literature*, I, 197, n. 4, I noted its use in the laments for the dead.

16. This sentence sums up the Egyptian concept of the good and blessed life. "Following the heart" (*šms-ib*) is to make the best and fullest use of what life holds; it is being active, generous, and joyful. Beneath the exhortation to enjoy life lay the continuous conflict between valuing life in all its transitoriness and the vision of an eternal afterlife, a vision that oscillated between hope and doubt. The debates stirred by this conflict are studied anew in J. Assmann's excellent article, "Fest des Augenblicks—Verheissung der Dauer" in *Otto Gedenkschrift*, pp. 55–84.

17. I.e., the grief of the people at large was as great as that of Nebneteru's relatives.

18. Lit., "Do not fret lest its like may happen." The meaning is, "Do not think about your death."

19. Lit., "Sadness is for him who lives with head-on-knee." "Head-on-knee" was the posture of mourning.

20. On *h3m-ib* see note 4.

21. Assuming the verb to be either *kni* of *Wb.*, 5,44.1, or *kn* of *Wb.*, 5,50.6.

22. I.e., "Be up when the sun is up, and when beer is available drink it."

23. A word play on *imn.t*, "the west," and *imn.t*, "concealment." Again the meaning is that to enjoy life is to forget death.

24. The Horus Eye, the symbol of offerings, offered at the feasts of the waxing moon.

25. Title of the high priest of the sun-god.

STATUE INSCRIPTION OF HARWA

Berlin Museum 8163

A block statue of black granite, 0.487 m high. It is one of eight known statues of Harwa, the High Steward of the "Divine Consort of Amun," Amenirdis, daughter of King Kashta. Under the Nubian kings of the Twenty-fifth Dynasty the office of "Divine Consort of Amun" at Thebes became especially prominent. Exercised by a king's daughter, and transmitted to a female successor by adoption, the position of High Priestess of Amun ensured the king's control over the Theban region.

The chief official of the "Divine Consort," who bore the title "High Steward," was an important personality in the administration. The prominence achieved by the Divine Consorts and by their High Stewards was also a corollary to the declining significance of the office of High Priest ("First Prophet") of Amun in the Nubian and Saite periods.

Perhaps the inscriptions in Harwa's sumptuous but badly damaged unpublished tomb (No. 37 at Thebes) contained allusions, however veiled, to the Nubian conquest of Egypt. The inscriptions on his eight statues, however, are limited to formulaic affirmations of his virtues and of the esteem in which he was held by his mistress, the Divine Consort of Amun, and by his master, the king. From the literary point of view these formulations are not without interest, for they combine traditional phrases with metaphors that appear to be of new, or recent, coinage.

The more one studies the Middle Egyptian idiom of Late Period inscriptions, the more does one realize the deliberateness that governs the choice of words. Far from being chosen at random, the phrases are composed for suitability to the underlying metrical schemes of the orational style, and for rhetorical effectiveness. And when one composition reappears with variations on another man's monument, we may assume that it had been deemed especially pleasing. Thus it is that many of the phrases of Harwa's Berlin statue also occur on his Louvre statue (A 84) and reappear on a statue of his successor, the High Steward Akhamenru.

Publication: B. Gunn and R. Engelbach, *BIFAO*, 30 (1931), 791–815 (the eight statues).   B. Gunn, *BIFAO*, 34 (1934), 135–142 (revised text of the Berlin statue and notes).

Comments on the eight statues: J. Clère, *BIFAO*, 34 (1934), 129–133. Ch. Kuentz, *BIFAO*, 34 (1934), 143–163.   G. Roeder, *BIFAO*, 34 (1934), 165–173.   H. Senk, *BIFAO*, 34 (1934), 175–187.

Translation: Otto, *Inschriften*, pp. 150–153 (the Berlin statue).

On the Divine Consorts of Amun see especially: Leclant, *Recherches*, pp. 353–386.

On the statue's right shoulder

The God's Hand, Amenirdis, justified.

On the left shoulder

The God's Hand, Mistress of the Two Lands, Amenirdis, justified.

On the front of the body in ten horizontal lines

(1) The prince, count, royal seal-bearer; true, beloved King's friend; keeper of the diadem of the God's Adoress;[1] royal servant[2] in the royal harem; embalmer-priest-of-Anubis of the God's Wife; prophet of the God's Adoress, Amenirdis, justified, in her *ka*-chapel; steward of the *ka*-priests; prophet of Osiris (3) Giver of Life; the Steward Harwa, son of the scribe Pedimut, justified, he says:

O prophets, divine fathers, priests, and lector-priests,
All who enter the temple of Amun of Ipet-sut,

To perform rites, to (5) make offerings,
To perform the service of the monthly priest:
The august god shall live for you,
You shall be pure to him,
He shall make you abide with his blessings,
If you will say:
An offering that the King gives,
A thousand of bread, beer, oxen, and fowl,
Alabaster, clothing, incense, and unguent,
(7) Everything good and pure—you shall say—
After the god has been satisfied with it,
For the King's friend Harwa, and for his *ka*.
For I am an excellent noble,
Equipped with his blessings,
One whose virtue the Two Lands know;
A refuge (9) for the wretched,
A float for the drowning,
A ladder for him who is in the abyss.[3]
One who speaks for the unhappy,
Who assists the unfortunate,[4]
Who helps the oppressed by his good deed;
The one honored by the King, Harwa.

On the right side in twelve horizontal lines

(1) The one honored by the King; the High Steward of the God's
Adoress; embalmer-priest-of-Anubis of the God's Wife; true, beloved
King's friend; master of the servants of the God's Adoress of Amun,
Harwa; he says:

O prophets, divine fathers, priests,
The whole temple-priesthood of Amun,
Everyone who passes by this (3) image:
That *ba* who is in Thebes[5] shall live for you,
The august god who presides over his secluded place,
If you will say:
A thousand of bread, beer, and all good things,
For the *ka* of the one honored by the God's Hand,
The King's friend, Harwa, justified, honored.
For I am a noble for whom one should act,
One sound of heart[6] to (5) the end of life.
I am one beloved of his city,
Praised of his district,
Kind-hearted to his towns.

I have done what people love and gods praise,
(As) one truly revered who had no fault,
Who gave bread to the hungry, clothes to the naked,
Removed pain, suppressed (7) wrongdoing;
Who buried the revered ones,[7] supported the old,
Removed the want of the have-not.
A shade for the child,
A helper for the widow,
One who gave rank to an infant.
I did these things knowing their weight,
And their reward from the Lord of Things:
To abide in men's mouth without (9) ever ending,
To be well remembered in after years.
The breath of your mouth profits the silent,
Without cost to your possessions;
Food-offering for his god is bread for its owner,[8]
The spirit is blessed by recalling his *ka*.[9]
The one honored by his lord, (11) Harwa, justified,
Who was untiring in the temple.
He who makes a monument is beloved,[10]
The *ka* of the beneficent is recalled
For his beneficence in his temple.

On the left side in twelve horizontal lines

(1) The prince, count, honored by his lord, in favor with his lady; kind of speech, sweet of words, well disposed to great and small; who gives advice to the timid in trouble,[11] when his witnesses stand up to accuse. (3) The open-handed who nourished all, who provided the have-not with what he lacked; the chief chamberlain of the God's Hand, the King's friend, Harwa, justified; he says:

I speak to you who will come (5) after,
New beings in millions of years:
My Lady made me great when I was a small boy,
She advanced my position when I was a child.
The King sent me on missions (7) as a youth,
Horus, Lord of the Palace, distinguished me.
Every mission on which their majesties sent me,
I accomplished it correctly,
And never told a lie about it.
I did not rob, (9) I did no wrong,
I maligned no one before them.
I entered the Presence to resolve difficulties,[12]

To assist the unfortunate.

I have given goods to the have-not,

(11) I endowed the orphan in my town.

My reward is being remembered for my beneficence,

My *ka* enduring because of my kindness—Harwa.

On the back in four columns

(1) An offering that the King gives (to) Mont, Lord of Thebes, that he may give provisions of bread, beer, cakes, oxen, fowl, alabaster and clothing, incense and unguent, all things good and pure whereon a god lives, which heaven gives, earth produces, and Hapy brings forth, from (3) the table of the Lord of Eternity, on the monthly feast, the half-monthly feast, on the Thoth feast, and on every feast, every day, to the *ka* of the one honored by Mont, Lord of Thebes, the true, beloved King's friend, Harwa.

NOTES

1. The three designations of the High Priestesses of Amun were "God's Wife," God's Adoress," and God's Hand."

2. Lit., "He who is at the feet of the King."

3. The three striking metaphors appear to be of new or recent coinage. They recur on Harwa's Louvre statue, and they were adopted along with other formulations, by the High Steward Akhamenru, who succeeded Harwa (see my article in *JNES*, 7 (1948), 163–179). Note the tristich form of these sentences. It is used repeatedly in Harwa's inscriptions. The third member of a tristich is usually longer than the preceding two and thus adds weight.

4. The phrase *snf nb-sp* is used again in line 10 of the left-side inscription, and *sp* alone occurs there in line 2. Though it has no qualifying adjective, *sp* here means "misfortune, trouble."

5. The god Amun.

6. I.e., "strong-minded, firm."

7. The deceased.

8. Note the phrasing of *t n nb.f df3w n ntr.f*, which Gunn rendered as: "Let bread be for its master, and food-offerings be for their god" (*BIFAO*, 34 [1934], 139). I suspect that the elliptic formulation is that of a proverb.

9. As Gunn observed (ibid.) the word *ka* here takes on the meaning "name," as it often does in Ptolemaic times.

10. Reading *ir mnw mrr(w) pw*. It is true that this is not the normal spelling of *mnw*; but it seems a more likely solution than Gunn's proposals (ibid.).

11. Literally, "when his trouble has happened." On *sp* see n. 4, above.

12. The same expression as in the inscription of Djedkhonsefankh; see p. 17, n. 9.

TWO STATUE INSCRIPTIONS OF MONTEMHET

The documentation for the high officials of Upper Egypt in the Post-Imperial Epoch is relatively rich. They built sumptuous tombs on the west bank of Thebes and placed quantities of their statues in the temples. Many of these statues escaped destruction through the ironic fact that, contrary to the wishes of their owners, they were periodically removed from the temples and buried in the ground, to be dug up only at the beginning of our century. Thus we can build up dossiers and compile genealogies. Unfortunately the direct historical content of these statue inscriptions is somewhat meager, owing to a reticence dictated both by the conventions of the autobiography and by prudence in the face of political change and turmoil.

The inscriptions of Montemhet typify this situation. Coming from a family of Theban notables, Montemhet played a leading role during many troubled years. He was "Count of Thebes" and "Governor of Upper Egypt," as well as "Fourth Prophet of Amun" under the Nubian kings Taharqa and Tantamani, and he was still in office in the reign of Psamtik I, the founder of the Saite Dynasty. His career spans the half-century from 700 to 650 B.C. He witnessed the recurring Assyrian invasions, including the climactic capture of Thebes in 663, an event that reverberated around the ancient world. After that, with King Tantamani having fled to Nubia and Psamtik I not yet in control of all of Egypt, the Thebaid was virtually autonomous under the governance of Montemhet and of his colleagues, the high stewards of the Divine Consort of Amun, the princess Shepenupet II. And when Psamtik I had attained full power he still retained the services of the aged Montemhet.

Montemhet's principal surviving (though much damaged) biographical inscription, that on a wall of a chamber in the temple of Mut at Karnak, yields a few allusions to historical events. We learn from it that Montemhet "had placed Upper Egypt on the right path when the whole land was upside down," and that he had "subdued the rebels in the southern nomes." For the most part, the inscription is devoted to relating his rebuilding of the temple of Mut and of other Theban monuments.

On his many statues only two achievements of his career are narrated: the rebuilding of monuments, and the general prosperity of the Thebaid brought about by his wise administration. The rest is prayers, hymns, requests for offerings, and affirmations of his worth, all phrased in traditional terms. But along with the formality and eclecticism of his inscriptions goes the fact that several of the statues are outstanding works of art by virtue of their powerful and expressive modeling. They reveal a vital artistic energy which is also found in the portrait sculpture of the Nubian kings. Furthermore, the relief fragments from Montemhet's badly damaged and plundered Theban tomb are exceptionally fine. The two statues whose inscriptions are translated here are conventional in style. The kneeling statue is in the manner of the New Kingdom, while the seated one harks back to the Middle Kingdom.

The sheer quantity and the artistic quality of Montemhet's surviving monuments make him one of the best-known personalities of the Late Period.

I. STATUE INSCRIPTION OF MONTEMHET

From the Temple of Karnak

Cairo Museum 42237

A statue of gray-green volcanic rock, 0.40 m high. Montemhet is kneeling and holds a stela in front of him. In this stelephorous pose, which derives from the New Kingdom, the stela held in front of the body is usually inscribed with a hymn. Though the style of the sculpture is conventional the workmanship is fine. The face is that of a youngish man. In the lunette of the round-topped stela is the winged sun-disk with the legend: "(Horus) of Behdet, the great god, lord of heaven." Below is the inscription in thirteen lines.

Publication: Legrain, *Statues*, III, 88–89 and pls. xlvi and xlviiA.   J. Leclant, *Montouemhat, quatrième prophète d'Amon, prince de la ville*, Institut français d'archéologie orientale, Bibliothèque d'étude, 35 (Cairo, 1961), pp. 32–38 and pl. vi, text, translation, notes, bibliography and general commentary.

Translation: Otto, *Inschriften*, pp. 158–159.

Comments: Kees, *Priestertum*, pp. 272–277. *Idem*, *ZÄS*, 87 (1962), 60–66.   Kitchen, *Third Intermediate*, pp. 390 and 395–398.

For additional bibliography see Leclant, *Montouemhat.*, p. 32.

(1) The fourth prophet of Amun, the count, governor of Upper Egypt, Montemhet, in health;[1] he says:

Hail to you, Amun,
Maker of mankind,
God who created all beings!
(3) Beneficent king,
First one of the Two Lands,
Who planned the eternity he made.
Great in power,
Mighty in awe,
Whose forms are exalted above other gods.
Mighty of strength,
Who smites (5) the rebels,
Whose horn attacks the evildoers.
I bow down to your name,[2]
May it be my physician,
May it remove my body's illness,
May it drive pain (7) away from me,
⌜May your horn be aflame, the arm moving.⌝

May he put love of me in people's hearts,
That everyone be fond of me.
May he grant me a good burial

(9) In the graveyard of my city,
The sacred land is in his grasp.
May he make my name last like heaven's stars,
My statue endure as one of his followers.
May my *ka* be remembered in (11) his temple night and day,
May I renew my youth like the moon.
May my name not be forgotten in after years ever,
(13) The name of[3] Amun's fourth prophet, count of the city,
Montemhet, in health.

NOTES

1. A cryptographic writing of *snb*; see Leclant, *Montouemhat*, pp. 34 and 248.
2. Or, "I rely on your name."
3. Emending *rn r* to *rn n*.

II. STATUE INSCRIPTION OF MONTEMHET

Berlin Museum 17271

A finely worked statue of gray granite, 0.50 m high. Montemhet is seated on a chair with arms folded and enveloped in a long mantle. The face is youthful. The stone block representing the chair is inscribed on all four sides. In addition, a column of text runs down the center of the mantle, and the back plinth is inscribed in two columns. The style of the statue is derived from Middle Kingdom prototypes.

Publication: W. Wreszinski, *OLZ*, 19 (1916), cols. 10−18 and pls. 1−2.   Leclant, *Montouemhat*, pp. 58−64 and pls. xii−xv.

For additional references see Leclant, op. cit., p. 58.

On the mantle in one column

(1) May all that comes from the altar of Amen-Re, Lord of Thrones-of-the-Two-Lands, and of his Ennead, be for the *ka* of the prince, count, fourth prophet of Amun, count of the city, governor of Upper Egypt, Montemhet.

On the right-edge front of the seat and
continuing on the right side and on the back
in twelve columns

(1) The prince, count, fourth prophet of Amun, count of the city, Montemhet, he says:

O all prophets and divine fathers,
Who enter to officiate[1] in this place!
Great Amun (3) will favor you,

He will make you continue in your children,
If you pronounce my name every day,
During the offering-rites for the city-god,
That are performed in this place.
For I am a noble (5) for whom one should act,
A truly august one, beloved of his lord.

I have renewed the temple of Mut-the-Great, Ashru's mistress,
So that it is more beautiful than before.
I adorned her bark[2] with electrum,
(7) All its images with genuine stones.[3]
I renewed the bark of Khons-the-Child,
And the bark of Bastet-residing-in-Thebes,
So as to satisfy her majesty with what she wishes.
I renewed the barks of the three Khons,
(9) The bark of Khons-reckoner-of-lifetime,[4]
The bark of Amun, Lord of Thrones-of-the-Two-Lands, of . . .[5]

I rebuilt the divine boat of Osiris in Abydos,
When I found it gone to ruin.
(11) My heart did not weary,
My arms did not slacken,
Until I had renewed what I found decayed.
Do what Amun, lord of heaven, loves,
Speak the name of the count, director of the temple,
Montemhet in the house of his god!

On the left edge of the front and on the left side
in six columns

(1) The prince, count, fourth prophet of Amun, governor of all of
Upper Egypt, Montemhet, he says:

I have acted for you in performing the rites,
Let me make you cognizant (3) of my good deeds:
I was count of the Theban nome,
And all of Upper Egypt was in my charge,
The southern boundary being at Yebu,
The northern one at Un.[6]
I bestowed (5) my benefits on Upper Egypt,
My love on Lower Egypt;
The citizens longed to see me,
Like Re when he shows himself,
So great was my beneficence,
So exalted was my excellence!

On the back plinth in two columns

(1) O city-god of the prince, count, fourth prophet of Amun, count of the city, governor of Upper Egypt, Montemhet:

Place yourself behind him,
While his *ka* is before him,
He is a Heliopolitan.[7]

NOTES

1. Lit., "to uncover the (divine) face."
2. The portable shrine in the form of a bark mounted on poles, in which the statues of the gods were carried in procession.
3. Semiprecious stones are meant.
4. The god Khons was worshiped in a number of different forms. In Montemhet's biographical inscription in the Mut temple at Karnak as many as seven forms of Khons are mentioned, while in this statue inscription allusion is made to five manifestations: "Khons-the-Child," "the three Khons," and "Khons-reckoner-of-lifetime" (*ḥsb ʿḥ*). The "three Khons" probably are the triad of Khons-in-Thebes *nfr ḥtp*, Khons *wn nḥw*, and Khons *p3 ir sḥr*, which appear together on a number of monuments; cf. Leclant, *Montouemhat*, pp. 62−63, note (q). The several manifestations of Khons were studied by G. Posener in *Annuaire du Collège de France*, 1965, pp. 342 f.; 1966, pp. 339−342; 1967, pp. 345−349; 1968, pp. 401−407; 1969, pp. 375−379; and 1970, pp. 391−396.
5. The meaning of *ʿrʿr* has not been established; see *Wb.* 1,210.5.
6. Montemhet's authority extended from Elephantine to Hermopolis Magna.
7. A formula which has been variously rendered and much discussed; the references are assembled by Leclant, *Montouemhat*, p. 15, note (a).

STATUE INSCRIPTION OF PEFTUANEITH

From Abydos

Louvre A93

A standing naophorous statue of gray granite, 1.69 m high. Peftuaneith, dressed in a long, tightly fitted garment, holds before him a small shrine (naos) with a figure of Osiris. The text in fourteen columns begins on the back plinth and continues on the left side of the slab that supports the advanced left leg. Peftuaneith relates that he carried out extensive restorations in the holy city of Abydos and in its district. He also tells of having given a donation of land and other revenue to the temple of Osiris so as to increase its income.

In the concluding prayer he begs Osiris to grant favors to him and to his master, King Amasis. On an earlier statue (British Museum 805 [83]) Peftuaneith speaks of having reorganized the administration of the temple of Heliopolis in his capacity of official of King Apries. Thus he is known to have served the two kings in succession. And his activities illustrate the restoring and reorganizing policies of the Saite kings.

Publication: Pierret, *Recueil*, II, 39–41.   Brugsch, *Thesaurus*, VI, 1252–1254 (abridged).   K. Piehl, *ZÄS*, 32 (1894), 118–122; and *idem*, *ZÄS*, 34 (1896), 81–83.   E. Jelinkova-Reymond, *ASAE*, 54 (1956/57), 275–287.

Translation: B*AR*, IV, §§ 1015–1025.   Otto, *Inschriften*, pp. 164–166.

Comments: G. Lefebvre, *RdÉ*, 1 (1933), 94–100.   H. Kees, *NGWG*, phil.-hist. Klasse, n.s. 1 (1935), 103–104.   A. H. Gardiner, *JEA*, 24 (1938), 165.

For additional references see Jelinkova-Reymond, *op. cit.*, p. 275.

(1) The prince, count, sole companion, administrator of the palace, chief physician, overseer of the two treasuries, grandee of the hall, great revered one in the palace, the high steward[1] Peftuaneith,[2] engendered by the controller of temples, administrator of Dep, prophet of Horus of Pe,[3] Sisobk, says:

O every priest who shall perform the rites,
Khentamenti will reward you
For reciting the offering to me,[4]
While kissing the ground to Khentamenti;
For you see me blessed before your god,
Valued by the majesty of my lord,
Above all his nobles.
I am a friend for whom one should act,[5]
An excellent craftsman who embellished his house.[6]

I reported the condition of Abydos,
To the palace, to his majesty's ear.
His majesty ordered me to do work in Abydos,
In order to rebuild Abydos;
I labored greatly in restoring Abydos,
I put everything belonging to Abydos in its place.
I lay awake seeking what was good for Abydos,
(3) I begged favors from my lord daily,
In order to restore Abydos.

I built the temple of Khentamenti,
As a solid work of eternity,
At his majesty's command,
That he might see prosperity in the affairs of Tawer.[7]
I surrounded it with walls of brick,
The shrine ʾrḳ-ḥḥ was of one block of granite,
The august chapel of electrum,
Ornaments, divine amulets, all sacred objects
Were of gold, silver, and all precious stones.

I built the *wpg*-sanctuary,[8] ⌈set up⌉ its braziers,
Dug its pond, planted with trees.

I provisioned the temple of Khentamenti,
Enlarged its income,
Established with daily supplies,
Its storehouse furnished with male and female slaves.
I gave it a donation of a thousand aruras,
In the countryside of Tawer,
Provided with people and herds of all kinds,
Its name being made "Osiris-town,"[9]
(5) So as to make a divine endowment of it for all time.
I renewed its divine endowment of bread, beer, oxen, and fowl,
Exceeding what it had been before.
I made for it an orchard,
Planted with all fruit trees,
Its gardeners being foreigners,
Brought in as prisoners.
Thirty pints of wine were given from it daily
To the altar of Khentamenti,
As an offering from it for all time.

I renewed the House of Life after its ruin,[10]
I established the sustenance (7) of Osiris,
I put all its procedures in order.
I built the god's boat of pine wood,
Having found (it) made of acacia wood.
I suppressed crime in Tawer,
I guarded Tawer for its lord,
I protected all its people.
I gave income from Tawer's desert to the temple,
Having found it in the hands of the count,
So that Abydenes (9) would have burials.[11]
I gave the ferryboat[12] of Tawer to the temple,
Having taken it away from the count,
. . . . . .[13]
His majesty praised me for what I had done.

May he give life to his son, *Amasis Son of Neith*,
May he give me favors from the King,
And reveredness before (11) the Great God!
O priest, praise god for me!
You who come from the temple blessed, say:
May the high steward Peftuaneith,
Born of Nanesbastet, be in the god's bark,
May he receive eternal bread at the head of the blessed!

NOTES

1. Peftuaneith's principal offices were those of chief physician, chief treasurer, and high steward, the last-named being the most important.

2. In its full form the name was Pef-tjau-awy-neith.

3. His father had held only priestly positions in the clergy of Horus of Buto, the town being called by its ancient names "Pe and Dep."

4. Throughout the text the suffix of the first person singular is not written.

5. In the phrase *ink smr n ir n.f* the writing *ir* stands for the infinitive *irt*. In this inscription the spelling *ir* also serves for *ir.i* (line 4) and *iry* (passive participle) in line 7.

6. "His house" probably refers to the temple of Osiris.

7. The nome of Abydos.

8. *Wb.* 1,306.2 raises the question whether *wpg* is identical with *w-pkr*, the sacred spot in Abydos where the tomb of Osiris was located.

9. Kerkeosiris. On place names formed with *grg* = *kerke*, see J. Yoyotte, *RdÉ*, 14 (1962), 83 ff.

10. This is one of the references to the institution called the "House of Life," which was first studied closely by Gardiner in *JEA*, 24 (1938), 157–179. Gardiner there defined its function too narrowly as that of a scriptorium where religious books were compiled. His conclusions were broadened by Volten, *Traumdeutung*, pp. 17–44, and by P. Derchain, *Le Papyrus Salt 825* (Brussels, 1965), pp. 18 ff. The principal subjects studied and practiced by the members of the House of Life were medicine, magic, theology, ritual, and dream interpretation.

11. This transfer of income from a "count" to the temple of Osiris was discussed by H. Kees (see bibliography). He saw in it a redistribution of revenues as part of the Saite dynasty's reorganization of landholdings. It is an interesting sidelight that this additional income was to be used to defray the burial costs of the inhabitants of Abydos.

12. This may mean the ferryboat tax.

13. An obscure sentence with a lacuna. Otto, following Kees, took it to mean, "for the benefit of Kerkeosiris." Jelinkova-Reymond rendered, "Qu'Osiris aime [. . .] selon que Sa Majesté, etc."

STATUE INSCRIPTION OF UDJAHORRESNE

Vatican Museum 158 [113]

A standing naophorous statue of green basalt. The head, shoulders, and arms have been restored in modern times. Without the restorations the statue is 0.70 m high. The naos contains a figure of Osiris. The inscription is distributed over the statue's body, the naos, the back plinth, and the base.

This is the most important biographical inscription from the time of the Persian domination of Egypt. Udjahorresne first served as a naval officer under Kings Amasis and Psamtik III. He witnessed the Persian invasion under Cambyses and the destruction of the Saite state. The Persian king made him a courtier and appointed him priest of Neith and chief physician. Through his good standing with Cambyses, Udjahorresne was able to obtain the reconsecration of the temple of Neith at Sais. and to help the people of Sais recover from the effects of the Persian invasion.

Omitting to mention the circumstances that brought him to Persia, he tells that King Darius I sent him back to Egypt in order to revive the activities of the House of Life. The text dates from the early years of the reign of Darius I.

Publication: Brugsch, *Thesaurus*, IV, 636–642 (text) and 682–698, translation.   G. Posener, *La première domination perse en Egypte*, Institut français d'archéologie orientale, Cairo, Bibliothèque d'étude, 11 (Cairo, 1936), pp. 1–26, text, translation, and comments.   A. Tulli in *Miscellanea Gregoriana*, pp. 211–280.

Translation: Otto, *Inschriften*, pp. 169–173.   Roeder, *Götterwelt*, pp. 75–86.

On the front and roof of the naos in six lines

(1) An offering that the King gives (to) Osiris-Hemag:[1] A thousand of bread, beer, oxen, and fowl, everything good and pure, for the *ka* of the one honored by the gods of Sais, the chief physician, Udjahorresne.

An offering that the King gives (to) Osiris who presides over the Palace:[2] A thousand of bread, beer, oxen, and fowl, clothing, myrrh, and unguent, and every good thing, for the *ka* of the one honored by all the gods, the chief physician, Udjahorresne.

(3) O Osiris, lord of eternity! The chief physician, Udjahorresne has placed his arms about you as protection.[3] May your *ka* command that all blessings be done for him, according as he protects your chapel forever.

Under the right arm in nine lines

(7) The one honored by Neith-the-Great, the mother of god,[4] and by the gods of Sais, the prince, count, royal seal-bearer, sole companion, true beloved King's friend, the scribe, inspector of council scribes, chief scribe of the great outer hall, administrator of the palace, (9) commander of the royal navy under the King of Upper and Lower Egypt, *Khenemibre*,[5] commander of the royal navy under the King of Upper and Lower Egypt, *Ankhkare*,[6] Udjahorresne; engendered by the administrator of the castles (of the red crown), chief-of-Pe priest, *rnp*-priest, priest of the Horus Eye, prophet of Neith who presides over the nome of Sais, Peftuaneith; (11) he says:

The Great Chief of all foreign lands, *Cambyses* came to Egypt, and the foreign peoples of every foreign land were with him. When he had conquered this land in its entirety, they established themselves in it, and he was Great Ruler of Egypt and Great Chief of all foreign lands.[7]

His majesty assigned to me the office of chief physician. (13) He made me live at his side as companion and administrator of the palace.

I[8] composed his titulary, to wit his name of King of Upper and Lower Egypt, *Mesutire*.[9]

I let his majesty know the greatness of Sais, that it is the seat of Neith-the-Great, the mother who bore Re and inaugurated birth when birth had not yet been; and the nature of the greatness of the temple of Neith, that it is heaven in its every aspect; and the nature of the greatness of the castles of Neith, (15) and of all the gods and goddesses who are there; and the nature of the greatness of the Palace,[10] that it is the seat of the Sovereign, the Lord of Heaven;[11] and the nature of the greatness of the Resenet and Mehenet sanctuaries;[12] and of the House of Re and the House of Atum, the mystery of all the gods.

Under the left arm in eight lines

(16) The one honored by his city-god and all the gods, the prince, count, royal seal-bearer, sole companion, true beloved King's friend, the chief physician, Udjahorresne, born of Atemirdis, he says:

I made a petition (18) to the majesty of the King of Upper and Lower Egypt, *Cambyses*, about all the foreigners who dwelled in the temple of Neith, in order to have them expelled from it, so as to let the temple of Neith be in all its splendor, as it had been before. His majesty commanded to expel all the foreigners (20) [who] dwelled in the temple of Neith, to demolish all their houses and all their unclean things that were in this temple.

When they had carried [all their] personal [belongings] outside the wall of the temple, his majesty commanded to cleanse the temple of Neith and to return all its personnel to it, (22) the − − − and the hour-priests of the temple. His majesty commanded to give divine offerings to Neith-the-Great, the mother of god, and to the great gods of Sais, as it had been before. His majesty commanded [to perform] all their festivals and all their processions, as had been done before. His majesty did this because I had let his majesty know the greatness of Sais, that it is the city of all the gods, who dwell there on their seats forever.

On the left side of the naos base in four lines

(24) The one honored by the gods of Sais, the chief physician, Udjahorresne, he says:

The King of Upper and Lower Egypt, *Cambyses*, came to Sais. His majesty went in person to the temple of Neith. He made a great prostration before her majesty, as every king has done. He made a great offering (26) of every good thing to Neith-the-Great, the mother of god, and to the great gods who are in Sais, as every beneficent king has done. His majesty did this because I had let his majesty know the greatness of her majesty Neith, that she is the mother of Re himself.

On the right side of the naos base in three lines

(28) The one honored by Osiris-Hemag, the chief physician, Udja-horresne, he says: His majesty did every beneficence in the temple of Neith. He established the presentation of libations to the Lord of Eternity[13] in the temple of Neith, as every king had done before. (30) His majesty did this because I had let his majesty know how every beneficence had been done in this temple by every king, because of the greatness of this temple, which is the seat of all the gods everlasting.

On the left wall of the naos and on the statue's garment
in six lines

(31) The one honored by the gods of the Saite nome, the chief physician, Udhahorresne, he says: I have established the divine offering of Neith-the-Great, the mother of god, according to his majesty's command for all eternity. I made a (pious) foundation for Neith, mistress of Sais, of every good thing, as does a servant (33) who is useful to his lord.

I am a man who is good in his town. I rescued its inhabitants from the very great turmoil when it happened in the whole land,[14] the like of which had not happened in this land. I defended the weak (35) against the strong. I rescued the timid man when misfortune came to him.[15] I did for them every beneficence when it was time to act for them.

On the right wall of the naos and on the statue's garment
in six lines

(37) The one honored by his city-god, the chief physician, Udja-horresne, he says: I am one honored by his father, praised by his mother, the intimate of his brothers. I established them in the office of prophet. I gave them a productive field by his majesty's command for (39) all eternity. I made a fine tomb for him who lacked one. I supported all their children. I established all their households. I did for them every beneficence as a father does for his son, when the turmoil happened in (41) this nome, in the midst of the very great turmoil that happened in the whole land.

On the back plinth in three columns

(43) The prince, count, royal seal-bearer, sole companion, prophet of those by whom one lives,[16] the chief physician, Udjahorresne, born of Atemirdis, he says: The majesty of the King of Upper and Lower Egypt, *Darius*, ever-living, commanded me to return to Egypt—when his majesty was in Elam and was Great Chief of all foreign lands and Great Ruler of Egypt—in order to restore the establishment of the House of Life – – –,[17] after it had decayed. The foreigners carried me

from country to country. They delivered me to Egypt as commanded by the Lord of the Two Lands.

I did as his majesty had commanded me. I furnished them[18] with all their staffs consisting of the wellborn, no lowborn among them. I placed them in the charge of every learned man (45) [⌜in order to teach them⌝] all their crafts. His majesty had commanded to give them every good thing, in order that they might carry out all their crafts. I supplied them with everything useful to them, with all their equipment that was on record, as they had been before.

His majesty did this because he knew the worth of this guild[19] in making live all that are sick, in making endure forever the names of all the gods, their temples, their offerings, and the conduct of their festivals.

On the right side of the statue base in one line

(46) The chief physician, Udjahorresne, he says: I was one who was honored by all his masters, my being . . . . . .[20] They gave me ornaments of gold and did for me every beneficence.

On the left side of the statue base in two lines

(47) One honored by Neith is he who shall say: "O great gods who are in Sais! Remember all the benefactions done by the chief physician, Udjahorresne. And may you do for him all benefactions! May you make his good name endure in this land forever!"

NOTES

1. A particular form of Osiris worshiped at Sais and elsewhere.

2. This is the *hwt-bit*, "mansion of the bee," the sanctuary in which Osiris was worshiped. Its precise relation to the temple of Neith at Sais is not clear; see H. Ranke, *MDIK*, 12 (1943), 118 (2), and G. Vittmann, *ZÄS*, 103 (1976), 144 (*a*).

3. This refers to the attitude of the naophorous statue, whose two arms hold a small shrine in which stands a figure of Osiris.

4. The sun-god Re.

5. Throne name of King Amasis.

6. Throne name of King Psamtik III.

7. This is Udjahorresne's very guarded account of the Persian conquest of Egypt.

8. The first-person suffix is missing several times in this inscription.

9. "Offspring of Re," the throne name of Cambyses.

10. The *hwt-bit*; see n. 2, above.

11. Osiris is meant.

12. On these two sanctuaries of Sais see now P. Kaplony in *Berlin Festschrift*, pp. 119 ff.

13. Osiris.

14. Another allusion to the Persian conquest; a third reference to it is in lines 40−41.

15. *Sp* = "misfortune, trouble," as in Harwa's inscription; see p. 28, n. 4.

16. I.e., the gods. This seems to be the most likely interpretation of the phrase *'nḫ im.sn*.

17. For the short lacuna after "House of Life" Posener had proposed the restoration "of Sais," while Gardiner (*JEA*, 24 [1938], 157−159) argued in favor of restoring *nw ir sinw* and rendering the whole phrase as "the department(s) of the House(s) of Life dealing with medicine." But medicine was only one of the several crafts practiced by the members of the House of Life. Moreover, the many occurrences of the term "House of Life" which Gardiner assembled in his study lack all qualifying epithets, except for the occasional epithet *n nb t3.wy*, "of the Lord of the Two Lands." It seems to me more likely that the lacuna contained a phrase such as "in all its parts."

18. Whatever stood in the lacuna discussed in the preceding note accounted for the plural pronoun here.

19. All translators have rendered *ḥmw.t* as "art." I believe it is the word "collectivity of craftsmen" (*Wb*. 3,85.5−8), for it is followed by Udjahorresne's summary of the various activities of the House of Life. This summary, though not a complete description, is highly instructive. The subjects and crafts studied and practiced by the members of the House of Life included medicine, theology, temple administration, and ritual. See also p. 36, n. 10.

20. Several unclear signs.

STELA OF SOMTUTEFNAKHT

Naples Museum 1035

Discovered in 1765 during the excavation of the temple of Isis at Pompeii, the stela is now in the Naples Museum. Originally it must have stood in the temple of Harsaphes at Heracleopolis Magna (Hnes). The stela measures 1.05 by 0.44 m and has twenty horizontal lines of inscription. Above the text is a relief frieze consisting of fourteen standing figures and four hieroglyphs. This frieze is a rebus which reads in translation: "Honored by Harsaphes, King of the Two Lands, ruler of the riverbanks, lord of Hnes." The person "honored" is, of course, Somtutefnakht, the owner of the stela.

Since no king is mentioned by name, the historical events to which Somtutefnakht alludes have been interpreted in various ways. The consensus now is that Somtutefnakht began his career under Nectanebo II (359−341), passed into the service of the Persians who had reconquered Egypt in 341, and, from the Persian side, witnessed the big battles in which Alexander the Great defeated Darius III. Thereafter, inspired by a dream in which Harsaphes, the god of his hometown, appeared to him, he returned to Egypt and resumed his priestly office,. Dreams in which a god gives directions to the dreamer are recorded in Egyptian texts since the New Kingdom and play an important role in the Late Period.

Publication: *Urk. II*, pp. 1−6.   P. Tresson, *BIFAO*, 30 (1931), 369−391 and three plates (text, translation, and commentary).

Translation: Roeder, *Götterwelt*, pp. 214−219.

For additional references see Tresson, *op. cit.*, pp. 371ff.

On dreams and dream interpretation see: Bonnet, *RÄRG*, pp. 835–838.   S. Sauneron in *Les songes et leur interprétation*, Sources orientales, 2 (Paris, 1959), 19–61.

(1) The prince, count, royal treasurer, sole companion; priest of Horus, lord of Hebnu; priest of the gods of the Oryx nome;[1] priest of Somtus of Yat-hehu;[2] divine mouth, supervisor of the riverbank; chief priest of Sakhmet in the whole land, Somtutefnakht; son of the master of grain, (3) the priest of Amen-Re, lord of Pershat, Djedsomtu-efankh, born of the lady Ankhet; he says:

O Lord of Gods, Harsaphes,[3]
King of the Two Lands,
Ruler of the shores,
Whose rising illumines the earth,
Whose right eye is the sun-disk,
Whose left eye is the moon,
Whose *ba* is (5) the sunlight,
From whose nostrils comes the northwind,
To make live all things!
I am your servant,
My heart is on your water,[4]
I have filled my heart with you.
I sustained no town except your town,
I failed not to place its fame before all;
My heart sought justice in your temple (7) night and day,
You rewarded me for it a million times.

You gave me access to the palace,
The heart of the Good God[5] was pleased by my speech.
You distinguished me before millions,
When you turned your back on Egypt.[6]
You put love of me in the heart of Asia's ruler,[7]
(9) His courtiers praised god for me.
He gave me the office of chief priest of Sakhmet,
In place of my mother's brother,
The chief priest of Sakhmet of Upper and Lower Egypt,
    Nekhthenb.

You protected me in the combat of the Greeks,
When you repulsed those of Asia.[8]
(11) They slew a million at my sides,
And no one raised his arm against me.
Thereafter I saw you in my sleep,

Your majesty saying to me:
"Hurry to Hnes, I protect you!"
I crossed the countries (13) all alone,
I sailed the sea unfearing,
Knowing[9] I had not neglected your word,
I reached Hnes, my head not robbed of a hair.[10]
As my beginning was good through you,
So have you made my end complete,
You gave me a long lifetime in gladness.[11]

(15) O every priest who serves this august god,
Harsaphes, King of the Two Lands,
Re-Harakhti, Lord-of-All,
Beneficent Ram in Hnes,
Atum, foremost in the *Naret* nome;[12]
High priest of the Ram, the primeval force,
Servant of the Ram, the begetting bull,
Scarf-wearer[13] of the lord of the shores,
His-beloved-son[14] of the King of the Two Lands,[15]
You who enter heaven[16] and behold those in it—
Harsaphes, King of the Two Lands,
Atum within his robing room,
Khnum, great god in the chapel,
And the King of Egypt, Wennofer—[17]
Your names will last on earth,
With the blessings of Harsaphes,
King of the Two Lands, for saying:
"May the gods and goddesses in Hnes bless you,
The one blessed by his lord,
Revered in his nome, Somtutefnakht."
It will be useful to yourselves,
Another will pronounce your names in afteryears.

NOTES

1. The 16th nome of Upper Egypt.
2. The god Somtus, "Uniter of the Two Lands," for whom Somtu-tefnakht was named, had a sanctuary named Yat-hehu at Heracleopolis Magna (Hnes). Depicted with a falcon head, he was often identified with Horus.
3. Represented as a ram, Harsaphes, "He who is upon his lake," was the principal god of Heracleopolis Magna, the metropolis of the 20th nome of Upper Egypt. Associated with other great gods, he is here invoked in terms applying to the sun-god Re.
4. Metaphorical expression for "loyalty" and "devotion."
5. The king, and this must be King Nectanebo II, the last native king of Egypt.

6. An allusion to the reconquest of Egypt by Artaxerxes III.

7. The Persian king.

8. Stationed on the Persian side, Somtutefnakht witnessed the victories of Alexander the Great over Darius III.

9. In *BIFAO*, 53 (1953), 103–105, H. de Meulenaere showed that the word is to be read *rḫ.kwi*.

10. As Tresson observed, the phrase recalls the biblical expression, "Not a hair shall fall from his head" (I Samuel xiv,45; II Samuel xiv,11; I Kings i,52; and Luke xxi,18).

11. So, rather than "May you give me a long lifetime in gladness." Somtutefnakht is looking back on many years of turbulence which he lived through unscathed.

12. Harsaphes is here identified with Re-Harakhti and Atum. The sacred *naret* tree was worshiped at Heracleopolis.

13. A priestly title.

14. A priestly title.

15. Harsaphes is also given the designation "King of Egypt."

16. The temple.

17. In his temple Harsaphes was worshiped together with Atum, Khnum, and Osiris.

FOUR INSCRIPTIONS FROM THE TOMB OF PETOSIRIS

In the Necropolis of Hermopolis

Discovered in 1919, this sumptuous tomb was found to have been built by Petosiris, high priest of Thoth, for himself and for the members of his family. The inscriptions allow us to trace the history of the family over five generations, beginning with the grandfather of Petosiris. In each generation the men held the office of high priest of Thoth at Hermopolis Magna, the town which was the foremost cult center of Thoth.

Though no kings are mentioned, the building and decoration of the tomb is to be assigned to the end of the fourth and the beginning of the third centuries B.C. The historical allusions in the inscriptions make it virtually certain that the grandfather of Petosiris, Djedthothefankh (Djed-Thoth-ef-ankh) and his father Sishu (or, Nes-Shu) held office under the kings of the Thirtieth Dynasty. The elder brother of Petosiris, Djedthothefankh II, and Petosiris himself witnessed the second Persian conquest of Egypt (341–332). During this time Petosiris succeeded his brother in the office of high priest of Thoth, and for a period of seven years he also held the office of controller of the temple. In that capacity he rebuilt the temples that had suffered in the war. He probably still served the temple in the years following Alexander the Great's conquest of Egypt. His son and his grandson continued to build and decorate the tomb in the time of Ptolemy I.

The tomb has the appearance of a small temple. It consists of a transverse hall (pronaos) with a colonnaded facade, and a chapel almost square in shape. Four pillars support the chapel's roof and divide the space into three sections. Near the center of the chapel's floor is the covered pit that leads to the subterranean burials. These were plundered in Roman times.

The reliefs and inscriptions in the transverse hall are devoted entirely to Petosiris. All scenes and texts relating to his family are in the chapel. The reliefs reveal a certain amount of Greek influence, especially in a scene showing the family gathered around the tomb to make a sacrifice. The inscriptions contain materials from all periods. There are chapters from the Pyramid Texts and the Book of the Dead, sun hymns, and newly composed texts. Of special interest are a series of texts expressing the religious philosophy of life of Petosiris and his family, cast in the form of speeches by Petosiris and by members of his family. They center on the concept of the "way of life," which is also called the "way of God," and provide the most elaborate statements of personal morality and philosophy that have survived from the Late Period (apart from the Demotic Instructions). The life lived on the "way of God" is a life of rectitude, piety, success, and happiness.

Publication: G. Lefebvre, *Le tombeau de Petosiris*, 3 vols. (Cairo, 1923–1924).

Translation of several inscriptions: Otto, *Inschriften*, pp. 174–184.

On the "way of life": B. Couroyer, "Le chemin de vie en Égypte et en Israël," *RB*, 56 (1949), 412–432.

THE LONG BIOGRAPHICAL INSCRIPTION OF PETOSIRIS

Inscription No. 81

East Wall of Chapel, 92 columns

(1) His beloved younger son,[1] owner of all his property, the Great one of the Five,[2] the master of the (holy) seats, the high priest who sees the god in his shrine, who carries his lord[3] and follows his lord, who enters into the holy of holies, who performs his functions together with the great prophets; the prophet of the Ogdoad,[4] chief of the priests of (5) Sakhmet, leader of the priests of the third and fourth phyles; the royal scribe who reckons all the property in the temple of Khmun; the second prophet of Khnum-Re, lord of Herwer, and of Hathor, lady of Nefrusi;[5] the phylarch of the second phyle of the temple of Herwer and that of Nefrusi, the prophet of Amen-Re and of the gods of those places, Petosiris, the revered, called ⟨An⟩khef(en)-khons, born of the lady Nefer-renpet, justified; he says:

(10) O every prophet, every priest, every scholar,
Who enter this necropolis and see this tomb,
Praise god for him who acts (for me),
Praise god for them who act (for me)![6]
For I was one honored by his father,
Praised by his mother,
Gracious to his brothers.
I built this tomb in this necropolis,
Beside the great souls who are there,
In order that my father's name be pronounced,

And that of my elder brother,
A man is revived when his name is pronounced!

The west is the abode of him who is faultless,
Praise god for the man who has reached it!
No man will attain it,
Unless his heart is exact in doing right.
The poor is not distinguished there from the rich,
Only he who is found free of (20) fault
By scale and weight before eternity's lord.
There is none exempt from being reckoned:
Thoth as Baboon in charge of the balance
Will reckon each man for his deeds on earth.

I was on the water of Khmun's lord since my birth,
I had all his plans in my heart.
⟨He⟩ chose me to administer (25) his temple,
Knowing I respected him in my heart.
I spent seven years as controller for this god,
Administering his endowment without fault being found,
While the Ruler-of-foreign-lands was Protector in Egypt,
And nothing was in its former place,
Since fighting had started (30) inside Egypt,
The South being in turmoil, the North in revolt;
The people walked with ⌈head turned back⌉,
All temples were without their servants,
The priests fled, not knowing what was happening.[7]

When I became controller for Thoth, lord of Khmun,
I put the temple of Thoth in (35) its former condition.
I caused every rite to be as before,
Every priest (to serve) in his proper time.
I made great his priests,
Advanced his temple's hour-priests;
I promoted all his servants,
I gave a rule to his attendants.
I did not reduce the offerings in his temple,
I filled (40) his granaries with barley and emmer,
His treasury with every good thing.
I increased what there had been before,
And every citizen praised god for me.
I gave silver, gold, and all precious stones,
So that I gladdened the hearts of the priests,
And of all those who work in the gold house,
And my heart rejoiced (45) in it.

I made splendid what was found ruined anywhere,
I restored what had decayed long ago,
And was no longer in its place.

I stretched the cord, released the line,
To found the temple of Re in the park.[8]
I built it of fine white limestone,
And finished with all kinds of work;
(50) Its doors are of pinewood,
Inlaid with Asian copper.
I made Re reside in it,
The nursling in the isle of fire.[9]

I built the house of the goddesses
Inside the house of Khnum,
Having found their house was old.
They dwell in the temple of Thoth, lord of Khmun,
(55) "Festive chapel of the goddesses," people call it,
Its face is turned east.[10]
I built the house of Nehmetaway, ⌈the one who-made-what-is⌉,
And the house of Hathor, lady of the southern sycamore,
⌈The like of⌉ Nehmetaway, the mother of god.
I built them of fine white limestone,
Finished with all kinds of work,
(60) I made these goddesses dwell there.

I made an enclosure around the park,
Lest it be trampled by the rabble,
For it is the birthplace of every god,
Who came into being in the beginning.
This spot, wretches had damaged it,
Intruders had traversed it;
The fruit (65) of its trees had been eaten,
Its shrubs taken to intruders' homes;
The whole land was in uproar about it,
And Egypt was distressed by it,
For the half of the egg[11] is buried in it.
I made a solid work of the wall of Khmun's temple,
To gladden the heart of (my) lady (70) Nehmetaway,
When she sees this work every day.

Now when I was before this goddess,
Heket, lady of Herwer,[12]
At her beautiful feast of the year's last month,
I being controller of Thoth,
She went to a spot in the north of this town,

To "House of Heket," as it is called by all,[13]
Which was ruined since time (75) immemorial.
The water had carried it off every year,
Till its foundation plan was no longer seen,
It only was called "House of Heket,"
While no brick nor stone was there,
Then the goddess halted there.[14]
I summoned the temple scribe of this goddess,
I gave him silver without counting,
To make a monument there from that day.
I built a great (80) rampart around it,
So that the water could not carry it off.
I was diligent in consulting the scholars,
So as to organize the rites,
By which this goddess is served,
And content her till she knew it was done.

My lord Thoth distinguished ⟨me⟩ above all ⟨my⟩ peers,
As reward for my enriching him,
With all good things, with silver and gold,
With (85) harvests and produce in granaries,
With fields, with cattle,
With orchards of grapes,
With orchards of all fruit trees,
With ships on the water,
With all good things of the storehouse.[15]
⟨I⟩ was favored by the ruler of Egypt,
I was loved by his courtiers.
May this too be given me as reward:
Length of lifetime in gladness of heart,
A good burial after old age,
My corpse interred in this tomb,
Beside my father and elder brother,
I being blessed by (90) the lord of Khmun,
And also all the gods of Un,
My house maintained by my children,
With son succeeding son!
May he who comes hereafter say:
"A servant of his god till veneration day!"[16]

NOTES

1. The text is inscribed in that section of the chapel which Petosiris had dedicated to his father Sishu. This is why he begins by identifying himself as his father's younger son.

2. Title of the high priest of Thoth at Hermopolis.

3. I.e., who carries the statue of the god in procession.

4. The eight primeval gods whose cult had originated at Hermopolis.

5. Herwer and Nefrusi were important towns in the Hare nome, the 15th nome of Upper Egypt, of which Hermopolis (Khmun, Un) had become the metropolis (see *AEO*, II, 79*–87*). Petosiris held priestly functions in all three towns.

6. "Acting" in the sense of worshiping and reciting the prayer for offerings.

7. This description of turmoil probably refers to the final years of Persian domination and the beginning of Macedonian rule, when order was restored. The Greek elements in the decoration make it certain that the tomb was built after Alexander's conquest of Egypt, and so unflattering an account of disorder under foreign rule would hardly have been written in Macedonian times if it were meant to refer to a Macedonian, rather than a Persian, ruler.

8. As a rule only Pharaoh could perform the temple-founding ceremonies which Petosiris here carried out himself.

9. A region of the eastern sky where the sun-god was born. On "fire island" and "fire lake" see H. Kees, *ZÄS*, 78 (1943), 41–53, and H. Altenmüller, *ZÄS*, 92 (1965/66), 86–95.

10. It is not clear who the goddesses were for whom Petosiris built a "festive chapel" within the precinct of the temple of Thoth. They do not seem to be identical with the goddesses Hathor and Nehmetaway whose temples he also built, as told in the next lines.

11. This is the egg from which the sun-god was born in the beginning of creation. The parallel text in Inscription No. 62 has "the two halves of the egg."

12. The goddess Heket of neighboring Herwer was represented as a frog and worshiped as a giver of life. She was associated with Nehmetaway of Hermopolis and with the eight primeval gods of that city.

13. Literally, "from mouth to mouth."

14. I.e., carried through the town in procession, the goddess halted at the spot where a temple of hers had been to indicate her wish that it be rebuilt.

15. The phrasing of lines 83–84 does not make it clear whether the goods enumerated in lines 84–87 were given by Petosiris to the temple of Thoth or by the god to Petosiris in reward for his many benefactions to the temples.

16. Literally, "till reveredness," i.e., "till death." The word serves both as a term for old age and as a euphemism for death.

TWO SPEECHES OF SISHU FATHER OF PETOSIRIS

I. Inscription No. 116

West Side of Pillar A in Chapel, 6 columns

(1) An offering that the King gives to Osiris-Khentamenti, the great god, lord of Abydos, that he may give [an offering of a thousand of bread and beer, oxen and fowl, alabaster and clothing, ointment and] incense, a thousand of everything good and pure to the *ka* of the owner of this tomb, the Great one of the Five, the master of the (holy) seats, the second prophet of Khnum-Re, lord of Herwer, and of Hathor, lady of Nefrusi; the phylarch of the second phyle of the temple of Herwer and that of Nefrusi, Sishu, justified; he says:

> O you who are alive on earth,
> And you who shall be born,
> Who shall come to this desert,
> Who shall see this tomb and pass by it:
> Come, let me lead (3) you to the way of life,
> That you may sail with good wind, without getting stranded,
> That you may reach the abode of generations,
> Without coming to grief!
> I am a worthy deceased without fault,
> If you hear ⟨my⟩ words,
> If you cleave to them,
> You will find their worth.
> Serving god is the good way,
> Blessed is he whose heart leads him to it!
> I speak to you of what happened to me,
> I let you perceive the plan of god,
> I let you discern knowledge of his might!

> I have come here to the city of eternity,
> Having done the good upon earth,
> Having filled my heart (5) with god's way,
> From my youth until this day!
> I lay down with his might in my heart,
> I rose up doing his *ka*'s wish;
> I did justice, abhorred falsehood,
> Knowing he lives by it (justice), is contented by it.
> I was pure as his *ka* desires,
> I joined not with him who ignores god's might,
> Relying on him who was loyal to him.
> I seized no goods from any man,
> I did no wrong to anyone,

All citizens praised god for me.
I did this remembering I would reach god after death,
Knowing the day of the lords of justice,
When they separate in judgment!
One praises god for him who loves god,
He will reach his tomb without grief.

II. Inscription No. 127

North Side of Pillar C in Chapel, 6 columns

(1) [The one honored by Osiris, lord of Mendes, Osiris the Ibis][1]
Osiris the Baboon;[2] the Great one of the Five, the master of the (holy)
seats, [the second prophet of] Khnum-Re, lord of Herwer, and of
Hathor, lady of Nefrusi; the phylarch of the second phyle of the
temple of Herwer and that of Nefrusi, Sishu, justified; son of the
Great one of the Five, the master of the (holy) seats, Djedthothefankh,
(2) [justified; he says]:

[O you who are alive on earth],
And you who shall come after;
O every man who reads writing,
Come, read these writings that are in this tomb!
I shall lead you to the way of life,
I shall teach you your conduct,
[That you may reach] (3) the abode of generations!
If you cleave to my words,
You will find their worth,
And will praise god for me on their account.

Drink till drunk while enjoying the feast day!
Follow your heart in the moment on earth!
It profits (4) [⌜a man to make use of his goods⌝].
As man departs his goods depart,[3]
He who inherits them does his wish in turn.
There is no sunlight for the rich,
No messenger of death takes bribes,
So as to forget what [he] was sent [to do],
(5) — — — — — —;
He goes quickly like a dream,
No one knows the day he comes,
It is god's skill to make the hearts forget it,
But a torn up plant is he who is taken young![4]
His storehouse is rich in everything,
(6) — — — — — his heart.

God puts it in the heart of him whom he hates,[5]
So as to give his goods to another whom he loves;
He is the master of his riches,[6]
He bestows them on their owner.
Blessed is he who fears[7] his god,
So as to put these things in his heart.

NOTES

1. There is a lacuna of five to six squares at the beginning of each text column, and these lacunae hinder the understanding. The text is nevertheless noteworthy for its juxtaposition of several basic themes: the exhortation to observe the "way of life"; the advice to enjoy life and make use of one's possessions, for they cannot be taken to the hereafter; the allusion to the hereafter as a land of darkness; the observation that death cannot be bribed (a thought often found in Greek epitaphs of the Greco-Roman period); a reference to the misfortune of premature death; and the assertion that only the god is the true owner, and bestower, of wealth. All the thoughts expressed here are representative of Egyptian religious thinking in its final phase. It is worth emphasizing that the urge to enjoy life was an integral part of this piety. It was only when the "make merry" motif was coupled with doubts about the reality of the afterlife, as in the Middle Kingdom *Harper's Song from the Tomb of King Intef*, that it became impious (see *Ancient Egyptian Literature*, I, 195).

2. Osiris is here identified with Thoth, the "Ibis" and the "Baboon."

3. The thought that man cannot take his goods to the hereafter, which had already been expressed in the *Harper's Song from the Tomb of King Intef*, is here formulated with the brief pithiness of a proverb: *šm s šm ḥt.f*.

4. The calamity of a premature death had befallen a son of Petosiris, as we learn from Inscription No. 56.

5. Owing to the lacuna, the passage should be used with caution when discussing Egyptian views on God's intervention.

6. The god is the "master of riches," or, "lord of things," (*nb ḫt*); the same expression occurs in the inscription of the Berlin statue of *Harwa*, see p. 27.

7. The word is misspelled. Lefebvre, *op. cit.*, I, 161, and II, 91, took it to be the verb *wdn*, "sacrifice"; I think it is *snd̲*, "fear."

SPEECH OF THOTHREKH SON OF PETOSIRIS

Inscription No. 56

On Door of Chapel, 11 columns

(1) Speech of the Osiris,[1] the Great one of the Five, the master of the (holy) seats, Thothrekh, justified, son of the Great one of the Five, the master of the (holy) seats, the priest Petosiris, the revered, born of the lady Nefer-renpet:

O you who are alive on earth,
Who shall come here to this desert,

All who come to offer in this graveyard:
Pronounce my name with abundant libation,
Thoth will favor you for ⟨it⟩!
It is rewarding to act for him who cannot act,
Thoth will requite the deed of him who acts for me!
[He who praises my *ka*], his *ka* will be praised,
He who harms me, [harm] will be done [to him],
I am a man whose name should be pronounced!

Who hears my speech, his heart will grieve for it,
For I am a small child snatched by force,
Abridged in years as an innocent one,
Snatched quickly as a little one,
Like a man carried off by sleep.
I was a youngster of − − −² years,
When taken to the city of eternity,
To the abode of the perfect souls;
I therefore reached the Lord of Gods,
Without having had my share.

I was rich in friends,
All the men of my town,
Not one of them could protect me!
(5) All the town's people, men and women,
Lamented very greatly,
Because they saw what happened to me,
For they esteemed me much.
All my friends mourned for me,
Father and Mother implored Death;
My brothers, they were head-on-knee,³
Since I reached this land of deprivation.⁴
When people were reckoned before the Lord of Gods,
No fault (of mine) was found;
I received bread in the hall of the Two Truths,
Water from the sycamore as (one of) the perfect souls.

You shall last in life, you shall follow Sokar,
You shall see the face of [Re] in the morning,
(10) On the New Year's feast when he rises
In the great house of the temple of Khmun;
You shall follow Thoth,
On that beautiful day of the start of Inundation,
You shall hear the jubilation in the temple of Khmun,

When the Golden one[5] appears to show her love,
If you say whenever you come to this desert:
"May your *ka* have all good things,
Little child whose time passed so quickly,
He could not follow his heart on earth!"

NOTES

1. I.e., the deceased Thothrekh; he had inherited the family's priestly rank but had died before holding office.

2. It is not clear whether a numeral stood in the small lacuna.

3. The posture of mourning.

4. The word is *g3w*, "narrowness, want." It is characteristic of the texts lamenting a premature death that they refer to the hereafter as a place where one suffers want while yet describing it in traditional terms. The tenses employed in this sentence and in the following one could also be understood as referring to the future and rendered: "When I shall reach . . . no fault (of mine) shall be found," etc., but this would not yield a suitable sense; for the point of these laments over premature death is that the dead is reporting on his condition in the hereafter, a condition that differs from those deceased who had lived a full life in that he continues to feel deprived; see the inscriptions of *Isenkhebe* and *Taimhotep*, where this continuing sorrow is brought out very clearly.

5. Hathor.

SARCOPHAGUS-LID INSCRIPTION OF WENNOFER

From Saqqara

Cairo Museum 29310

The finely carved sarcophagus-lid is of white limestone and over two meters long. It dates from the Ptolemaic period. The sarcophagus itself has not been found. The surface of the lid is covered with reliefs and a long biographical inscription. The upper third of the lid has relief scenes arranged in five registers. They depict the sky and the adoration of the sun by numerous divinities. The biographical inscription begins below the fifth register and runs down the center of the lid in nine long vertical columns. Below it, in eight horizontal lines, is an additional text, not translated here, which is spoken by the knife-carrying demons that flank the central text on the right and left.

The presence of a biographical text on a sarcophagus is unusual. As a rule, the sarcophagi of the Late Period were inscribed with chapters of the Book of the Dead or other mortuary texts. The gist of Wennofer's autobiography is that he enjoyed his life.

Publication: Brugsch, *Thesaurus*, IV, 741–743.   G. Maspero, H. Gauthier, and A. Bayoumi, *Sarcophages des époques persane et ptolémaique*, Vol. II, Catalogue général . . . du Musée du Caire (Cairo, 1939), pp. 42–55 and pls. xiii–xv.

Translation: Otto, *Inschriften*, pp. 194–196.

Translation, with comments, of lines 3–5: F. Daumas, ZÄS, 95 (1968), 16–17.

(1) Speech of the prophet of Osiris, the royal scribe, Wennofer, born of Nephthys, justified:

> O my lord Osiris-Khentamenti,
> Great god, lord of Abydos, lord of Busiris,
> All the gods, and Maat, and the Great Council,
> Who are in the following of Osiris!
> And Horus in Roau,[1] Anubis, lord of Sepa,
> And Ptah in the eastern Memphite nome!
> I was one honored by his father,
> Praised by his mother,
> Gracious to his brothers,
> I did not do what you abhor upon earth.
> Give me incense for the city of eternity,
> Water for the graveyard of the west,
> For I am a man for whom one should act!

> (2) I was true-of-heart, impartial, trusted,
> One who walked on the water of god.[2]
> I was one praised in his town,
> Beneficent in his nome,
> Gracious to everyone.
> I was well-disposed, popular,[3]
> Widely loved, cheerful.
> I was self-controlled in the year of distress,
> Sweet-tongued, well-spoken.
> I was a good shelter for the needy,
> One on whom every man could lean.
> I was one who ⌜welcomed the stranger⌝,[4]
> A helpful advisor, excellent guide.
> I was one who protected the weak from the strong,
> So as (3) to be a ferryboat for everyone.
> I was a worthy noble who did the gods' wish,
> I was one gracious to his companions.
> I was open-handed to the have-not,
> My heart did not say, "Give me!"
> I was one who loved justice,
> Who hated wrongdoing,
> For I knew the god abhors it.

> I was a lover of drink, a lord of the feast day,
> It was my passion[5] to roam the marshes.
> I spent life on earth in the King's favor,
> I was beloved by his courtiers.

Dwelling in Ainu of the eastern Memphite nome
(4) —Roau it is called by name—[6]
I gathered my relations all together,
And every man of my town,
So that they were with me in heart's content,
And were wont to do what I said.

I fulfilled my life on earth in heart's content,
By the grace of the gods;
No worry entered the room I was in,
No sorrow arose in my dwelling.
Singers and maidens gathered together,
Made acclaim like that of Meret,[7]
Braided, (5) beauteous, tressed, high-bosomed,[8]
Priestesses richly adorned,
Anointed with myrrh, perfumed with lotus,
Their heads garlanded with wreaths,
All together drunk with wine,[9]
Fragrant with the plants of Punt,
They danced in beauty, doing my heart's wish,
Their rewards were on their limbs.[10]
I followed my heart inside the garden,
I roamed the marshes as I wished.

They know I am righteous, the prophets and priests,
(6) And the worthy ancestors of Egypt.
I did not take what belongs to gods and goddesses,
I always did what was good.
Slanderers conspired against their lord,
And slandered me before the judge;
When they saw my face they all shrank back,
They were condemned by the King in his time,[11]
His coiled uraeus[12] raged against them.
I left the King's house as one justified,
By the grace of the gods.

(7) Hail to you, gods of the Two Truths,
Excellent nobles, lords of the court,
Osiris-Sepa, most august of On's Souls,
Apis-Osiris-Khentamenti, gods of this holy place!
And Horus in Roau, Anubis, lord of Sepa,
And Ptah in the eastern Memphite nome!
Recall my good name[13] before Re when he rises,
And Atum as he sets in life, saying:
"O prophet of Osiris, royal scribe, Wennofer,

Born of Nephthys, the justified!
May incense be given you in the palace,
Libations in the Obelisk House![14]
May your bread be from the Souls of On,
May you receive loaves in the hall of the Two Truths,
Beside the great god in the graveyard;
May you receive libation in the southern necropolis,
Beside the lord of Rostau!
May you come and enter the bark of Re,
Your entry not barred by the revered ones;
May your *ba* alight in heaven behind Re's *ba*,
May your shadow walk upon earth!
The great graveyard extends her arms to receive you,
She unites you with the worthy ones.
Re, may he give you radiance,
May his rays flood your eye!
(9) Shu, may he give you sweet northwind,
Breath to your nose for life!
May Geb give you all his fruits to live on,
May Osiris give you Hapy to live and repeat your youth!
May your good name stay stay, last last
In the temple of Horus in Roau forever!
May your children's children stay after you,
Without ever ceasing on earth!
May he who comes hereafter say:
'A revered one who followed his god!' "

NOTES

1. The modern Tura, on the east side of the river across from Memphis. It contained the quarries from which the fine white limestone came. Sepa may have been within Tura; see Gardiner, *AEO*, II, 126*–128*.

2. I.e., One who was loyal to his god. Being on someone's water was a frequent metaphor for devotion and loyalty.

3. Lit., "good to see."

4. Lit., "I was an *'k h3* to him who was strange to him." *Wb.* does not list a word *h3* determined with the sign of the way (hieroglyph N31); perhaps it is only an unusual writing of *h3*, "hall."

5. Since *hm* does not really mean "majesty" it is not suitable to render *hr.t hm.i* as "the necessity of my majesty." *Hm* often means no more than "person" or "self" (cf. J. Spiegel, *ZÄS*, 75 (1939), 112–121).

6. The relation of Ainu to Roau was discussed by Gardiner, *AEO*, II, 128*–130*. Gardiner concluded that Ainu was "either an earlier synonym of Ro-au or else a rather more extended term for Ro-au and its neighbourhood." See also W. Helck, *Die altägyptischen Gaue* (Wiesbaden, 1974), pp. 148–149.

7. A goddess of music.

8. This rendering of the line is based on the remarks by P. Derchain, *RdÉ*, 21 (1969), 24–25.

9. The word for wine here is "the green Horus Eye."

10. I.e., they were rewarded with jewels. According to Daumas, *op. cit.*, the festivity described here was a Hathor festival.

11. I.e., the reigning king.

12. Lit., "His Mehenet-serpent," i.e., the serpent on his crown.

13. Lit., "Recall my name to good."

14. Lit., "Pyramidion House," i.e. the temple of Re at Heliopolis, or specifically its inner sanctum. The *bnbn* is the pyramidion on the top of the obelisk.

STELA OF ISENKHEBE

Leiden Museum V 55

A round-topped limestone stela of good workmanship, 0.52 m high. In the upper half the deceased, shown as a young girl, is worshiping Osiris and Isis. There are two text columns on the right behind the girl and two text columns on the left behind the gods. The two text columns on the left comprise the beginning of the main text which continues below the scene in six horizontal lines. In Boeser's publication the stela is included among the Saite monuments, while Erman believed it to be of Ptolemaic date. In Munro's recent study of Late Period stelae, where the stelae are arranged by probable provenience and date based on archeological criteria, the stela is classified as having come from the workshops of Abydos and as belonging to the early Saite period (ca. 650–630 B.C.).

Publication: C. Leemans, *Description raisonnée des monuments égyptiens du musée d'antiquités des Pays Bas à Leide* (Leiden, 1840), No. V 55, p. 281. P. A. A. Boeser, *Beschreibung der aegyptischen Sammlung des Niederländischen Reichsmuseums der Altertümer in Leiden*, Vol. VII (Leiden, 1915), No. 13, p. 5 and pl. xv.   A. Erman in *Sachau Festschrift*, pp. 103–107, text, translation, and comments.

Translation: Otto, *Inschriften*, pp. 187–188.

Archeological classification: P. Munro, *Die spätägyptischen Totenstelen*, Ägyptologische Forschungen, 25 (Glückstadt, 1973), pp. 284–285.

Behind the girl and behind the gods in four columns

(1) The one justified before Osiris, Isenkhebe,[1] justified; daughter of the stolist in Thebes, Nes-Shu-Tefnut, justified. (3) May there be bread for the belly, water for the throat, sweet breath for the nose of the one justified before Osiris, Isenkhebe, justified.

Below the scene in six lines

(1) She says:
I worship your *ka*, O Lord of Gods,
Though I am but a child!
Harm is what befell me,[2]

When I was but a child!
A faultless one reports it.
I lie in the vale, a young girl,
I thirst with water beside me![3]
I was driven from childhood too early!
Turned away from my house as a youngster,
Before I had my fill in it!
The dark, a child's terror, engulfed me,
While the breast was in my mouth![4]
The demons (5) of this hall bar everyone from me,
I am too young to be alone![5]
My heart enjoyed seeing many people,
I was one who loved gaiety!
O King of Gods, lord of eternity, to whom all people come!
Give me bread, milk, incense, water that come from your altar,
I am a young girl without fault!

NOTES

1. I.e., "Isis in Chemmis," a name common in the Late Period. For studies of the name see G. Vittmann, *ZÄS*, 103 (1976), 145, note b).

2. The sentence *ḥḏ nn ḥr.i* was rendered by Erman as "(Dich) der dieses an(?) mir schädigte," and by Otto as "Das (d.h. das Leben) wurde mir vermindert(?)." As Erman observed, *ḥḏ* is used as a circumlocution for death. This is also the case in the *Harper's Song from the Tomb of King Intef* (see *Ancient Egyptian Literature*, I, 197, n. 4). Thus the meaning is clear though the formulation is somewhat ambiguous.

3. The same sentence occurs in the stela of *Taimhotep* (see p. 63). It is one of several complaints expressing the idea that a person who has died young has been treated cruelly by the gods and finds no peace in the afterlife.

4. As we know from other texts, children were nursed till the age of three. But here the expression may have been used hyperbolically.

5. Lit., "Who is not in the right time for being alone."

STELA OF TAIMHOTEP

British Museum 147

A tall round-topped stela dating from the reign of Cleopatra VII. The relief scene at the top shows the lady Taimhotep worshiping Osiris and five other gods who stand behind him. Below the scene is the text in twenty-one horizontal lines. Taimhotep had been born in the reign of Ptolemy XII Neos Dionysos (Auletes). At the age of fourteen she had married Psherenptah, the high priest of Ptah at Memphis. She had borne him three daughters and at last the long-awaited son, and had died in the reign of Cleopatra VII at the age of thirty. On the mortuary stela erected for her by her husband she recounts these events and mourns her early death in the longest and most explicit of such laments over death found in Egyptian biographical inscriptions. The text should be seen together with the two earlier examples of this type, the speech of *Thothrekh son of Petosiris*, and the stela of *Isenkhebe*. Additional remarks on this genre have been made in the Introduction.

On his own biographical stela, dedicated by his son (British Museum 886), Psherenptah relates his accession to the high priesthood of Ptah, the birth of his son by Taimhotep, and his own death at the age of forty-nine, in the year following the death of his wife.

Publication: R. Lepsius, *Auswahl der wichtigsten Urkunden des aegyptischen Alterthums* (Leipzig, 1842), pl. 16.   G. Maspero, *Journal Asiatique*, 15 (1880), 411−416 (excerpts).   Brugsch, *Thesaurus*, V, 918−927. *A General Introductory Guide to the Egyptian Collections in the British Museum*, by H. R. Hall (London, 1930), p. 216, photograph.

Translation: Otto, *Inschriften*, pp. 190−194.

The final portion with the lament on death has often been translated, e.g.: Müller, *Liebespoesie*, pp. 35−36.   Erman in *Sachau Festschrift*, pp. 107−112 (with text).   Schott, *Liebeslieder*, pp. 144−145.   Bresciani, *Letteratura*, pp. 543−544.

Comments: P. Munro, *Die spätägyptischen Totenstelen* (Glückstadt, 1973), p. 165 and pl. 217.   D. Wildung, *Imhotep und Amenhotep*, Münchner ägyptologische Studien, 36 (Munich, 1977), pp. 68−70 and pl. 13 (photograph).

On the high priests of Ptah: J. Quaegebeur, *Ancient Society*, 3 (1972), 77−109.   E. A. E. Reymond and J. W. B. Barns, *Orientalia*, 46 (1977), 1−33.

For additional references see Wildung, *Imhotep und Amenhotep*, p. 68.

(1) A royal offering to Sokar-Osiris,
The god who presides over Sokar's chapel,
The great god in Rutisut;[1]
(To) Apis-Osiris-Khentamenti, King of Gods,
Lord of eternity, ruler of everlastingness;
(To) Isis-the-Great, the mother of god,
The eye of Re, the lady of heaven,
The mistress of all the stars;
(To) Nephthys, the sister of the god;
(To) Horus, champion-of-his-father,
The great god in Rutisut;
(To) Anubis upon his mountain,
The embalmer who presides over the shrine,
(And to) all the gods in Rostau,[2]
The beautiful west of Memphis:
May they give an offering of bread, beer, oxen, fowl,
Incense, ointment, and clothing,
And everything good from their altar
To the *ka* of (3) the Osiris, the princess,

Greatly valued, greatly praised,
Full of charm, well-disposed,
Much beloved by everyone,
Highly praised by her friends,
The worthy young woman, skilled in speech,
Whose words please, whose counsel helps,
Taimhotep, the justified;
Daughter of the god's beloved, god's father, King's friend,
Prophet of Ptah, priest of the gods of Memphis,
Prophet of Min, lord of Panopolis,
Of Khnum-Re, lord of Ptolemais,
Prophet of Horus, lord of Letopolis,
The initiate in Iatbaket,
The initiate in Letopolis and Iyet, Khahapi;
Born of the good musician of great Ptah South-of-his-Wall,
Lord of Ankhtawi,[3] Herankh; (5) she says:
O all dignitaries, all ritualists,
All grandees, all nobles,
All people who shall enter this tomb,
Come, listen to what happened to me!
Year 9, day 9 of Khoiak,
Under the majesty of the Lord of the Two Lands,
The God Father-loving Brother-loving Young Osiris,
The Son of Re, Lord of Crowns, *Ptolemaios, ever-living,*[4]
Beloved of Ptah and Isis,
That was the day I was born.
Year 23, day 1 of Epiphi,
Under the majesty of this Lord of the Two Lands,
My father gave me as wife to the Prophet of Ptah,
The scribe of the god in the house of books,
The prophet of the robing-chamber,
The priest of the gods of Memphis,
The chief prophet of the gods and goddesses of Egypt,
The eyes of the King of Upper Egypt,
The ears of the King of Lower Egypt,
The second after the King at the erection of the Djed-pillar,
The staff of the King in the temples,
(7) The prince in the seat of Geb,
The lector-priest in the seat of Thoth,
Who reenacts the creation by Khnum,
Who . . . . . .
⌜And the great god is born in their joining⌝,[5]

The Chief of the Master-Craftsmen,[6] Psherenptah,
Son of the like-ranked[7] Pedibast, the justified,
Born of the musician, the great ornament,
The singer of Ptah South-of-his-Wall,
Lord of Ankhtawi, Herankh, the justified.

The heart of the high priest rejoiced over it greatly. I was pregnant by him three times but did not bear a male child, only three daughters. I prayed together with the high priest (9) to the majesty of the god great in wonders, effective in deeds, who gives a son to him who has none: Imhotep Son of Ptah.[8]

He heard our pleas, he hearkened to his prayers. The majesty of this god came to the head of the high priest in a revelation.[9] He said: "Let a great work be done in the holy of holies of Ankhtawi, the place were my body is hidden. As reward for it I shall give you a male child."

When he awakened from this he kissed the ground to the august god. He gave the orders to the prophets, (11) the initiates, the priests, and to the sculptors of the gold-house also. He ordered them to carry out an excellent work in the holy of holies. They did as he had said. He performed the opening of the mouth for the august god. He made a great sacrifice of all good things. He rewarded the sculptors on behalf of the god. He gladdened their heart with all good things. In return he (the god) made me conceive a male child.

He was born in year 6, day 15 of Epiphi, in the 8th hour of the day, under the majesty of the Queen, the Lady of the Two Lands, *Cleopatra*, life-prosperity-health. (13) It was on the Offering-feast of the august god Imhotep Son of Ptah. His (the child's) appearance was like that of the Son of South-of-his-Wall.[10] There was jubilation over him by the people of Memphis. He was given the name Imhotep and was also called Pedibast. Everyone rejoiced over him.

Year 10, day 16 of Mekhir, was the day of my death.[11] My husband, the prophet of Ptah, prophet of Osiris, lord of Rostau, prophet of King *Ptolemaios*, the justified,[12] initiate of the temple of Ptah, initiate of heaven, earth, and netherworld, initiate of Rostau, initiate of Rutisut, the high priest Psherenptah brought me to the west. (15) He performed for me all the rites for a worthy deceased. He buried me in a beautiful burial. He made me lie in his tomb behind Rutisut.

O my brother, my husband,
Friend, high priest!
Weary not of drink and food,
Of drinking deep and loving!

Celebrate the holiday,
Follow your heart day and night,
Let not care into your heart,
Value the years spent on earth![13]

The west, it is a land of sleep,
Darkness weighs on the dwelling-place,[14]
Those who are there sleep in their mummy-forms.[15]

(17) They wake not to see their brothers,
They see not their fathers, their mothers,
Their hearts forgot their wives, their children.

The water of life which has food for all,
It is thirst for me;[16]
It comes to him who is on earth,
I thirst with water beside me![17]

I do not know the place it is in,[18]
Since (I) came to this valley,
Give me water that flows!

Say to me: "You[19] are not far from water!"
Turn my face to the northwind at the edge of the water,
Perhaps my heart will then be cooled in its grief!

As for death, "Come!" is his name,[20]
All those that he calls to him
Come to him immediately,
Their hearts afraid through dread of him.

Of gods or men no one beholds him,
Yet great and small are in his hand,
None restrains his finger from all his kin.

He snatches the son from his mother
Before the old man who walks by his side;[21]
Frightened they all plead before him,
He turns not his ear to them.

He comes not to him who prays for him,
(21) He hears not him who praises him,
He is not seen that one might give him any gifts.

O you all who come to this graveyard,
Give me incense on the flame,
Water on every feast of the west!

The scribe, sculptor, and scholar; the initiate of the gold-house in Tenent,[22] the prophet of Horus, Imhotep, son of the prophet Khahapi, justified, has made it.[23]

NOTES

1. On the reading of this Memphite place name see J. Quaegebeur, *CdÉ*, 49 (1974), 66, n. 1. The stela was discovered in the Memphite necropolis. I have found no evidence for the thesis of E. A. E. Reymond, *op. cit.*, p. 13, that Taimhotep and her husband had originally been buried in Alexandria.

2. Name for the necropolis and specifically that of Memphis.

3. Memphis.

4. I.e., Theos Philopator Philadelphos Neos Dionysos Ptolemy XII (Auletes). Taimhotep was born on December 17, 73 B.C.

5. It is not clear what ritual is described in this passage.

6. The title of the High Priest of Ptah at Memphis.

7. I.e., his father had also been high priest of Ptah.

8. The deified Old Kingdom sage whose cult was prominent in the Late Period, when he was given the rank of "Son of Ptah," and had a sanctuary at Memphis where he was buried.

9. The expression *m wp(.t) m3˹.t* has been much discussed. The most recent study is that of R. Anthes in *JNES*, 16 (1957), 176−185, where he rendered it as "determination of right." I continue to believe that B. Gunn (*JEA*, 27 [1941], 2−3) was right in thinking that it meant a "revelation" in a dream. See now the new discussion of the passage by Wildung, *Imhotep und Amenhotep*, pp. 69−72. The text does not specify where the high priest received his dream. We have encountered the inspiration through dream in the stela of *Somtutefnakht*.

10. I.e., like Imhotep Son of Ptah.

11. Taimhotep died on February 15, 42 B.C.

12. I.e., the high priest of Ptah was also the mortuary priest of the now deceased Ptolemy XII.

13. There are many different translations of this sentence. Erman, *op. cit.*, p. 108, interpreted the word written *i̱tw* as being *iwty*, "without," and rendered, "What are they, the years that are not on earth?" This translation was adopted by Otto and Schott, but it is not convincing. In my opinion, the context requires a sentence continuing the exhortation to enjoy life which is expressed in the preceding sentences. Moreover, the existence in the hereafter was not reckoned in "years," hence an expression "years not on earth" is improbable. Furthermore, the initial word *i̱hy* need not be the interrogative particle *i̱h*, "what," but is probably the verb *3ḫ*. On the *Naucratis Stela of Nectanebo I*, line 3, *3ḫw*, "benefits," is spelled *i̱ḫw*. Lastly, *i̱tw* is probably the verb *i̱ti* in the well-known sense of "spend, pass time."

14. Either the verb *dns* could be used transitively, or a preposition is missing. Again differing from Erman and others, I take *n nty imw* to stand for *n3 nty imw* and to form the beginning of the next sentence, not the end of this one.

15. This is probably the word *sm*, "form, image," rather than the word *sm*, "occupation."

16. I.e., "It is what I am thirsting for."

17. We have encountered this sentence in the inscription of *Isenkhebe*. The underlying idea, that those who have died young thirst for the "water of life," here receives its fullest development.

18. Or, "the place I am in." In either case the text needs to be emended.

19. On the word *ḥm*, here in the feminine form, see p. 57, n. 5.

20. As Erman observed (*op. cit.*, p. 111) this is a good wordplay on Coptic *mou—amou*, reflecting the actual pronunciation of the words in the Ptolemaic period.

21. I.e., Death, being cruel, even prefers the child to the old man. Note the rhyming pair, "his mother—his side," *mwt.f—rwt.f*.

22. A Memphite sanctuary.

23. The signature of the scribe and sculptor who composed the text and designed the stela.

II. *Royal Inscriptions*

The great *Victory Stela of King Piye*, on which the king narrates his conquest of all of Egypt, is the foremost historical inscription of the Late Period. It equals the New Kingdom Annals of Thutmosis III in factualness and surpasses them in vividness. It also paints the portrait of a Nubian king who was forceful, shrewd, and generous. He meant to rule Egypt but he preferred treaties to warfare, and when he fought he did not glory in the slaughter of his adversaries in the manner of an Assyrian king. Like all members of his egyptianized dynasty, he was extremely pious and especially devoted to Amun, whom he worshiped in his Nubian residence, Napata, and of course in the god's own hallowed city, Thebes.

Nubian rule over Egypt lasted less than a hundred years, and was succeeded by the rule of the vigorous Egyptian dynasty hailing from Sais, the Twenty-sixth Dynasty, which rebuilt a strongly centralized and prosperous state. Relations with Nubia were at first peaceful, but in 592 B.C. Psamtik II attacked Nubia and claimed a victory. A reconquest of northern Nubia by Egypt was out of the question, and just what prompted the king to attack is not known. In any event, the campaign recorded on the *Victory Stela of King Psamtik II* may be viewed as an act of revenge.

The *Naucratis Stela of King Nectanebo I* is a monument to the prosperous reign of the Thirtieth Dynasty, the last native dynasty of Egypt. Nectanebo I built extensively, and the quality of his monuments is high. Erected in the temple of the goddess Neith, in the predominantly Greek town of Naucratis, the stela bears witness to the material wealth contributed by the Greeks in their capacity as traders and manufacturers.

THE VICTORY STELA OF KING PIYE

Cairo Museum 48862

The large round-topped stela of gray granite was discovered in 1862 in the ruins of the temple of Amun at Napata, the Nubian capital at the foot of Gebel Barkal. The temple of Amun, erected in the New Kingdom, had been much enlarged by Piye. The stela measures 1.80 by 1.84 m and the sides are 0.43 m thick. It is inscribed on all four sides with a total of one hundred and fifty-nine lines.

The relief in the lunette shows on the left Amun enthroned, with Mut standing behind him and King Piye before him. Behind Piye King Namart of Hermopolis leads up a horse. With him is his wife whose right arm is raised in a gesture of prayer. In the register below are the prostrate figures of Kings Osorkon IV, Iuput II, and Peftuaubast. Behind them, also kissing the ground, are five rulers: the prince Pediese and four chiefs of the Libyan Ma (or, Meshwesh): Patjenfi, Pemai, Akanosh, and Djedamenefankh. The words inscribed before these subjected rulers are mostly destroyed.

Piye, King of Nubia, was in control of Upper Egypt, with an army of his stationed there. While at Napata, the news reached him that Tefnakht of Sais, the Great Chief of the Ma, who ruled the entire western Delta, was extending his conquests southward. He had formed an alliance with a number of chiefs, including King Namart of Hermopolis, and had turned south to besiege Heracleopolis whose ruler, Peftuaubast, was allied with Piye. Piye first decided to send reinforcements to his army in Egypt, and when this army failed to win decisive victories, he himself led another army into Egypt.

In the twentieth year of his reign, ca. 734 B.C., Piye sailed to Egypt. After halting at Thebes to celebrate the Opet festival of Amun, he tightened the siege of Hermopolis until King Namart surrendered. He then rescued the besieged Peftuaubast at Heracleopolis and received his homage. Thereafter he proceeded to capture the strongholds that stood between him and Memphis. The great walled city of Memphis, which refused to surrender, was stormed in heavy fighting. Then the rulers of the Delta hastened to surrender; only Tefnakht of Sais still held out. Eventually Tefnakht admitted defeat and, treating through an envoy, made his submission. Loaded with booty, a triumphant Piye sailed home to Napata.

The direct factual style of the inscription makes it a historical document of the first order. It is also the most important in a series of royal inscriptions of the Nubian Twenty-fifth Dynasty.

In recent years several scholars reached the conclusion that the name of the king, hitherto read Piankhy, was really Pi or Piye. In the latest discussion of the name G. Vittmann proposed that, whereas the Nubian form was Pi or Piye, the Egyptians understood it as Piankhy. Thus some scholars now write Pi(ankhy). I have after some hesitation chosen Piye.

Publication: Mariette, *Mon. div.*, pls. 1–6.   *Urk. III*, pp. 1–56.

Additional fragments: G. Loukianoff, *Ancient Egypt*, n.v. (1926), 86–89 and 2 plates.   D. Dunham, *The Barkal Temples* (Boston, 1970), pp. 12, 48, 77–81.

Translation: BAR, IV, §§ 796–883.   Bresciani, *Letteratura*, pp. 470–484.

Textual comments: A. H. Gardiner, *JEA*, 21 (1935), 219–223. K. H. Priese, *ZÄS*, 98 (1972), 99–124.   T. J. Logan and J. G. Westenholz, *JARCE*, 9 (1971/72), 111–119.

The reading of the king's name: J. Leclant, *OLZ*, 61 (1966), 152. R. A. Parker, *ZÄS*, 93 (1966), 111–114.   J. J. Janssen, *JEA*, 54 (1968), 172.   K. H. Priese, *MIO*, 14 (1968), 166–175.   J. von Beckerath, *MDIK*, 24 (1969), 58–62.   G. Vittmann, *Orientalia*, n.s. 43 (1974), 12–16.

Studies of the historical situation: J. Yoyotte in *Mélanges Maspero I*, 4 (1961), 121–181.   K. H. Priese, *ZÄS*, 98 (1972), 16–32.   K. Baer, *JNES*, 32 (1973), 4–25.   Kitchen, *Third Intermediate*, pp. 362–398. F. Gomaà, *Die libyschen Fürstentümer des Deltas*, Beihefte zum Tübinger

Atlas des vorderen Orients, Reihe B (Geisteswissenschaften), No. 6
(Wiesbaden, 1974).
For additional references to older studies see *PM*, VII, 217.

(1) Year 21, first month of the first season, under the majesty of the
King of Upper and Lower Egypt, *Piye beloved-of-Amun*, ever living.
Command spoken by my majesty:

"Hear what I did, exceeding the ancestors,
I the King, image of god,
Living likeness of Atum!
Who left the womb marked as ruler,
Feared by those greater than he!
His father knew, his mother perceived:
He would be ruler from the egg,[1]
The Good God, beloved of gods,
The Son of Re, who acts with his arms,
Piye beloved-of-Amun."

Tefnakht's advance

One came to say to his majesty: "The Chief of the West, the count
and grandee in Netjer,[2] Tefnakht, is in the nome of − − −,[3] (3) in the
nome of Xois,[4] in Hapy,[5] in − − −,[6] in Ayn,[7] in Pernub,[8] and in the
nome of Memphis. He has conquered the entire West from the coastal
marshes to Itj-tawy,[9] sailing south with a numerous army, with the
Two Lands united behind him, and the counts and rulers of domains
are as dogs at his feet.

"No stronghold has closed [its gates in] the nomes of Upper Egypt.
Mer-Atum,[10] Per-Sekhemkheperre,[11] Hut-Sobk,[12] Permedjed,[13]
Tjeknesh,[14] all towns of the West[15] have opened the gates for fear of
him. When he turned around to the nomes of the East they opened to
him also: Hut-benu,[16] Teudjoi,[17] Hut-nesut,[18] Per-nebtepih.[19]

"Now [he is] (5) besieging Hnes.[20] He has encircled it completely,[21]
not letting goers go, not letting entrants enter, and fighting every day.
He has measured it in its whole circuit. Every count knows his wall.[22]
He has made every man besiege his portion, to wit the counts and
rulers of domains." His majesty heard [it] with delight, laughing
joyously.

Then those chiefs, the counts and generals who were in their
towns,[23] sent to his majesty daily, saying: "Have you been silent in
order to forget the Southland, the nomes of Upper Egypt, while
Tefnakht conquers (all) before him and finds no resistance? *Namart*,[24]
[ruler of Hermopolis], (7) count of Hutweret,[25] has demolished the
wall of Nefrusi.[26] He has thrown down his own town[27] out of fear of

him who would seize it for himself in order to besiege another town. Now he has gone to be at his (Tefnakht's) feet; he has rejected the water of his majesty.[28] He stays with him like one of [his men in] the nome of Oxyrhynchos. He (Tefnakht) gives him gifts to his heart's content of everything he has found."

Piye orders his troops in Egypt to attack
and sends reinforcements

His majesty wrote to the counts and generals who were in Egypt, the commander Purem, and the commander Lemersekny, and every commander of his majesty who was in Egypt: "Enter combat, engage in battle; surround − − −, (9) capture its people, its cattle, its ships on the river! Let not the farmers go to the field, let not the plowmen plow. Beset the Hare nome; fight against it daily!" Then they did so.

Then his majesty sent an army to Egypt and charged them strictly:[29] "Do not attack by night in the manner of draughts-playing; fight when one can see.[30] Challenge him to battle from afar. If he proposes to await the infantry and chariotry of another town, then sit still until his troops come. Fight when he proposes. Also if he has allies in another town, let (11) them be awaited. The counts whom he brings to help him, and any trusted Libyan troops, let them be challenged to battle in advance, saying: 'You whose name we do not know, who musters the troops! Harness the best steeds of your stable, form your battle line, and know that Amun is the god who sent us!'[31]

"When you have reached Thebes at Ipet-sut, go into the water. Cleanse yourselves in the river; wear the best linen.[32] Rest the bow; loosen the arrow. Boast not (13) ⌈to⌉ the lord of might, for the brave has no might without him.[33] He makes the weak-armed strong-armed, so that the many flee before the few, and a single one conquers a thousand men! Sprinkle yourselves with water of his altars; kiss the earth before his face. Say to him:

'Give us the way,
May we fight in the shade of your arm!
The troop you sent, when it charges,
May the many tremble before it!' "

Then they placed themselves on their bellies before his majesty:

"It is your name that makes our strength,
Your counsel brings your army into port;
Your bread is in our bellies on every way,
Your beer (15) quenches our thirst.

It is your valor that gives us strength,
There is dread when your name is recalled;
No army wins with a cowardly leader,
Who is your equal there?

You are the mighty King who acts with his arms,
The chief of the work of war!"

They sailed north and arrived at Thebes; they did as his majesty had said.

Sailing north on the river they met many ships going south with soldiers and sailors, all kinds of fighting troops from Lower Egypt, equipped with weapons of warfare, (17) to fight against his majesty's army. Then a great slaughter was made of them, whose number is unknown. Their troops and ships were captured, and taken as prisoners to where his majesty was.[34]

Battle at Heracleopolis

They proceeded toward Hnes and challenged to battle. List of the counts and kings of Lower Egypt:

King *Namart* and King *Iuput*.

Chief of the Ma, Sheshonq of Per-Usirnebdjedu.[35]

And Great Chief of the Ma, Djedamenefankh of Per-Banebdjedet.[36]

And his eldest son, the commander of Per-Thoth-weprehwy.[37]

The troops of Prince Bakennefi and his eldest son, the Count and Chief of the Ma, (19) Nesnaisu of Hesbu.[38] Every plume-wearing chief of Lower Egypt.

And King *Osorkon* of Perbast[39] and the district of Ranofer.[40]

All the counts, all the rulers of domains in the west, in the east, and in the isles of the midst were united in their allegiance at the feet of the great Chief of the West, the Ruler of the domains of Lower Egypt, the prophet of Neith, mistress of Sais, the *setem*-priest of Ptah, Tefnakht.

They went forth against them; they made a great slaughter of them, exceedingly great. Their ships on the river were captured. The remnant made a crossing and landed on the west side in the vicinity of Perpeg. At dawn of the next day the troops of his majesty crossed over (21) against them and troops mingled with troops. They slew many of their men and countless horses. Terror befell the remnant and they fled to Lower Egypt from the blow that was great and exceedingly painful.

List of the slaughter made of them. Men: − − −.[41]

King *Namart* fled upstream southward when he was told, "Khmun is faced with war from the troops of his majesty; its people and its cattle are being captured." He entered into Un,[42] while his majesty's army was on the river and on the riverbanks (23) of the Hare nome. They heard it and surrounded the Hare nome on its four sides, not letting goers go, not letting entrants enter.

Piye resolves to go to Egypt

They wrote to report to the majesty of the King of Upper and Lower Egypt, *Piye beloved of Amun*, given life, on every attack they had made, on every victory of his majesty. His majesty raged about it like a panther: "Have they left a remnant of the army of Lower Egypt, so as to let some of them escape to report the campaign, instead of killing and destroying the last of them? I swear, as Re loves me, as my father Amun favors me, I shall go north myself! I shall tear down (25) his works. I shall make him abandon fighting forever!

"When the rites of New Year are performed, and I offer to my father Amun at his beautiful feast, when he makes his beautiful appearance of the New Year, he shall send me in peace to view Amun at his beautiful feast of Ipet.[43] I shall convey him in his processional bark to Southern Ipet at his beautiful feast of "Night of Ipet," and the feast of "Abiding in Thebes," which Re made for him in the beginning. I shall convey him to his house, to rest on his throne, on the day of "Bringing in the God," in the third month of the inundation, second day. And I shall let Lower Egypt taste the taste of my fingers!"

Then the army that was here in (27) Egypt heard of the anger his majesty held against them. They fought against Permedjed of the Oxyrhynchite nome; they captured it like a cloudburst. They wrote to his majesty—his heart was not appeased by it.

Then they fought against "the Crag Great-of-Victories."[44] They found it filled with troops, all kinds of fighters of Lower Egypt. A siege tower was made against it; its wall was overthrown. A great slaughter was made of them, countless numbers, including a son of the Chief of the Ma, Tefnakht. They wrote of it to his majesty—his heart was not appeased by it.

(29) Then they fought against Hut-benu; its interior was opened; his majesty's troops entered it. They wrote to his majesty—his heart was not appeased by it.

Piye goes to Egypt and besieges Hermopolis

First month of the first season, day 9, his majesty went north to Thebes. He performed the feast of Amun at the feast of Ipet. His majesty sailed north to the harbor of the Hare nome. His majesty came out of the cabin of the ship. The horses were yoked, the chariot was mounted, while the grandeur of his majesty attained the Asiatics and every heart trembled before him.

His majesty burst out to (31) revile his troops, raging at them like a panther: "Are you continuing to fight while delaying my orders? It is the year for making an end, for putting fear of me in Lower Egypt, and inflicting on them a great and severe beating!"

He set up camp on the southwest of Khmun. He pressed against it every day. An embankment was made to enclose the wall. A siege tower was set up to elevate the archers as they shot, and the slingers as they hurled stones and killed people there each day.

Days passed, and Un was a stench to the nose, for lack of air to (33) breathe.[45] Then Un threw itself on its belly, to plead before the king. Messengers came and went with all kinds of things beautiful to behold: gold, precious stones, clothes in a chest, the diadem from his head, the uraeus that cast his power,[46] without ceasing for many days to implore his crown.

Then they sent his wife, the royal wife and royal daughter, Nestent, to implore the royal wives, the royal concubines, the royal daughters, and the royal sisters. She threw herself on her belly in the women's house before the royal women: "Come to me, royal wives, royal daughters, royal sisters, that you may appease Horus, lord of the palace, great of power, great of triumph! Grant (35) ──────.[47]

(51) "Lo, who guides you, who guides you?[48] Who then guides you, who guides you? ⌜You have abandoned⌝ the way of life! Was it the case that heaven rained arrows?[49] I was [⌜content⌝] that Southerners bowed down and Northerners (said), 'Place us in your shade!' Was it bad that ─── with his gifts?[50] The heart is the rudder. It capsizes its owner through that which comes from the wrath of god. ⌜It sees fires as coolness⌝───. (55) ⌜He is not grown old who is seen with his father⌝. Your nomes are full of children."

He[51] threw himself on his belly before his majesty, [saying: "Be appeased], Horus, lord of the palace! It is your power that has done it to me. I am one of the King's servants who pays taxes into the treasury. ─── (57) their taxes. I have done for you more than they." Then he presented silver, gold, lapis lazuli, turquoise, copper, and all kinds of precious stones. The treasury was filled with this tribute. He brought a horse with his right hand, and in his left hand a sistrum of gold and lapis lazuli.[52]

His majesty arose in splendor (59) from his palace and proceeded to the temple of Thoth, lord of Khmun. He sacrificed oxen, shorthorns, and fowl to his father Thoth, lord of Khmun, and the Ogdoad in the temple of the Ogdoad.[53] And the troops of the Hare nome shouted and sang, saying:

"How good is Horus at peace in (61) his town,
The Son of Re, *Piye*!

You make for us a jubilee,
As you protect the Hare nome!"

His majesty proceeded to the house of King *Namart*. He went through all the rooms of the palace, his treasury and his storehouse. He (Namart) presented (63) the royal wives and royal daughters to him. The saluted his majesty in the manner of women, while his majesty did not direct his gaze at them.

His majesty proceeded to the stable of the horses and the quarters of the foals. When he saw they had been [left] (65) to hunger he said: "I swear, as Re loves me, as my nose is refreshed by life: that my horses were made to hunger pains me more than any other crime you committed in your recklessness!⁵⁴ ⌜I would teach you to respect your neighbors⌝. (67) Do you not know god's shade is above me and does not let my action fail? Would that another, whoever he might be, had done it for me! I would not have to reprimand him for it.⁵⁵ I was fashioned in the womb, created in the egg of the god! (69) The seed of the god is in me! By his *ka*, I act not without him; it is he who commands me to act!"

Then his goods were assigned to the treasury, and his granary to the endowment of Amun in Ipet-sut.⁵⁶

Heracleopolis reaffirms its loyalty, other towns surrender

There came the ruler of Hnes *Peftuaubast*,⁵⁷ bearing tribute (71) to Pharaoh: gold, silver, all kinds of precious stones, and the best horses of the stable. He threw himself on his belly before his majesty and said:

"Hail to you, Horus, mighty King,
Bull attacking bulls!
The netherworld seized me,
I foundered in darkness,
O you who give me (73) the rays of his face!
I could find no friend on the day of distress,
Who would stand up on battle day,
Except you, O mighty King,
You drove the darkness from me!
I shall serve with my property,
Hnes (75) owes to your dwelling;
You are Harakhti above the immortal stars!
As he is king so are you,
As he is immortal you are immortal,
King of Upper and Lower Egypt, *Piye* ever living!"

His majesty sailed north to the entrance of the canal beside Re-hone,[58] and found Per-Sekhemkheperre with its wall raised, its gate closed, and filled with all kinds of fighters of Lower Egypt. Then his majesty sent to them, saying: "O you who live in death, you who live in death; you poor wretches, you who live in death! If the moment passes without your opening to me, you will be counted slain according to the King's judgment. Do not bar the gates of your life, so as to be brought to the block this day! Do not desire death and reject life! (79) — — — before the whole land."

Then they sent to his majesty, saying:

> "Lo, god's shade is above you,
> Nut's Son gave you his arms!
> Your heart's plan happens instantly,
> Like the word of mouth of god.
> Truly, you are born of god,
> For we see (it) by the work of your arms!
> Lo, your town and its gates
> — — — — — —;
> May entrants enter, goers go,
> May his majesty do as he wishes!"

They came out with a son of the Chief of the Ma, Tefnakht. The troops of his majesty entered it, and he did not slay one of all the people he found. (81) — — — — — and treasurers, in order to seal its possessions. Its treasuries were allocated to the treasury, its granaries as endowment to his father Amen-Re, lord of Thrones-of-the-Two-Lands.

His majesty sailed north. He found Mer-Atum, the house of Sokar, lord of Sehedj, closed and unapproachable. It had resolved to fight. — — — — — —; fear of (his) grandeur sealed their mouth. His majesty sent to them, saying: "Look, two ways are before you; choose as you wish. Open, you live; close, you die. My majesty will not pass by a closed town!" Then they opened immediately. His majesty entered the town. (83) He sacrificed — — — — — —, [to] Menhy, foremost of Sehedj. Its treasury was allocated to the treasury, its granary as endowment to Amun in Ipet-sut.

His majesty sailed north to Itj-tawy. He found the rampart closed, the walls filled with valiant troops of Lower Egypt. Then they opened the gates and threw themselves on their bellies before [his majesty, saying to] his majesty:

> "Your father gave you his heritage,
> Yours are the Two Lands, yours those in it,
> Yours is all that is on earth!"

His majesty went to offer a great sacrifice to the gods of this town: oxen, shorthorns, fowl, and everything good and pure. Its storehouse was allocated to the treasury, its granary as endowment to (85) his father Amen-Re.

Capture of Memphis

[His majesty proceeded to] Memphis. He sent to them, saying: "Do not close, do not fight, O home of Shu since the beginning! Let the entrant enter, the goer go; those who would leave shall not be hindered! I shall offer an oblation to Ptah and the gods of Memphis. I shall sacrifice to Sokar in Shetit. I shall see South-of-his-Wall.[59] And I shall sail north in peace! − − − − − −. [The people of] Memphis will be safe and sound; one will not weep over children. Look to the nomes of the South! No one was slain there, except the rebels who had blasphemed god; the traitors were executed."

They closed their fort. They sent out troops against some of his majesty's troops, consisting of artisans, builders, and sailors (87) [who had entered] the harbor of Memphis. And the Chief of Sais[60] arrived in Memphis by night to charge his soldiers, his sailors, all the best of his army, consisting of 8,000 men, charging them firmly:

"Look, Memphis is filled with troops of all the best of Lower Egypt, with barley, emmer, and all kinds of grain, the granaries overflowing; with weapons [of war] of all kinds. A rampart [surrounds it]. A great battlement has been built, a work of skilled craftsmanship. The river surrounds its east side; one cannot fight there. The stables here are filled with oxen; the storehouse is furnished with everything: silver, gold, copper, clothing, incense, honey, resin. I shall go to give gifts to the chiefs of Lower Egypt. I shall open their nomes to them.[61] I shall be (89) − − −, [in a few] days I shall return." He mounted a horse (for) he did not trust his chariot,[62] and he went north in fear of his majesty.

At dawn of the next day his majesty arrived at Memphis. When he had moored on its north, he found the water risen to the walls and ships moored at [the houses of] Memphis. His majesty saw that it was strong, the walls were high with new construction, and the battlements manned in strength. No way of attacking it was found. Every man of his majesty's army had his say about some plan of attack. Some said: "Let us blockade (91) − − −, for its troops are numerous." Others said: "Make a causeway to it, so that we raise the ground to its wall. Let us construct a siege tower, setting up masts and using sails as walls for it. You should divide it thus on each of its sides with ramparts and [ᒥa causewayᒧ] on its north, so as to raise the ground to its wall, so that we find a way for our feet."

Then his majesty raged against them like a panther, saying: "I swear, as Re loves me, as my father Amun favors me, ... according to the command of Amun! This is what people say: (93) ' — — — and the nomes of the South opened to him from afar, though Amun had not put (it) in their hearts, and they did not know what he had commanded. He (Amun) made him in order to show his might, to let his grandeur be seen.' I shall seize it like a cloudburst, for [Amen-Re] has commanded me!"

Then he sent his fleet and his troops to attack the harbor of Memphis. They brought him every ship, every ferry, every *shry*-boat, all the many ships that were moored in the harbor of Memphis, with the bow rope fastened to its houses. (95) [There was not] a common soldier who wept among all the troops of his majesty. His majesty himself came to line up the many ships.

His majesty commanded his troops: "Forward against it! Mount the walls! Enter the houses over the river! When one of you enters the wall, no one shall stand in his vicinity, no troops shall repulse you! To pause is vile. We have sealed Upper Egypt; we shall bring Lower Egypt to port. We shall sit down in Balance-of-the Two-Lands!"[63]

Then Memphis was seized as by a cloudburst. Many people were slain in it, or brought as captives to where his majesty was.

Now (97) [when] it dawned on the next day his majesty sent people into it to protect the temples of god for him. The arm was raised over the holy of holies of the gods. Offerings were made to the Council (of the gods) of Memphis. Memphis was cleansed with natron and incense. The priests were set in their places.

His majesty proceeded to the house of [Ptah]. His purification was performed in the robing room. There was performed for him every rite that is performed for a king when he enters the temple. A great offering was made to his father Ptah South-of-his-Wall of oxen, shorthorns, fowl, and all good things. Then his majesty went to his house.

Then all the districts in the region of Memphis heard (it). Hery-pedemy, (99) Peninewe, Tower-of-Byu, Village-of-Byt, they opened the gates and fled in flight, and it was not known where they had gone.

Three rulers surrender

Then came King *Iuput*,[64] and the Chief of the Ma, Akanosh,[65] and Prince Pediese,[66] and all counts of Lower Egypt, bearing their tribute, to see the beauty of his majesty.

Then the treasuries and granaries of Memphis were allocated as endowment to Amun, to Ptah, and to the Ennead in Memphis.

Piye visits the sanctuaries of Heliopolis

At dawn of the next day his majesty proceeded to the East. (101) An offering was made to Atum in Kheraha,[67] the Ennead in Per-Pesdjet,[68] and the cavern of the gods in it,[69] consisting of oxen, shorthorns, and fowl, that they might give life-prosperity-health to the King of Upper and Lower Egypt, *Piye* ever living.

His majesty proceeded to On over that mountain of Kheraha on the road of Sep[70] to Kheraha. His majesty went to the camp on the west of Iti.[71] His purification was done: he was cleansed in the pool of Kebeh; his face was bathed in the river of Nun, in which Re bathes his face. He proceeded to the High Sand[72] in On. A great oblation was made on the High Sand in On before the face of Re at his rising, consisting of white oxen, milk, myrrh, incense, and all kinds of (103) sweet-smelling plants.

Going in procession to the temple of Re.[73] Entering the temple with adorations. The chief lector-priest's praising god and repulsing the rebels from the king.[74] Performing the ritual of the robing room; putting on the *sdb*-garment; cleansing him with incense and cold water; presenting him the garlands of the Pyramidion House; bringing him the amulets.

Mounting the stairs to the great window to view Re in the Pyramidion House. The king stood by himself alone. Breaking the seals of the bolts, opening the doors; viewing his father Re in the holy Pyramidion House; ⌐adorning⌐[75] the morning-bark of Re and the evening-bark of Atum. Closing the doors, applying the clay, (105) sealing with the king's own seal, and instructing the priests: "I have inspected the seal. No other king who may arise shall enter here." They placed themselves on their bellies before his majesty, saying: "Abide forever without end, Horus beloved of On!"

Entering the temple of Atum. Worshiping the image of his father Atum-Khepri, Great one of On.

Then came King *Osorkon*[76] to see the beauty of his majesty.

Piye holds court at Athribis

At dawn of the next day his majesty proceeded to the harbor at the head of his ships. He crossed over to the harbor of Kemwer.[77] The camp of his majesty was set up on the south of Keheny, in the east (107) of Kemwer.

Then came those kings and counts of Lower Egypt, all the plume-wearing chiefs, all viziers, chiefs, king's friends from the west, the east, and the isles in their midst, to see the beauty of his majesty. Prince Pediese threw himself on his belly before his majesty, saying: "Come to Athribis, that you may see Khentikhety,[78] that Khuyet[79] may protect you, that you may offer an oblation to Horus in his house, of oxen shorthorns, and fowl. When you enter my house, my treasury will be open to you. I shall present you with my father's possessions. I shall give you gold as much as you wish, (109) turquoise heaped before you, and many horses of the best of the stable, the choicest of the stall."

His majesty proceeded to the house of Horus Khentykhety. An offering of oxen, shorthorns, and fowl was made to his father Horus Khentykhety, lord of Athribis. His majesty went to the house of Prince Pediese. He (Pediese) presented him with silver, gold, lapis lazuli, and turquoise, a great quantity of everything, and clothing of royal linen of every number,[80] couches laid with fine linen, myrrh and ointment in jars, and stallions and mares, all the best of his stable.

He purified himself by a divine oath before these kings and great chiefs of (111) Lower Egypt: "Anyone who hides his horses and conceals his ⌜wealth⌝[81] shall die the death of his father! I have said this in order that you bear out your servant with all that you know of me. Tell if I have concealed from his majesty anything of my father's house: gold ⌜bars⌝, precious stones, vessels of all kinds, armlets, bracelets of gold, necklaces, collars wrought with precious stones, amulets for every limb, headbands, earrings, all royal adornments, all vessels for the king's purification of gold and precious stones. All these I have presented (113) to the King, and garments of royal linen by the thousands of the very best of my house. I know you will be satisfied with it. Proceed to the stable, choose what you wish, all the horses you desire!" Then his majesty did so.

Then said these kings and counts to his majesty: "Let us go to our towns to open our treasuries, that we may choose according to what your heart may desire, and bring to you the best of our stables, the finest of our horses." Then his majesty did so.

List of the northern rulers

List of their names:[82]

King *Osorkon* in Perbast and the district of Ranofer,[83]

King *Iuput* in Tentremu and Taan,[84]

Count Djedamenefankh (115) in Per-Banebdjedet[85] and Granary-of-Re,[86]

His eldest son, the general in Per-Thoth-weprehwy,[87] Ankh-hor,

Count Akanosh in Tjeb-neter, Per-hebyt, and Sema-behdet,[88]

Count and Chief of the Ma, Patjenfi in Per-Sopd and Granary-of-Memphis,[89]

Count and Chief of the Ma, Pemai in Per-Usirnebdjedu,[90]

Count and Chief of the Ma, Nesnaisu in Hesbu,[91]

Count and Chief of the Ma, Nekhthor-neshnu in Per-gerer,[92]

Chief of the Ma, Pentweret,

Chief of the Ma, Pentbekhent,[93]

Prophet of Horus, lord of Khem,[94] (117) Pedihorsomtus,

Count Herbes in Per-Sakhmet-nebetsat and in Per-Sakhmet-nebetrehsa,[95]

Count Djedkhiu in Khentnefer,[96]
Count Pebes in Kheraha and Per-Hapy,[97]
with all their good tribute [of] gold, silver, [precious stones], couches
laid with fine linen, myrrh in (119) jars, $-----$ of good value,
horses $-----$.

$---$ [after] this one came to tell (121) his majesty: " $------$
the wall $------$. He has set fire to [his] treasury [and to the ships]
on the river. He has garrisoned Mesed (123) with soldiers $------$."[98]
Then his majesty sent soldiers of his to see what was happening there,
he being the protector of Prince Pediese. They returned to report
(125) to his majesty, saying: "We have slain every man we found
there." Then his majesty gave it (the town) to Prince Pediese as a gift.

Tefnakht announces his submission

The Chief of the Ma, Tefnakht, heard it[99] (127), and a messenger
was sent to where his majesty was with cajoling words, saying: "Be
gracious! I cannot see your face in the days of shame; I cannot stand
before your flame; I dread your grandeur! For you are Nubti,
foremost of the Southland,[100] and Mont, (129) the mighty bull!
Whatever town you turn your face to, you will not be able to find your
servant there, until I have reached the islands of the sea! For I fear
your wrath on account of those fiery words which are hostile to me!

"Is your majesty's heart (131) not cooled by the things you did to
me? While I am under a just reproach, you did not smite me in
accordance with (my) crime. Weigh in the balance, count by weight,
and multiply it against me threefold! (But) leave the seed, that you
may gather it in time. Do not cut down (133) the grove to its roots!
Have mercy! Dread of you is in my body; fear of you is in my bones!

"I sit not at the beer feast; the harp is not brought for me. I eat the
bread of the hungry; I drink the water of (135) the thirsty, since the
day you heard my name! Illness is in my bones, my head is bald, my
clothes are rags, till Neith is appeased toward me! Long is the course
you led against me, and your face is against me yet! It is a year (137)
that has purged my *ka* and cleansed your servant of his fault! Let my
goods be received into the treasury: gold and all precious stones, the
best of the horses, and payment of every kind.[101] Send me (139) a
messenger quickly, to drive the fear from my heart! Let me go to the
temple in his presence, to cleanse myself by a divine oath!"

His majesty sent the chief lector-priest Pediamen-nest-tawy and the
commander Purem. He (Tefnakht) presented (141) him with silver
and gold, clothing and all precious stones. He went to the temple; he
praised god; he cleansed himself by a divine oath, saying: "I will not
disobey the King's command. I will not thrust aside (143) his majesty's
words. I will not do wrong to a count without your knowledge. I will

only do what the King said. I will not disobey what he has commanded." Then his majesty's heart was satisfied with it.

Final surrenders, Piye returns to Nubia

One came to say (145) to his majesty: "Hut-Sobk[102] has opened its gate; Meten[103] has thrown itself on its belly. No nome is shut against his majesty, of the nomes of the south and the north. The west, the east, and the islands in the midst are on their bellies in fear of him, (147) and are sending their goods to where his majesty is, like the subjects of the palace."

At dawn of the next day there came the two rulers of Upper Egypt and the two rulers of Lower Egypt, the uraeus wearers,[104] to kiss the ground to the might of (149) his majesty. Now the kings and counts of Lower Egypt who came to see his majesty's beauty, their legs were the legs of women. They could not enter the palace because they were uncircumcised (151) and were eaters of fish, which is an abomination to the palace. But King *Namart* entered the palace because he was clean and did not eat fish. The three stood (153) there while the one entered the palace.

Then the ships were loaded with silver, gold, copper, and clothing; everything of Lower Egypt, every product of Syria, and all plants of god's land.[105] His majesty (155) sailed south, his heart joyful, and all those near him shouting. West and East took up the announcement, shouting around his majesty. This was their song of jubilation:

"O mighty ruler, O mighty ruler,
(157) Piye, mighty ruler!
You return having taken Lower Egypt,
You made bulls into women!
Joyful is the mother who bore you,
The man who begot you!
The valley dwellers[106] worship her,
The cow (159) that bore the bull!
You are eternal,
Your might abides,
O ruler loved of Thebes!"

NOTES

1. I.e., born to be a ruler.
2. Netjer, not identified with certainty, may be the region of Buto; see Yoyotte, *op. cit.*, pp. 154 f.
3. The scribe did not fill in the nome sign. Probably the Harpoon nome, the 7th nome of Lower Egypt, in the northwest corner of the Delta, was meant; see Yoyotte, *op. cit.*, p. 154.

4. The 6th nome of Lower Egypt.

5. A name for the double nome of Sais; see Yoyotte, *op. cit.*, p. 155.

6. The sign is destroyed; a territory adjacent to Hapy must be meant.

7. A name for the marshy regions of Imau (or, Iamu), the metropolis of the 3d nome of Lower Egypt.

8. This town has not been identified.

9. The old residence of the Middle Kingdom, south of Memphis. It marked the southern boundary of Tefnakht's domains at the beginning of his new campaign.

10. Meidum in the Fayyum.

11. "House of Osorkon I," near El-Lahun and Gurob; see Yoyotte, *op. cit.*, p. 135, n. 1.

12. Crocodilopolis, the capital of the Fayyum.

13. Oxyrhynchos, the metropolis of the 19th nome of Upper Egypt.

14. A town in the 19th nome of Upper Egypt.

15. I.e., on the west bank of the Nile. The towns are listed from north to south.

16. A town in the 18th nome of Upper Egypt.

17. Town in the 18th nome of Upper Egypt, modern El-Hiba.

18. Another town in the 18th nome.

19. Aphroditopolis (modern Atfih), the metropolis of the 22d nome of Upper Egypt. These four towns on the east bank are listed from south to north, thus showing that Tefnakht had made a circular sweep.

20. Heracleopolis Magna, the metropolis of the 20th nome of Upper Egypt.

21. Lit., "He made himself into a tail-in-the-mouth," i.e., he encircled the town like a coiled snake.

22. I.e., each chief allied with him was encamped before a section of the wall.

23. I.e., the Egyptian petty rulers of Upper Egypt who were loyal to Piye.

24. Namart of Hermopolis was one of four Egyptian rulers who claimed the title "king" at this time. His domain was the Hare nome, the 15th nome of Upper Egypt.

25. Hutweret is Herwer, an important town in the Hare nome.

26. Another town in the Hare nome.

27. The fortress of Nefrusi.

28. I.e., Namart has joined Tefnakht and repudiated his allegiance to Piye.

29. Piye's charge to his army was explained by Gardiner, *JEA*, 21 (1935), 219–223.

30. I.e., they should not attack by stealth as in a game where one party tries to outwit the other.

31. The aim of Piye's charge was that his troops should fight a few large decisive battles rather than many small skirmishes. And he was confident that Amun was on his side.

32. I take this to be the word *tpy* of *Wb.* 5,292.15–16, rather than *Wb.* 5,291.17.

33. Gardiner rendered, "Boast not of being lords of might." But *nb*, "lord," is in the singular, and the "lord of might" is Amun, who is referred to in the next sentence.

34. I.e., to Napata.

35. Busiris, the metropolis of the 9th nome of Lower Egypt.

36. Mendes, the metropolis of the 16th nome of Lower Egypt.

37. Hermopolis Parva, the metropolis of the 15th nome of Lower Egypt.

38. The 11th nome of Lower Egypt.

39. King Osorkon IV of Bubastis.

40. Ranofer has not been definitely localized; see Gomaà, *op. cit.*, pp. 132–134.

41. A blank space.

42. Khmun and Un together formed Hermopolis Magna.

43. I.e., after celebrating the New Year's feast at Napata, Piye would proceed to Thebes in time for the feast of Ipet (Opet), one of the principal feasts of Amun at Thebes.

44. A fortress in the 18th nome; cf. *AEO*, II, 93*.

45. Priese, *op. cit.*, p. 124, discussed the various translations of this sentence and proposed to render: "When the third day had begun—Hermopolis having become rotten to the nose in that it lacked the free breath of its nose—Hermopolis placed itself on its belly." I do not find this convincing. Neither the reading "three days" is probable, nor the reading *m sp n ndm fnd.s*, which is too wordy to suit the terseness and economy of this narrative style. I read *m hnm fnd.s*. Furthermore, it is not likely that the decisive result of the siege, i.e., the town's turning too foul to be habitable, would be told in a parenthesis; and *iw* probably introduces the main clause, since this is classical Egyptian.

46. I.e., King Namart's crown.

47. A long lacuna: lines 35–50 are almost entirely destroyed. This missing portion contained the intercession of Piye's women, Piye's acceptance of the surrender of Hermopolis, and King Namart's appearance before him.

48. Piye is speaking.

49. Piye makes the point that his rule of Egypt had been benign. He had not oppressed the people and had contented himself with the loyalty of their rulers.

50. Perhaps restore: "Was it bad that the King of the Hare nome came with gifts?"

51. King Namart.

52. This is how Namart is depicted on the scene at the top of the stela, only the hands are reversed.

53. The eight primeval gods whose cult center was Hermopolis.

54. In *ZÄS*, 87 (1962), 115–116, E. Hornung discussed the meaning of *kf3-ib* and proposed "profligacy, recklessness" for this instance. This is suitable here but not in some other cases. In *Ancient Egyptian Literature*, I, 77–78, n. 27, I suggested that two different roots of *kf3* may be involved.

55. If this is the correct translation, the meaning is obscure.

56. In all conquered towns Piye allocated part of the booty to Amun of Thebes.

57. The ruler of Heracleopolis was one of the four rulers who claimed the title "king" and the only one who had remained loyal to Piye.

58. Modern El-Lahun; cf. *AEO*, II, 116*.

59. Ptah.

60. Tefnakht.

61. This probably means that Tefnakht would restore to the northern

chiefs the towns he had captured from them, in order to gain their help for the defense of Memphis and the Delta.

62. In *JNES*, 36 (1977), 296, M. Gilula pointed out that *nḥty* is the root *nḥt*, "believe, trust," and not *nḥi*, "wish, ask for."

63. Memphis.

64. Iuput II, ruler of Leontopolis (*T3-rmw*, *Ṯnt-rmw*), one of the four "kings."

65. This important Libyan chief ruled in Sebennytos (*Ṯb-ntr*), the metropolis of the 12th nome of Lower Egypt, and controlled a large territory around it, including the towns of Iseopolis (Per-hebyt) and Diospolis Inferior (Sema-behdet) see Yoyotte, *op. cit.*, pp. 159—161, and Gomaà, *op. cit.*, pp. 69—71. He had not joined Tefnakht's alliance, and along with Iuput and Pediese, he now came to make his submission.

66. The ruler of Athribis. He too appears to have remained neutral; see Yoyotte, *op. cit.*, pp. 162—163.

67. A town south of Heliopolis called "Babylon" by the Greeks. In *AEO*, II, 131*—144* Gardiner discussed it at length.

68. Ibid., pp. 141*—142* Gardiner examined the question whether Per-Pesdjet, the "House of the Ennead," was a place distinct from Kheraha or merely another name for it, and he leaned to the latter view.

69. The "cavern" means a source of the inundation. In addition to the "twin sources" of the Nile at Elephantine, Kheraha claimed possession of a source.

70. A god of the region, spelled Sepa in earlier texts.

71. Name of the canal of Heliopolis.

72. An often-mentioned sacred place in Heliopolis.

73. The principal temple of Heliopolis.

74. A symbolic act.

75. It is not clear whether the word is *ḏsr* and just what ritual act the king is performing.

76. Osorkon IV of Bubastis, the last of the four kings to surrender.

77. The 10th nome of Lower Egypt, the metropolis of which was Athribis.

78. The principal god of Athribis who was identified with Horus.

79. A local goddess.

80. Perhaps a reference to the number of threads in a fabric by which its fineness was determined.

81. Assuming that *š3w*, "worth, value, weight," could be used in the sense of a person's material worth, i.e., his wealth.

82. The list is arranged according to rank.

83. See nn. 39—40 and 76.

84. See n. 64. Taan has not been identified.

85. See n. 36.

86. Not localized with certainty; see Gomaà, *op. cit.*, p. 88.

87. Hermopolis Parva, see n. 37. On the two rulers see Gomaà, *op. cit.*, pp. 86—89.

88. See n. 65.

89. Patjenfi's residence, Per-Sopd (modern Saft el-Henna) was the metropolis of the 22d nome of Lower Egypt. His other town, "Granary-of-Memphis," has not been localized. This chief had not participated in Tefnakht's alliance. On the rulers of Per-Sopd see Gomaà, *op. cit.*, pp. 101—104.

90. Pemai was the ruler of Busiris. His predecessor, Sheshonq, had been a member of Tefnakht's coalition. On these dynasts of Busiris see Yoyotte, *op. cit.*, pp. 165–172, and Gomaà, *op. cit.*, pp. 60–67.

91. See n. 38. Nesnaisu had been an important member of Tefnakht's coalition.

92. This chief has not been mentioned previously. His town in the eastern Delta has not been localized with certainty; see Gomaà, *op. cit.*, pp. 105–106.

93. Two minor chiefs not previously mentioned.

94. Khem = Letopolis was the metropolis of the 2d nome of Lower Egypt.

95. Two fortresses in the 2d nome.

96. A town in the nome of Memphis; see Gardiner, *AEO*, II, 120*–122*, and Gomaà, *op. cit.*, p. 51.

97. Twin towns south of Heliopolis; see *AEO*, II, 131*–144.

98. I.e., Tefnakht had occupied the town of Mesed (Mosdai) north of Athribis, on the border of Pediese's realm.

99. When Tefnakht heard that the resistance of Mesed had been crushed he surrendered but without appearing in person.

100. The god Seth.

101. Or, "equipped with everything," referring to the horses.

102. See n. 12.

103. The nome of Aphroditopolis, the 22d nome of Upper Egypt.

104. The four kings: Namart, Peftuabast, Iuput II, and Osorkon IV.

105. This term for foreign regions south and east of Egypt seems to refer specifically to wooded areas. It could also be employed for woodlands within Egypt, as in the *Victory Stela of Psamtik II*; see p. 86, n. 2.

106. The inhabitants of Upper Egypt.

A VICTORY STELA OF KING PSAMTIK II

From Shellal

Found at the village of Shellal, near Assuan, in 1964, this stela turned out to be the duplicate of a previously known stela of Psamtik II found at Karnak. Whereas the Karnak stela is a fragment, the Shellal stela is complete. It is a round-topped stela of red granite, 2.53 m high. In the lunette, under the winged sun-disk, are the cartouches of the king. Below is the inscription in twelve columns.

It is an important monument, for it sheds further light on Psamtik II's Nubian campaign, a campaign already known from other sources, notably from Herodotus II, 161, from a fragmentary stela found at Tanis in 1937, from the Karnak stela fragment mentioned above, and from the graffiti which the king's foreign mercenary troops inscribed on two of the colossi of Ramses II at Abu Simbel.

The historical situation has been elucidated by J. Yoyotte and S. Sauneron in two articles (see below). In the earlier article Yoyotte pointed out that the numerous erasures of royal names of the Nubian Twenty-fifth Dynasty on their monuments in Egypt must have been the work of Psamtik II. These erasures and the campaign are evidence of renewed hostility between Egypt and the Nubian kingdom.

Nubian rule of Egypt had collapsed under the onslaught of the Assyrians. In the wake of that collapse relations between Nubia and Egypt had been peaceful. In rebuilding a strong unified state, the Twenty-sixth (Saite) Dynasty had at first viewed its Asiatic neighbors in the east, and not Nubia in the south, as the potential source of trouble. Now, perhaps following a Nubian move, Psamtik II not only went to war but undertook to wipe out the memory of the Nubian kings who had ruled Egypt. The time when Egypt could dominate Nubia had long passed, and the campaign did not change the fact that Nubia had become a strong independent kingdom with the capability of invading Egypt. In any event, Psamtik's erasures of Nubian royal names and his prideful victory stela may be seen as the somewhat delayed Egyptian reaction to the period of Nubian domination.

In addition to its historical interest, the text has some noteworthy literary features, notably the description of the king's sightseeing tour in the region of Elephantine with its evocation of a pleasant landscape of water and trees. The king had not himself led the army into Nubia, but had remained in this peaceful setting, and it was here that he received the report of the successful battle, a report which contains the remarkable expression "wading in blood as in water."

Publication: H. S. K. Bakry, *Oriens Antiquus*, 6 (1967), 225–244 and plates lvi–lix.

Studies of the historical background: J. Yoyotte, *RdÉ*, 8 (1951), 215–239.   S. Sauneron and J. Yoyotte, *BIFAO*, 50 (1952), 157–207 and four plates.

(1) Year 3, 2d month of summer, day 10 under the majesty of Horus: *Menekhib*; King of Upper and Lower Egypt, Two Ladies: Mighty-of-arm; Gold-Horus who graces the Two Lands: *Neferibre*; Son of Re, of his body: *Psamtik* ever-living; beloved of Khnum, lord of the cataract region, of Satis, lady of Yebu, of Anukis, presiding over Nubia. Good god, effective of counsel; (3) valiant king, successful in deeds; strong-of-arm who smites the Nine Bows.

His majesty was roaming the marshes at lake Neferibre,[1] circling its inundated land, traversing its two islands, viewing the sycamores of god's land[2] on its mud bank, his heart eager (5) to see the goodness (or, beauty), like the Great God traversing the primeval water. Then one came to tell his majesty:

"The troops your majesty sent to Nubia have reached the hill-country of Pnubs.[3] It is a land lacking a battlefield,[4] a place lacking horses. (7) The Nubians of every hill-country rose up against him,[5] their hearts full of rage against him.[6] His attack took place,[7] and it was misery for the rebels. His majesty has done a fighter's work. When the battle was joined the rebels turned their backs. The arrows did not stray from[8] piercing them. (9) The hand did not let loose.[9] One waded in their blood as in water. Not one bound pair escaped of the 4,200 captives. A successful deed has been done!"

Then the heart of his majesty was happy beyond anything. His majesty presented (11) a great sacrifice of oxen and shorthorns to all the gods of Upper and Lower Egypt, and an offering to the gods of the palace in the palace chapel. May he be given all life, stability, dominion, all health and happiness like Re forever!

NOTES

1. Since the titulary invokes the three gods of the border region, it is clear that the locality of the king's sightseeing was the region of Assuan and Elephantine, and that he had remained there to await the report of his army. This is confirmed by the Greek inscription which his generals Potasimto and Amasis left at Abu Simbel; see Sauneron and Yoyotte, *op. cit.*, pp. 187–188.

2. Here the term "god's land" can only refer to the woodlands of this area; see p. 84, n. 105.

3. It seems that Pnubs was located in the region of the third cataract, see Sauneron and Yoyotte, *op. cit.*, pp. 163 ff.

4. I.e., lacking a flat plain.

5. I.e., against King Psamtik. As so often in addressing the king, the report uses both the second and the third persons.

6. I believe that the word which Bakry left unread is a preposition, perhaps *m-ḫnt.f.*

7. I.e., the attack of the king's army.

8. Read *nwdw*, as clearly written on the Karnak stela.

9. Here, as in some other instances, *wnḫ* means "loosen," not "put on" (see *Ancient Egyptian Literature*, II, 211, n. 1).

THE NAUCRATIS STELA OF KING NECTANEBO I

Cairo Museum

Situated on the east bank of the Canopic branch of the Nile, some fifty miles from the open sea and ten miles from Sais, Naucratis had become the chief Greek town in Egypt. It had risen to this position as the result of the monopoly on Greek trade bestowed on the town by King Amasis, as we know from Herodotus II, 177. Though the monopoly as such had been ended by the Persian occupation of Egypt—for Persian dominion led to a dispersal of the Greek settlements there—Naucratis was still the foremost Greek town and a center of trade and manufacture in the time of the Thirtieth Dynasty.

Besides Greeks the town had a native Egyptian population and, belonging to the nome of Sais, it had a temple of Neith, the goddess of Sais. The stela of Nectanebo was found in the temple precinct.

It is a round-topped finely carved stela of black granite, measuring 1.58 x 0.68 m. In the lunette, under the winged sun-disk, King Nectanebo is shown presenting offerings to the enthroned goddess Neith in two symmetrical scenes. Below is the inscription in fourteen columns.

The orthographic peculiarities of the inscription, which impeded its understanding, were explained by the successive studies of Maspero, Erman, Sethe, Piehl, Kuentz, Posener, Gunn, and de Meulenaere which are listed below. Thus it seemed as if Gunn's translation of 1943 represented a more or less definitive rendering, except for two additional corrected readings contributed by de Meulenaere in 1959. Yet I have had occasion to show that, along with all other translators, Gunn had misunderstood the crucial portion of the text, the passage in lines 8–10 in which the king specified the terms of his donation to the temple of Neith. This passage had been taken to mean that the king was granting to the temple the entire proceeds of customs dues levied at Naucratis on imported goods at a rate of ten percent, as well as the proceeds of a tax, also assessed at the rate of ten percent, on all goods manufactured in the town. The true facts, however, are that the king's decree granted the temple one-tenth of the revenue derived from the seaborne imports that were subject to a customs tax, and one-tenth of the revenue obtained from the tax on locally manufactured goods, *the rate at which the two taxes were levied remaining unspecified*. Hence the belief of the translators, subsequently repeated in many books, that the Naucratis stela is evidence for the existence of a ten percent customs tax and a ten percent tax on trades is erroneous.

Publication: G. Maspero in E. Grébaut, *Le Musée égyptien*, Vol. I (Cairo, 1890–1900), pp. 40–44 and pl. 45, and in *CRAIBL*, 27 (1899), 793–795.   A. Erman and U. Wilcken, *ZÄS*, 38 (1900), 127–135.   H. Brunner, *Hieroglyphische Chrestomathie* (Wiesbaden, 1965), pls. 23–24, excellent photographs.

Translation: B. Gunn, *JEA*, 29 (1943), 55–59.   Roeder, *Götterwelt*, pp. 86–94.

Comments: K. Sethe, *ZÄS*, 39 (1901), 121–123.   K. Piehl, *Sphinx*, 6 [1902], 89–96.   Ch. Kuentz, *BIFAO*, 28 (1929), 103–106.   G. Posener, *ASAE*, 34 (1934), 141–148.   H. de Meulenaere, *ZÄS*, 84 (1959), 78–79.   M. Lichtheim in *Studies in Honor of George R. Hughes*, Studies in Ancient Oriental Civilization, 39 (Chicago, 1977), pp. 139–146.

(1) Year 1, fourth month of summer, day 13 under the majesty of Horus: Mighty-of-arm; King of Upper and Lower Egypt, Two Ladies: Who benefits the Two Lands; Gold-Horus who does the gods' wish: *Kheperkare*; Son of Re, *Nekhtnebef*,[1] ever-living, beloved of Neith, mistress of Sais. Good god, Re's image, Neith's beneficent heir.

She raised his majesty above millions,
Appointed him ruler of the Two Lands;
She placed her uraeus upon his head,
Captured for him the nobles' hearts;
She enslaved for him the people's hearts,
And destroyed all his enemies.

Mighty monarch guarding Egypt,
Copper wall (3) enclosing Egypt;
Powerful one with active arm,
Sword master who attacks a host;

Fiery-hearted at seeing his foes,
Heart gouger of the treason-hearted.

Who does good to him who is loyal,
They can slumber until daylight,
Their hearts full of his good nature,
And they stray not from their path.
Who makes green all lands when he rises,
Who sates every man with his bounty;
All eyes are dazzled by seeing him,
Like Re when he rises in lightland.
Love of him greens in each body,
He has given life to their bodies.

Whom the gods acclaim (5) when they have seen him,
Who wakes to seek what serves their shrines;
Who convokes their prophets to consult them
On all the functions of the temple;
Who acts according to their words,
And is not deaf to their advice.
Right-hearted on the path of god,
Who builds their mansions, founds their walls,
Supplies the altar, heaps the bowls,[2]
Provides oblations of all kinds.

Sole god of many wonders,
Served by the sun-disk's rays;
Whom mountains tell their inmost,
Whom ocean offers its flood;[3]
Whom foreign lands bring (7) their bounty,
That he may rest their hearts in their valleys.

His majesty rose in the palace of Sais, and set in the temple of
Neith.[4] The king entered the mansion of Neith, and rose in the Red
Crown beside his mother.[5] He poured a libation to his father, the lord
of eternity,[6] in the mansion of Neith. Then his majesty said:
"Let there be given one in 10 (of) gold, of silver, of timber, of (9)
worked wood, of everything coming from the Sea of the Greeks,[7] of all
the goods (or: being all the goods) that are reckoned to the king's
domain in the town named Hent;[8] and one in 10 (of) gold, of silver, of
all the things that come into being in Pi-emroye, called ⟨Nau⟩cratis,
on the bank of the Anu,[9] that are reckoned to the king's domain, to be
a divine offering for my mother Neith for all time (11) in addition to
what was there before.[10] And one shall make one portion of an ox, one
fat goose, and five measures of wine from them as a perpetual daily

offering, the delivery of them to be at the treasury of my mother Neith. For she is the mistress of the sea; it is she who gives its abundance.

"My majesty has commanded to preserve and protect the divine offering of my mother Neith, (13) and to maintain everything done by the ancestors, in order that what I have done be maintained by those who shall be for an eternity of years."

His majesty said: "Let these things be recorded on this stela, placed in Naucratis on the bank of the Anu. Then shall my goodness be remembered for all eternity!"

On behalf of the life, prosperity, and health of the King of Upper and Lower Egypt, *Kheperkare*, Son of Re, *Nekhtnebef*, ever-living. May he be given all life, stability, dominion, all health and happiness like Re forever!

NOTES

1. Nectanebo I, the founder of the Thirtieth Dynasty.
2. Lit., "who multiplies the sacred vessels." The Egyptian phrase consists of two words, hence the lexically precise translation would destroy the rhythmic pattern.
3. The usual meanings of *rḏw* are "liquid," "fluid," "moisture."
4. The king's exit from his palace and entry into the temple are told in the words denoting the rising and setting of the sun.
5. The goddess Neith.
6. Osiris.
7. Whether *ḥ3w-nbw* here means Greeks or Phoenicians, the Mediterranean Sea is meant.
8. A town "Hent" (i.e., "canal" or "watercourse") is not known from other records. Perhaps it was the harbor of Naucratis.
9. The Canopic branch of the Nile.
10. As I pointed out in the article cited above, this passage means that the temple of Neith was to receive one-tenth of the royal revenues collected at Naucratis from customs dues on imported goods and from a trades tax on locally manufactured goods. The rate at which the taxes were assessed is not stated.

III. *Two Pseudepigrapha*

The two monumental inscriptions known as the *Bentresh Stela* and the *Famine Stela* are examples of a genre that appears to have been favored in the Late Period. They are propagandistic works composed by priests that are disguised as royal inscriptions of much earlier times, the purpose of the disguise being to enhance their authority.

THE BENTRESH STELA

From Karnak

Louvre C 284

A stela of black sandstone, 2.22 × 1.09 m, found in 1829 in a small, no longer extant, Ptolemaic sanctuary near the temple of Khons erected at Karnak by Ramses III. The stela was brought to Paris in 1844. The scene in the lunette shows King Ramses II offering incense before the bark of Khons-in-Thebes-Neferhotep. Behind the king, a priest offers incense before the smaller bark of Khons-the-Provider-in-Thebes. Below the scene is the text in twenty-eight horizontal lines.

Though made to appear as a monument of Ramses II, the stela is in fact a work of either the Persian or the Ptolemaic period. It tells a wondrous tale of healing performed by the Theban god Khons-the-Provider. If the tale had been written on papyrus it would rank with other stories told about the gods. But in the guise of a monument of Ramses II it possessed a propagandistic purpose. Just what the purpose was does not emerg very clearly. Was it meant to glorify the two principal manifestations of the Theban god Khons: Khons-the-Merciful (*nfr-ḥtp*) and Khons-the-Provider (*p3 ir sḥr*)? Or did it project a rivalry between their two priesthoods? Was it also designed to recall the glory of Egypt's native kings at a time of foreign—Persian or Ptolemaic—domination?

Publication: P. Tresson, *RB*, 42 (1933), 57–78 and pl. I.   A. de Buck, *Egyptian Readingbook* (Leiden, 1948), pp. 106–109.   Kitchen, *Inscriptions*, II, 284–287.

Translation: *BAR* III, §§ 429–447.   Lefebvre, *Romans*, pp. 221–232.   J. A. Wilson in *ANET*, pp. 29–31.   Brunner-Traut, *Märchen*, pp. 163–167.   Bresciani, *Letteratura*, pp. 533–536.

Comments: A. Erman, *ZÄS*, 21 (1883), 54–60.   W. Spiegelberg, *RT*, 28 (1906), 181.   G. Posener, *BIFAO*, 34 (1934), 75–81.   G. Lefebvre, *CdE*, 19 (1944), 214–218.   S. Donadoni, *MDIK*, 15 (1957) 47–50.

For additional references see Lefebvre, *Romans*, pp. 224–225.

(1) Horus: Mighty bull, beautiful of crowns; Two Ladies: Abiding in kingship like Atum; Gold-Horus: Strong-armed smiter of the Nine Bows; the King of Upper and Lower Egypt, Lord of the Two Lands: *Usermare-sotpenre*; the Son of Re, of his body: *Ramesse beloved of Amun*,[1] beloved of Amen-Re, lord of Thrones-of-the-Two-Lands, and of the Ennead, mistress of Thebes.

> Good god, Amun's son,
> Offspring of Harakhti,
> Glorious seed of the All-Lord,
> Begotten by Kamutef,
> King of Egypt, ruler of Red Lands,
> Sovereign who seized the Nine Bows;
> Whom victory was foretold as he came from the womb,
> Whom valor was given while in the egg,
> Bull firm of heart as he treads the arena,
> Godly king going forth like Mont on victory day,
> Great of strength like the Son of Nut!

When his majesty was in Nahrin according to his annual custom,[2] the princes of every foreign land came bowing in peace to the might of his majesty from as far as the farthest marshlands. Their gifts of gold, silver, lapis lazuli, (5) turquoise, and every kind of plant of god's land[3] were on their backs, and each was outdoing his fellow. The prince of Bakhtan[4] had also sent his gifts and had placed his eldest daughter in front of them, worshiping his majesty and begging life from him. The woman pleased the heart of his majesty greatly and beyond anything. So her titulary was established as Great Royal Wife *Nefrure*.[5] When his majesty returned to Egypt, she did all that a queen does.

It happened in year 23,[6] second month of summer, day 22, while his majesty was in Thebes-the-victorious, the mistress of cities, performing the rites for his father Amen-Re, lord of Thrones-of-the-Two-Lands, at his beautiful feast of Southern Ipet, his favorite place since the beginning, that one came to say to his majesty: "A messenger of the prince of Bakhtan has come with many gifts for the queen." He was brought before his majesty with his gifts and said, saluting his majesty: "Hail to you, Sun of the Nine Bows! Truly, we live through you!" And kissing the ground before his majesty he spoke again before his majesty, saying: "I have come to you, O King, my lord, on account of Bentresh,[7] the younger sister of Queen *Nefrure*. A malady has seized her body. May your majesty send a learned man to see her!"

His majesty said: "Bring me the personnel of the House of Life[8] and the council (10) of the residence." They were ushered in to him immediately. His majesty said: "You have been summoned in order to hear this matter: bring me one wise of heart with fingers skilled in writing from among you." Then the royal scribe Thothemheb came before his majesty, and his majesty ordered him to proceed to Bakhtan with the messenger.

The learned man reached Bakhtan. He found Bentresh to be possessed by a spirit; he found him to be an enemy whom one could fight.[9] Then the prince of Bakhtan sent again to his majesty, saying: "O King, my lord, may your majesty command to send a god [to fight against this spirit!" The message reached] his majesty in year 26, first month of summer, during the feast of Amun while his majesty was in Thebes. His majesty reported to Khons-in-Thebes-Neferhotep, saying: "My good lord, I report to you about the daughter of the prince of Bakhtan." Then Khons-in-Thebes-Neferhotep proceeded to Khons-the-Provider, the great god who expels disease demons.[10] His majesty spoke to Khons-in-Thebes-Neferhotep: "My good lord, if you turn your face to (15) Khons-the-Provider, the great god who expels disease demons, he shall be dispatched to Bakhtan." Strong approval twice.[11] His majesty said: "Give your magical protection to him, and I shall dispatch his majesty to Bakhtan to save the daughter of the prince of Bakhtan." Very strong approval by Khons-in-Thebes-Neferhotep. He made magical protection for Khons-the-Provider-in-Thebes four times. His majesty commanded to let Khons-the-Provider-in-Thebes proceed to the great bark with five boats and a chariot, and many horses from east and west.[12]

This god arrived in Bakhtan at the end of one year and five months.[13] The prince of Bakhtan came with his soldiers and officials before Khons-the-Provider. He placed himself on his belly, saying: "You have come to us to be gracious to us, as commanded by the King of Upper and Lower Egypt, *Usermare-sotpenre!*" Then the god proceeded to the place where Bentresh was. He made magical protection for the daughter of the prince of Bakhtan, and she became well instantly.

Then spoke the spirit who was with her[14] to Khons-the-Provider-in-Thebes: "Welcome in peace, great god who expels disease demons! Bakhtan is your home, its people are your servants, I am your servant! (20) I shall go to the place from which I came, so as to set your heart at rest about that which you came for. May your majesty command to make a feast day with me and the prince of Bakhtan!" Then the god motioned approval to his priest, saying: "Let the prince of Bakhtan make a great offering before this spirit."

Now while this took place between Khons-the-Provider-in-Thebes and the spirit, the prince of Bakhtan stood by with his soldiers and was very frightened. Then he made a great offering to Khons-the-Provider-in-Thebes and the spirit; and the prince of Bakhtan made a feast day for them. Then the spirit went in peace to where he wished, as commanded by Khons-the-Provider-in-Thebes. The prince of Bakhtan rejoiced very greatly together with everyone in Bakhtan.

Then he schemed with his heart, saying: "I will make the god stay here in Bakhtan. I will not let him go to Egypt." So the god spent three years and nine months in Bakhtan. Then, as the prince of Bakhtan slept on his bed, he saw the god come out of his shrine as a falcon of gold and fly up to the sky toward Egypt. (25) He awoke in terror and said to the priest of Khons-the-Provider-in-Thebes: "The god is still here with us! He shall go to Thebes! His chariot shall go to Egypt!" Then the prince of Bakhtan let the god proceed to Egypt, having given him many gifts of every good thing and very many soldiers and horses.

They arrived in peace in Thebes. Khons-the-Provider-in-Thebes went to the house of Khons-in-Thebes-Neferhotep. He placed the gifts of every good thing which the prince of Bakhtan had given him before Khons-in-Thebes-Neferhotep, without giving anything to his (own) house.[15] Khons-the-Provider-in-Thebes arrived in his house in peace in year 33, second month of winter, day 19, of the King of Upper and Lower Egypt, *Usermare-sotpenre*, given eternal life like Re.

NOTES

1. The two principal royal names are those of Ramses II, but the Horus, Two-Ladies, and Gold-Horus names are mistakenly composed, being derived from the titulary of Thutmosis IV.

2. The land of Mitanni on the Upper Euphrates had been reached by Thutmosis I and III, but Ramses II had never been there.

3. On "god's land" meaning wooded regions see pp. 84, n. 105 and 86, n. 2.

4. It has been surmised that the name "Bakhtan" is a corrupted Egyptian version of the name of Bactria; see Lefebvre, *Romans*, p. 222.

5. The historical marriage of Ramses II with a Hittite princess who was given the Egyptian name Maatnefrure is the basis for this fictional marriage.

6. The scribe wrote "year 15," but the easy emendation to "year 23," first proposed by Erman, is very probable in view of the dates given later.

7. This may be a Canaanite name (see Lefebvre, *Romans*, p. 222, n. 7).

8. On the "House of Life" see p. 36, n. 10.

9. The learned scribe Thothemheb diagnosed the malady as one that might be cured, but he himself could not effect the cure, i.e., expel the demon.

10. The Theban god Khons was worshiped under several distinct manifestations, with Khons-in-Thebes-Neferhotep occupying the leading position, while the most outstanding trait of Khons-*p3-ir-shr* was that of a healer. The epithet *p3 ir shr* has been translated in various ways, including "he who determines fate." Bearing in mind that we do not know the exact shade of meaning, I have preferred "the Provider." See also p. 33, n. 4.

11. A movement on the part of the god's statue signifying approval.

12. The chariot and horses were needed for the overland part of the journey.

13. The remoteness of the land of Bakhtan is indicated in fairy-tale manner by the extreme length of the journey.

14. I.e., "who had been in her."

15. I.e., Khons-the-Provider delivered all the presents to his superior, Khons-in-Thebes-Neferhotep, without keeping anything for his own temple.

THE FAMINE STELA

On Sehel Island

The inscription is carved in thirty-two columns on the face of a granite rock where it was given the shape of a rectangular stela. The rock face is split by a broad horizontal fissure, which already existed when the inscription was carved. After the carving, further ruptures occurred in the rock, and they have caused a number of textual lacunae. Above the text is a relief scene showing King Djoser offering to Khnum-Re, Satis, and Anukis, the gods of the cataract region.

The stela purports to be a decree by King Djoser of the Third Dynasty addressed to a "Governor of the South" stationed at Elephantine. In it the king informs the governor that, distressed over the country's seven-year famine, he had consulted a priest of Imhotep. After a study of the sacred books, the priest had informed him in detail about the temple of Khnum at Elephantine, and how Khnum controlled the flow of the inundation. The priest had also named to him all the minerals, precious stones, and building stones found in the border region. In the following night the king had seen Khnum in his dream, and the god had promised him an end to the famine. In gratitude to the god, the king now issues a decree granting to the temple of Khnum of Elephantine a share of all the revenue derived from the region extending from Elephantine south to Takompso, a distance of "twelve *iter*." In addition, a share of all Nubian imports was to be given to the temple. The governor was charged with carrying out the decree.

In its present form, the text is undoubtedly a work of the Ptolemaic period. Some scholars have surmised that it was based on a genuine Old Kingdom decree from the time of Djoser. Others take it to be a complete fiction. In any case, the text puts forth a claim to revenue on behalf of the Khnum temple of Elephantine.

Who stood behind this claim? According to P. Barguet, it was Ptolemy V who issued the decree as a means of proclaiming Ptolemaic control of this Nubian region. H. de Meulenaere countered this suggestion by asking whether the "governor of the south," who bore the non-Egyptian name Mesir, may not have been a Nubian chief ruling the area in defiance of the Ptolemaic king. The most plausible hypothesis, it seems to me, is the one that sees the inscription as the work of the priesthood of the Khnum temple, who were anxious to strengthen their privileges in the face of the encroaching claims made by the clergy of Isis of Philae.

The extent of the "12-*iter* land" or, Dodekaschoinos, has also been much discussed, for the location of Takompso, mentioned as its southern limit, is not known, and the length of the *iter* appears to have varied. The problem now seems to have been settled in favor of an *iter* usually averaging 10.5 km, except for a much shorter *iter* indicated by the boundary stelae of Akhenaten at El-Amarna (see the new studies of A. Schwab-Schlott). Thus, the "12-*iter* land" would designate the northern half of Lower Nubia, extending south from Elephantine for a length of about eighty miles.

Barguet's good edition has greatly advanced the understanding of this difficult text. There remain a number of problems and uncertainties.

Publication: H. K. Brugsch, *Die biblischen sieben Jahre der Hungersnoth* (*Leipzig, 1891*).   P. Barguet, *La stèle de la famine à Séhel*, Institut français d'archéologie orientale, Bibliothèque d'étude, 34 (Cairo, 1953).

Translation: G. Roeder, *Urkunden zur Religion des alten Ägypten* (Jena, 1915), pp. 177–184.

Translation of excerpts: J. Vandier, *La famine dans l'Égypte ancienne*, Institut français d'archéologie orientale, Recherches, 7 (Cairo, 1936), pp. 38–44 and 132–139.   J. A. Wilson in *ANET*, pp. 31–32.

Studies and comments: K. Sethe, *Dodekaschoinos das Zwölfmeilenland an der Grenze von Aegypten und Nubien*, Untersuchungen, II/3 (Leipzig, 1901; reprint Hildesheim, 1964).   K. Sethe, *ZÄS*, 41 (1904), 58–62.   W. Schubart, *ZÄS*, 47 (1910), 154–157.   H. de Meulenaere, *Bibliotheca Orientalis*, 14 (1957), 33–34, review of Barguet's publication.   H. Brunner, "Die Hungersnotstele" in *Kindler's Literatur Lexikon*, III (Zurich, 1967), cols. 2255–2256.   D. Wildung, *Die Rolle ägyptischer Könige im Bewusstsein ihrer Nachwelt*, Vol. I, Münchner ägyptologische Studien, 17 (Berlin, 1969), pp. 85–91.   A. Schwab-Schlott, *Die Ausmasse Ägyptens nach altägyptischen Texten*. Dissertation, University of Tübingen, 1969; *idem, MDIK*, 28 (1972), 109–113; *idem*, "Dodekaschoinos" in *Lexikon der Ägyptologie*, Vol. I (Wiesbaden, 1975), cols. 1112–1113.   M. Lichtheim in *Studies in Honor of George R. Hughes*, Studies in Ancient Oriental Civilization, 39 (Chicago, 1977), pp. 142–144.

On the stones and metals consult: Harris, *Minerals*.

(1) Year 18 of Horus: *Neterkhet*; the King of Upper and Lower Egypt: Neterkhet; Two Ladies: Neterkhet; Gold-Horus: *Djoser*; under the Count, Prince, Governor of the domains of the South, Chief of the Nubians in Yebu, Mesir.[1] There was brought to him this royal decree. To let you know:

I was in mourning on my throne,
Those of the palace were in grief,
My heart was in great affliction,
Because Hapy had failed to come in time

In a period of seven years.[2]
Grain was scant,
Kernels were dried up,
Scarce was every kind of food.
Every man robbed (3) his twin,[3]
Those who entered did not go.[4]
Children cried,
Youngsters fell,
The hearts of the old were grieving;
Legs drawn up, they hugged the ground,
Their arms clasped about them.
Courtiers were needy,
Temples were shut,
Shrines covered with dust,
Everyone was in distress.

I directed my heart to turn to the past,
I consulted one of the staff of the Ibis,
The chief lector-priest of Imhotep,
Son of Ptah South-of-his-Wall:[5]
"In which place is Hapy born?
Which is the town of the Sinuous one?
Which god dwells there?
That he might join with (5) me."

He stood: "I shall go to Mansion-of-the-Net,[6]
⌜It is designed to support a man in his deeds⌝;[7]
I shall enter the House of Life,
Unroll the Souls of Re,[8]
I shall be guided by them."

He departed, he returned to me quickly,
He let me know the flow of Hapy,
[⌜His shores⌝] and all the things they contain.
He disclosed to me the hidden wonders,
To which the ancestors had made their way,
And no king had equaled them since.
He said to me:
"There is a town in the midst of the deep,
Surrounded by Hapy, (7) Yebu by name;
It is first of the first,
First nome to Wawat,[9]
Earthly elevation, celestial hill,
Seat of Re when he prepares

To give life to every face.
Its temple's name is 'Joy-of-life,'
'Twin Caverns' is the water's name,
They are the breasts that nourish all.

It is the house of sleep of Hapy,[10]
He grows young in it in [his time],
[⌈It is the place whence⌉] he brings the flood:
Bounding up he copulates,
As man copulates with woman,
Renewing his manhood with joy;
Coursing twenty-eight cubits high,
He passes Sema-behdet (9) at seven.[11]
Khnum is the god [⌈who rules⌉] there,
[⌈He is enthroned above the deep⌉],[12]
His sandals resting on the flood;
He holds the door bolt in his hand,
Opens the gate as he wishes.
He is eternal there as Shu,[13]
Bounty-giver, Lord-of-fields,
So his name is called.
He has reckoned the land of the South and the North,[14]
To give parts to every god;
It is he who governs barley, [emmer],
Fowl and fish and all one lives on.
Cord and scribal board are there,
The pole is there with its beam
. . . . . .[15]
(11) His temple opens southeastward,
Re rises in its face every day;
Its water rages on its south for an *iter*,
A wall against the Nubians each day.[16]
There is a mountain massif in its eastern region,
With precious stones and quarry stones of all kinds,
All the things sought for building temples
In Egypt, South and North,[17]
And stalls for sacred animals,
And palaces for kings,
All statues too that stand in temples and in shrines.

"Their gathered products are set before the face of Khnum and around him; likewise (13) tall plants and flowers of all kinds that exist between Yebu and Senmut,[18] and are there on the east and the west.

"There is in the midst of the river—covered by water at its annual flood—a place of relaxation for every man who works the stones on its two sides.

"There is in the river, before this town of Yebu, a central elevation of difficult body which is called *grf-3bw*.[19]

"Learn the names of the gods and goddesses of the temple of Khnum: Satis, Anukis, Hapy, Shu, Geb, Nut, Osiris, Horus, Isis, Nephthys.

"Learn the names of (15) the stones that are there, lying in the borderland:[20] those that are in the east and the west, those [on the shores] of Yebu's canal, those in Yebu, those in the east and west, and those in the river: *bḫn*,[21] *mṯ3y*,[22] *mḥtbtḥ*,[23] *rˁgs*, *wtšy*[24] in the east; *prḏn*[25] in the west; *tšy*[26] in the west and in the river.

"The names of the precious stones of the quarries that are in the upper region—some among them at a distance of four *iter*—are: gold, silver, copper, iron, lapis lazuli, turquoise, *ṯḥnt*,[27] red jasper, *kˁ*,[28] *mnw*,[29] emerald,[30] *tm-ikr*.[31] In addition, *nšmt*,[32] *t3-mḥy*,[33] *ḥm3gt*,[34] (17) *ibht*,[35] *bḳs-ˁnḫ*,[36] green eye-paint, black eye-paint, carnelian,[37] *shrt*,[38] *mm*,[39] and ochre[40] are within this township."

When I heard what was there my heart ⸢was guided⸣. Having heard of the flood ⟨I⟩ opened the wrapped books.[41] ⟨I⟩ made a purification; ⟨I⟩ conducted a procession of the hidden ones; ⟨I⟩ made a complete offering of bread, beer, oxen, and fowl, and all good things for the gods and goddesses in Yebu whose names had been pronounced.

As I slept in peace, I found the god standing before me. ⟨I⟩ propitiated him by adoring him and praying to him. He revealed himself to me with kindly face; he said:

> "I am Khnum, your maker!
> My arms are around you,
> To steady your body,
> To (19) safeguard your limbs.[42]
> I bestow on you stones upon stones,
> ⸢That were not found⸣ before,
> Of which no work was made,
> For building temples,
> Rebuilding ruins,
> Inlaying statues' eyes.
>
> For I am the master who makes,
> I am he who made himself,
> Exalted Nun, who first came forth,
> Hapy who hurries at will;

Fashioner of everybody,
Guide of each man in his hour,
Tatenen, father of gods,
Great Shu, high in heaven!

The shrine I dwell in has two lips,[43]
When I open up the well,[44]
I know Hapy hugs the field,
A hug that fills each nose with life,
(21) For when hugged the field is reborn!
I shall make Hapy gush for you,
No year of lack and want anywhere,
Plants will grow weighed down by their fruit;
With Renutet ordering all,
All things are supplied in millions!
I shall let your people fill up,
They shall grasp together with you!
Gone will be the hunger years,
Ended the dearth in their bins.
Egypt's people will come striding,
Shores will shine in the excellent flood,
Hearts will be happier than ever before!"

The Donation

I awoke with speeding heart. Freed of fatigue I made (23) this decree on behalf of my father Khnum. A royal offering to Khnum, lord of the cataract region and chief of Nubia:

In return for what you have done for me, I offer you Manu as western border, Bakhu as eastern border,[45] from Yebu to Kemsat,[46] being twelve *iter* on the east and the west, consisting of fields and pastures, of the river, and of every place in these miles.

All tenants[47] who cultivate the fields, and the vivifiers who irrigate the shores and all the new lands that are in these miles, their harvests shall be taken to your granary, in addition to (25) your share which is in Yebu.[48]

All fishermen, all hunters, who catch fish and trap birds and all kinds of game, and all who trap lions in the desert—I exact from them one-tenth of the take of all of these, and all the young animals born of the females in these miles [in their totality].

One shall give the branded animals for all burnt offerings and daily sacrifices; and one shall give one-tenth[49] of gold, ivory, ebony, carob wood, ochre, carnelian, *shrt*, *diw*-plants, *nfw*-plants, all kinds of timber,

(being) all the things brought by the Nubians of Khent-hen-nefer[50]
⟨to⟩ Egypt, and (by) every man (27) ⌐who comes with arrears from
them.⌐

No officials are to issue orders in these places or take anything from
them, for everything is to be protected for your sanctuary.

I grant you this domain with (its) stones and good soil. No person
there − − − − − − anything from it. But the scribes that belong to you
and the overseers of the South shall dwell there as accountants, listing
everything that the *kiry*-workers, and the smiths, and the master
craftsmen, and the goldsmiths, and the . . . ,[51] (29) and the Nubians,
and the crew of Apiru,[52] and all corvée labor who fashion the stones,
shall give of gold, silver, copper, lead, baskets of . . . ,[53] firewood, the
things that every man who works with them shall give as dues, namely
one-tenth of all these. And there shall be given one-tenth of the
precious stones and quarrying stones that are brought from the
mountain side, being the stones of the east.

And there shall be an overseer who measures the quantities of gold,
silver, copper, and genuine precious stones, the things which the
sculptors shall assign to the gold house, (31) ⟨to⟩ fashion the sacred
images and to refit the statues that were damaged, and any imple-
ments lacking there. Everything shall be placed in the storehouse until
one fashions anew, when one knows everything that is lacking in your
temple, so that it shall be as it was in the beginning.

Engrave this decree on a stela of the sanctuary in writing, for it
happened as said, (and) on a tablet, so that the divine writings shall be
on them in the temple twice.[54] He who spits (on it) deceitfully shall be
given over to punishment.

The overseers of the priests and the chief of all the temple personnel
shall make my name abide in the temple of Khnum-Re, lord of Yebu,
ever-mighty.

NOTES

1. The reading of the name is not quite certain, and the name is
probably not an Egyptian one.

2. When the inscription was first published, the description of a
seven year famine was believed to be connected with the biblical story of
a seven-year famine in Egypt (Genesis 41). Since then it has been shown
that a tradition of seven years of famine was widespread in the litera-
tures of the ancient Near East; see C. H. Gordon, *Orientalia*, n.s., 22
(1953), 79−81.

3. Barguet, *op. cit.*, p. 15, took *ḥtr* to be the word for "revenue," while
I take it to be the word for "twin."

4. The meaning seems to be that those who had entered a house
were too weak to leave it again.

5. The "staff of the Ibis" designates the corporation of scribes whose

patron was Thoth. As Barguet, *op. cit.*, p. 16, pointed out, the king consults a priest of Imhotep, not the god Imhotep himself, as previous translators had thought. The earlier view is now argued anew by D. Wildung, *Imhotep und Amenhotep* (Munich, 1977), pp. 149–152.

6. *Ḥwt-ibṯ.t*, the "Mansion of the Net," appears to have been a name for the temple of Thoth at Hermopolis Magna. The logic of the tale would seem to require that the king's consultation with the priest of Imhotep takes place in the capital, i.e., at Memphis, which was also the cult center of Imhotep. Since the priest is said to have returned "quickly," or "immediately," poetic license might stretch this to include a quick trip from Memphis to Hermopolis, but surely not a voyage to the Khnum temple of Elephantine. Hence the "Mansion of the Net," if it does not here refer to the temple of Hermopolis, could only designate a sanctuary in, or close to, Memphis.

7. A somewhat obscure sentence which rendered literally would be: "gathered for the steadfastness of everyone for what they do," which I take to refer to the sanctuary, whereas Barguet construed it as referring to the priest.

8. The "Souls of Re" are the sacred books kept in the temple's "House of Life."

9. I.e., Elephantine, in the first nome of Upper Egypt, faces toward Lower Nubia (Wawat).

10. The passage gives the traditional view that the inundation rose from twin caverns at Elephantine.

11. I.e., by the time the inundation has reached the Delta town of Sema-behdet, the metropolis of the 17th nome of Lower Egypt, its height of twenty-eight cubits above low water has diminished to seven cubits.

12. I have restored the lacuna merely to indicate that some such meaning is required. It is Khnum, the creator, who releases Hapy, the inundating Nile.

13. The identification of Khnum with Shu also occurs in other texts of the Ptolemaic period, notably at Esna.

14. Lit., "the land of Upper Egypt and Lower Egypt."

15. Despite Barguet's explanation I fail to understand the words used to describe the instrument, its location, and its relation to Shu. Barguet, *op. cit.*, pp. 20–21 translated: "Il y a là un support de bois et sa croix faite de poutres *swt*, pour son peson, qui sont sur la rive; à cela est affecté Chou, fils de Re, en tant que 'maître de largesse'," and he discussed the instrument further in *CdE*, 28, no. 56 (1953), 223–227.

16. I.e., the first cataract of the Nile, which was an effective boundary throughout Egypt's history.

17. Literally, "temples of Upper and Lower Egypt."

18. The island of Biggah, south of Elephantine and opposite Philae.

19. The two elevations described here, a pleasant one and a difficult one, have been identified with the "two mountains called Crophi and Mophi," mentioned in Herodotus II,28. See Barguet, *op. cit.*, p. 22, where Crophi is identified with *grf-3bw*.

20. Since many of the stones have not been identified, it is not clear to what extent the list may have been accurate.

21. On the much discussed *bḫn* stone see now Harris, *op. cit.*, pp. 78–82, where the translation "greywacke" is favored.

22. Harris (ibid., p. 74) thinks it probable that $m\underline{t}3y$ was merely another spelling of $m3\underline{t}$, "granite."

23. An unidentified material seemingly of golden color; see ibid., p. 88.

24. The stones $r\cdot gs$ and $wt\check{s}y$ have not been identified; see ibid, pp. 85 and 89.

25. According to Harris (ibid., p. 105), this may be the Greek *prason*, "prase."

26. An unidentified stone, see ibid., p. 92.

27. This is both a precious stone and a term for faience, glass, and glaze, see ibid., pp. 135−138.

28. An unidentified stone, see ibid., pp. 133 and 232.

29. Harris (ibid., pp. 110−111) thinks it probable that this is "quartz."

30. Or perhaps "beryl," see ibid., p. 105.

31. An unidentified stone, see ibid, p. 92.

32. According to Harris (ibid., p. 115), this term usually designates "green felspar."

33. According to Harris (ibid., p. 154), this is a writing of $\underline{t}mhy$ and signifies a species of "red ochre."

34. Harris (ibid., pp. 118−120) thinks it probable that this is "garnet."

35. An unidentified stone, see ibid., pp. 96−97.

36. Harris (ibid., pp. 168 and 233−234) concludes that this stone, originally called $bi3\ \underline{k}sy$, is haematite and possibly also magnetite.

37. On $hrst$, "carnelian," see ibid., pp. 120−121.

38. Harris (ibid., pp. 130−131) concludes that this was a semiprecious stone probably of green color.

39. Mm or $mimi$ is known as a word for seed-grain, but that does not suit here.

40. On sty and $t3$-sty, "ochre," see ibid., pp. 150−152.

41 I.e., the king consulted the manuals that taught how to perform the temple ritual.

42. The speech of the god abounds in assonances, which I have imitated whenever possible.

43. The "lips" suggest some kind of gate or lid made of two sections which, when opened, releases the water.

44. I take this to be the word for "well" rather than "sieve."

45. Lit., "your west as Manu, your east as Bakhu," the two names for the mountain ranges bordering the Nile valley on the west and east.

46. The Greek Takompso, the locality that marked the southern limit of the Dodekaschoinos.

47. Barguet, *op. cit.*, p. 29, read $imy\ s\ nb$; I wonder if it might be $imy\ n\d{h}b$ nb, meaning the $n\d{h}b$ of Wb. 2,293.15.

48. Barguet, ibid., read the name as "Ville du Piège" (Hermopolis). I think it is merely another writing of "Yebu."

49. Barguet, *op. cit.*, p. 30, read the signs as $\cdot rf$, "sack," rather than di r-10. I have retained the reading $di\ r$-10 and have discussed the problem of the whole donation in my article on the *Naucratis Stela* in *Studies in Honor of George R. Hughes* (Chicago, 1977), pp. 142−144.

50. A region of Nubia south of the second cataract; see C. Vandersleyen, *Les guerres d'Amosis* (Brussels, 1971), pp. 64−68.

51. I wonder if the unread word might be $hnrw$, "prisoners"?

52. A recent article with extensive bibliography on the much debated Apiru is by M. B. Rowton, *JNES*, 35 (1976), 13–20.

53. It is not clear what word is written, see Barguet, *op. cit.*, p. 31. Since the edible produce has been listed separately, a species of grain is hardly suitable.

54. What is written is: "in the temples twice on it."

IV. *Hymns and Lamentations*

The hymns translated in *Ancient Egyptian Literature*, Vols. I and II, came from private funerary monuments—tombs, stelae, and statues—or were preserved on papyrus. By contrast, the hymns given here are inscribed on the walls of temples. That is to say, they were cult hymns that formed part of the temple ceremonial. The well-preserved temples of the Greco-Roman period, notably those of Philae, Edfu, Dendera, and Esna, are especially rich in such hymns.

The *Lamentations of Isis and Nephthys*, addressed to Osiris, also came from the temple cult of the god. But the work translated here is written on papyrus and adapted to the use of an individual person.

A HYMN TO IMHOTEP

In the Temple of Ptah at Karnak

In addition to deifying the kings—that is to say, a whole class of persons—the Egyptians accorded divine worship to a few deceased individuals who had been especially beneficent and wise. The beginnings of such deification of deceased individuals lie in the Old Kingdom. In the New Kingdom these cults became prominent, and in the Late Period they achieved their fullest expression.

The most prominent of the deified individuals were Imhotep, the vizier and architect of King Djoser, and Amenhotep son of Hapu, the architect and courtier of King Amenhotep III.

Imhotep was originally worshiped at Memphis, where he had lived and died. In the Late Period he became a god of healing, was associated with the great god Ptah as his "son," and his cult spread throughout Egypt. We have seen him as the benefactor who granted a son to the lady *Taimhotep*, and, in the *Famine Stela*, as the patron of the scribe to whom King Djoser turned for instruction. The hymn in the Ptah temple at Karnak documents his worship at Thebes.

Amenhotep son of Hapu had a remarkable career under Amenhotep III. At his death he possessed a mortuary temple, located behind that of his king, on the west bank of Thebes, and there he was worshiped by the populace as a benefactor and healer. His cult, less widespread than that of Imhotep, appears to have been limited to the Theban region. In the Theban area the two divine healers were worshiped together as "brothers."

The *Hymn to Imhotep* is inscribed in six columns on the right (southern) doorpost of the fourth door of the temple of Ptah at Karnak. A hymn to Amenhotep son of Hapu is on the left (northern) post of the same door. Both hymns are works of the Roman period, and both end with the name of the emperor Tiberius. Unfortunately, the hymn to Amenhotep son of Hapu has suffered much damage, and it is therefore not translated here.

Publication: G. Legrain, *ASAE*, 3 (1903), 61–62.   *Urk. VIII*, p. 145. S. Sauneron, *BIFAO*, 63 (1965), 73–87 and pl. V, text, translation and commentary.

On the cult of Imhotep and Amenhotep son of Hapu: K. Sethe, *Imhotep der Asklepios der Aegypter*, Untersuchungen, II/4 (Leipzig, 1902; reprint Hildesheim, 1964).   J. B. Hurry, *Imhotep, the Vizier and Physician of King Zoser* (London, 1926; 2d ed. 1928).   E. Otto, *ZÄS*, 78 (1943), 28–40.   A. Varille, *Inscriptions concernant l'architecte Amenhotep fils de Hapou*, Institut français d'archéologie orientale. Bibliothèque d'étude, 44 (Cairo, 1968).   D. Wildung, *Imhotep und Amenhotep*, Münchner ägyptologische Studien, 36 (Munich, 1977), especially pp. 206–209.

(1) Hail to you, kind-[hearted] god,
Imhotep son of Ptah!
Come to your house, your temple in Thebes,
May its people[1] see you with joy!
Receive what is presented there,
Inhale the incense,
Refresh your body with libation!

This your seat is your favored seat,
More splendid for you than the seats of other towns;
You see Amun in the seasons' feasts,
For your seat is next to his.[2]
You join life in the joiner-of-life,[3]
It faces your house at Manu.[4]
Your arm is sustained by Mont, lord of Thebes,[5]
You catch the northwind southbound by your house.
You see the sun shining in rays of gold
At the upper doors of the lord of glory![6]
You view (3) the gods' houses on your house's four sides,[7]
You receive the offerings that come from their altars;
You moisten your throat with water,
When your prophets bring this libation.
Your endowment priests offer to you of all good things,
All food supplies for every day:
Wine, beer, milk,
Burnt-offerings at nightfall.
May your *ba* swoop from heaven to your house every day,
At the welcoming voice of your priestly singer!
May you hear the chantings of your steward,
As he sets things before your *ka*![8]

Men applaud you,[9]
Women worship you,
One and all exalt your kindness!
For you heal them,
You revive them,
You renew your father's (5) creation.[10]
They bring you their donations,
Bear to you their gifts,
Proffer you their goods;
That you eat the offering loaves,
That you swallow the beer,
With your brothers, the elder gods,
And feed the worthy spirits with your surpluses.[11]
The learned ones praise god for you,
Foremost among them your brother,
Who loves you, whom you love,
Amenhotep son of Hapu.
He abides with you,
He parts not from you;
Your bodies form a single one,
Your *ba*'s receive the things you love,[12]
Brought you by your son, *Caesar Augustus.*[13]

NOTES

1. I read the word as ʿ*ḥ* , "multitude of people." Sauneron, *op. cit.,* p. 78, note (e), preferred to read *shmw*, "divine powers."

2. This passage describes how the temple of Ptah was surrounded on all sides by the other sanctuaries of Karnak, beginning with the great temple of Amun on its south.

3. The necropolis on the westbank.

4. The western mountain. On *snty=sty* see *Wb.* 4,332.7–10.

5. The temple of Mont lay to the north.

6. I.e., the east side of the temple of Amun, which received the rays of the morning sun.

7. Assonances abound in the whole text and are especially prominent in the section which begins here. Being a junior god, Imhotep receives offerings that have first been presented to the great gods of the temples around him.

8. Imhotep has his own priesthood consisting of "prophets," "endowment priests," a "musician-priest," and a "steward."

9. Having described the regular temple cult of Imhotep, the hymn now speaks of the worship of the populace who bring their personal gifts to the god and seek his help.

10. As healer and "son of Ptah," Imhotep renews the life-giving creativity of Ptah.

11. The "worthy spirits" are the deceased persons whose temple statues received offerings that had first been presented to the gods.

12. The word "body" and the word "*ba*" are both in the singular.
13. I.e., Tiberius.

HYMNS TO HATHOR IN THE TEMPLE OF DENDERA

Dendera (Iunet), the metropolis of the 6th nome of Upper Egypt, was the cult center of the goddess Hathor. The huge temple of Greco-Roman date that has survived there records in detail the worship of the goddess in its daily ritual and during festivals. Among the many texts that accompany the ritual scenes there are a number of hymns that have poetic merit. They were assembled, translated, and discussed by H. Junker. A cycle of four short hymns taken from his edition is translated here.

The four hymns form part of a long text inscribed in vertical columns on the rear wall of the Hall of Offerings. The text accompanies a scene showing the king offering a wine jug (the *mnw*-jug) to the enthroned goddess. The first nine lines describe the contents of the jug. With line 10 begin the hymns.

The hymns bring out that aspect of Hathor which made her the counterpart of Aphrodite: she is the "golden" goddess of love who is worshiped with wine, music, and dancing.

Publication: Mariette, *Dendérah*, I (Paris, 1870), 31. II. Junker, *ZÄS*, 43 (1906), 101–127.

Translation of four of the hymns: Schott, *Liebeslieder*, pp. 76–79.

On Hathor hymns at Philae: F. Daumas, *ZÄS*, 95 (1968), 1–17.

On Hathor at Dendera: F. Daumas, *Dendara et le temple de Hathor*, Institut français d'archéologie orientale, Recherches d'archéologie, de philologie et d'histoire, 29 (Cairo, 1969).

I

The King, Pharaoh, comes to dance,
He comes to sing;
   Mistress, see the dancing,
   Wife of Horus, see the skipping!

He offers it to you,
This jug;
   Mistress, see the dancing,
   Wife of Horus, see the skipping!

His heart is straight, his inmost open,
No darkness[1] is in his breast;
   Mistress, see the dancing,
   Wife of Horus, see the skipping!

II

O Golden one, how good is this song!
Like the song of Horus himself;

Re's son sings as master singer,
He is the Horus-child, the musician![2]

He diminishes not your bread,
He reduces not your loaf;
His heart is straight, his inmost open,
No darkness is in his breast!

He abhors the sorrow of your *ka*,
He abhors (your) hunger and thirst,
He abhors the distress of the goddess![3]

III

O beauteous one, O cow, O great one,
O great magician, O splendid lady, O queen of gods![4]
The King reveres you, Pharaoh, give that he live!
O queen of gods, he reveres you, give that he live!

Behold him, Hathor, mistress, from heaven,
See him, Hathor, mistress, from lightland,
Hear him, flaming one, from ocean!
Behold him, queen of gods, from sky, from earth,
From Nubia, from Libya, from Manu, from Bakhu,[5]
From each land, from each place, where your majesty shines!

Behold what is in his inmost,
Though his mouth speaks not;
His heart is straight, his inmost open,
No darkness is in his breast!
He reveres you, O queen of gods,
Give that he live!

IV

He comes to dance,
He comes to sing!
  His bread is in his hand,
  He defiles not the bread in his hand,
  Clean are the foods in his arms,
  They have come from the Horus Eye,
  He has cleansed what he offers to her!

He comes to dance,
He comes to sing!
  His bag[6] is of rushes,
  His basket of reeds,[7]
  His sistrum of gold,
  His necklace of malachite.[8]

His feet hurry to the mistress of music,
He dances for her, she loves his doing!

NOTES

1. *Snk*, "darkness," in the sense of "malice."
2. Reading the sign as *iḥy* rather than *ntr ꜥ3*; cf. *Wb.*, 1,121.
3. The *itn.t*, the "sun-goddess," title of Hathor.
4. Or, "gold of gods."
5. I.e., south, north, west, and east.
6. Read *k3r.f*, see *Wb.*, 5,12.1.
7. I have rendered the *twn* and *nnt* plants freely as "rushes" and "reeds." It is not known what plants are meant by these terms. The relation of the verse to Pyramid Texts utterance 342 was studied by A. Gutbub in *Mélanges Maspero I*, 4 (1961), 31–72.
8. On *w3ḏ*, "malachite," see Harris, *Minerals*, pp. 102–104.

TWO HYMNS TO KHNUM IN THE TEMPLE OF ESNA

Just as the temple of Dendera records the cult of Hathor, so the temple of Esna (Iunyt, Latopolis), also of Greco-Roman date, furnishes a rich documentation for the cult of Khnum. The masterful publication of the Esna temple by S. Sauneron provides searching studies of the annual festivals in which the cult found its fullest expression. This monumental work guides through the intricacies of Egyptian temple ceremonies and the programs of the various feasts, and leads toward an overview of Egyptian religious thought and practice in the final centuries of paganism.

From the large number of hymns sung at the various festivals, I have selected two for translation here, a *Morning Hymn*, which served to awaken the god in his shrine, and the *Great Hymn to Khnum*, which glorified Khnum as creator-god.

The morning hymn is a genre known through a number of texts from different temples and addressed to various gods. It is characterized by a clear strophic form, achieved by means of anaphoras and refrains, or anaphoras only. This strophic arrangement distinguishes it from the general hymns of praise, for these lack strophic structure, though distinct changes of content must have entailed pauses in the recitation, pauses that we indicate by paragraphs. The temple of Esna contains several morning hymns. The one included here was addressed to Khnum on the feast of the 20th day of the month of Epiphi.

The original cult center of Khnum was the town of Elephantine, where, as the *Famine Stela* describes it, the god ruled the cataract region and controlled the caverns from which sprang Hapy, the inundating Nile. Subsequently, Khnum achieved the status of a creator-god, specifically one who fashioned mankind on the potter's wheel. As a major god, he was associated with other great gods, notably Amun, Re, Shu, and Horus. In the *Morning Hymn* he is first identified with Amun, then with Shu, the warlike son of Re, who fights the battles that the sun-god must wage. But it is the role of creator which is brought out most forcefully in the hymns of the Esna temple, in particular in the *Great Hymn to Khnum*, sung at the feast of installing the potter's wheel, which was celebrated on the first day of the month of Phamenot. Dating from the Roman period, the text is modeled on a hymn of Ptolemaic date, also inscribed in the Esna temple, but now in a poor state of preservation.

Publication: *A Morning Hymn to Khnum: Esna*, Vol. III, No. 261, 15–18, pp. 157–158, text.   *Esna*, Vol. V, pp. 364–366, translation.

Study of morning hymns: A. M. Blackman and H. W. Fairman in *Miscellanea Gregoriana*, pp. 397–428.   *Esna*, Vol. V, pp. 84–87.

The Great Hymn to Khnum: Esna, Vol. III, No. 250,6–21, pp. 130–134, text.   *Esna*, Vol. V, pp. 94–107, translation and commentary.   J. Assmann, *Ägyptische Hymnen und Gebete* (Zurich, 1975), No. 145, pp. 344–346, translation of excerpts.

A MORNING HYMN TO KHNUM

Awakenings of Khnum; say:

Wake well in peace, wake well in peace,
Khnum-Amun, the ancient,
Issued from Nun,
In peace, awake peaceably!

Wake, lord of fields,
Great Khnum,
Who makes his domain in the meadow,
In peace, awake peaceably!

Wake, lord of gods and men,
Lord of the war cry,[1]
In peace, awake peaceably!

Wake, mighty planner,
Great power in Egypt,
In peace, awake peaceably!

Wake, lord of life,
Wooer of women,
To whom come gods and men as he bids,
In peace, awake peaceably!

Wake, ram great of majesty,
Tall-plumed, sharp-horned,
In peace, awake peaceably!

Wake, great lion,
Slayer of rebels,
In peace, awake peaceably!

Wake, crocodile-king,
Mighty victor,

Who conquers as he wishes,
In peace, awake peaceably!

Wake, veiled-faced one,
Who shuts his eyes to his foes,
As he bears arms,
In peace, awake peaceably!

Wake, leader of herdsmen,
Who grasps the stick,
Smites his attacker,
In peace, awake peaceably!

Wake, great crocodile who says,
"Each of you shall slay his fellow,"[2]
In peace awake, peaceably!

Wake, Shu, strong-armed,
His father's champion,
Slayer of rebels,
In peace, awake peaceably!

Wake, fighting ram who chases his foes,
Herdsman of his followers,
In peace, awake peaceably!

Wake, multiform one,
Who changes shape at will,
In peace, awake peaceably!

Wake, Khnum who fashions as he wishes,
Who sets every man in his place!

NOTES

1. Literally, "Strong of war cry."
2. An allusion to the sun-god's battles against his enemies in which he is supported by Shu and other gods. Here Khnum, identified with Shu, fights on behalf of the sun-god. "His fellow" must mean his opponent in battle.

THE GREAT HYMN TO KHNUM

The hymn consists of three parts. In the first part Khnum is viewed as the creator of mankind who continually creates men and women on his potter's wheel and endows the human body with all its parts and functions. In the second part, the god is adored as the creator of all peoples and as the maker of all animals and plants. The third part describes the different manifestations of the god by virtue of which he is identical with the other creator-gods.

The parallelism of members underlying the metrical scheme is rein-
forced by numerous assonances.

Khnum creator of bodies

(250,6) Another hymn to Khnum-Re,
God of the potter's wheel,
Who settled the land by his handiwork;
Who joins in secret,
Who builds soundly,[1]
Who nourishes the nestlings by the breath of his mouth;
Who drenches this land with Nun,
While round sea and great ocean surround him.

He has fashioned gods and men,
He has formed flocks and herds;
He made birds as well as fishes,
He created bulls, engendered cows.

He (8) knotted the flow of blood to the bones,
Formed in his ⌈workshop⌉ as his handiwork,
So the breath of life is within everything,
⌈Blood bound with semen⌉ in the bones,[2]
To knit the bones from the start.

He makes women give birth when the womb is ready,
So as to open − − − as he wishes;
He soothes suffering by his will,
Relieves throats, lets everyone breathe,
To give life to the young in the womb.

He made hair sprout and tresses grow,
Fastened the skin over the limbs;
He built the skull, formed the cheeks,
To furnish shape to the image.[3]
He opened the eyes, hollowed the ears,
He made the body inhale air;
(10) He formed the mouth for eating,
Made the ⌈gorge⌉ for swallowing.

He also formed the tongue to speak,
The jaws to open, the gullet to drink,
The throat to swallow and spit.
The spine to give support,
The testicles to ⌈move⌉,
The ⌈arm⌉ to act with vigor,
The rear to perform its task.

The gullet to devour,
Hands and their fingers to do their work,
The heart to lead.
The loins to support the phallus
In the act of begetting.
The frontal organs to consume things,
The rear to aerate the entrails,
Likewise to sit at ease,
And sustain the entrails at night.
The male member to beget,
The womb to conceive,
And increase generations in Egypt.
The bladder (12) to make water,
The virile member to eject
When it swells between the thighs.
The shins to step,
The legs to tread,
Their bones doing their task,
By the will of his heart.

Khnum creator of all peoples and all life

Formed all on his potter's wheel,
Their speech differs in each region,
And clashes with that of Egypt.[4]
He created precious things in their lands,
That they might bear their products abroad,
For the lord of the wheel is their father too,
Tatenen[5] who made all that is on their soil.
They produce their supplies—thus the people of Ibhat—[6]
To nourish themselves and their children.
As his mouth spat out they were born straightaway,
Without pause henceforth the wheel turns (14) every day.

All your creatures give you thanks,
You are Ptah-Tatenen, creator of creators,
Who in Iunyt brought forth all that is.
He feeds the chick in the nest in its time,
He makes its mother eject it in time.
He made mankind, created gods,
He fashioned flocks and herds.
He made birds, fishes, and reptiles all,
By his will Nun's fishes leap from the caverns,
To feed men and gods in his time.

He made plants in the field,
He dotted the shores with flowers;
He made fruit trees bear their fruit,
To fill the needs of men and gods.
(16) He opened seams in the bellies of mountains,
He made the quarries spew out their stones.

The diverse forms of Khnum

In "First-of-towns" he is Ba-of-Re,[7]
Fashioning people throughout this land;
At Iunyt he is Ba-of-Shu,
Modeling people on his wheel.
He has fashioned men, engendered gods,
They live by that which comes from him,
He makes breathe those who rest in their tombs.

In Shas-hotep he is Ba-of-Osiris,
Making all herds by his handiwork;
In Herwer he is Ba-of-Geb,
Fashioning all beings in this land.
He is Horus-Metenu in Semenhor,
Making birds from the sweat of his body.

He changes his form (18) to Lord-of-the-booth,[8]
To wrap Osiris in the place of embalmment;
He models all things between his hands,
To guard Osiris on his right side,
Save him from the water by his Twins,[9]
Guard the King on his left side, ever-living.

He changes his form to Suwadjenba of Pi-neter,[10]
Who makes all things in his field,
He grows trees, he raises crops,
To nourish all by his products.
He alters his form to beneficent Nourisher,
On top of nestling-hill,
To fashion all men and beasts.

They[11] have placed their four Mesekhnet[12] at their sides,
To repel the designs of evil by incantations;
They stand as lords of the shrines of South and North,
At the place of creation of all that (20) exists.
Beneficent god,
Contenting god,

God who forms bodies,
God who equips nostrils,
God who binds the Two Lands,
So that they join their natures.

When Nun and Tatenen first came into being,
They appeared as lotus on his back,
As heir to Djed-shepsy at the start.[13]
Their *ka* will not perish,
None shall hinder their action,
No land is lacking in all that he made.
They are concealed among mankind,[14]
Creating all beings since god's time,
They are alive and abiding,
Like Re rising and setting,
May your fair face be kind to *Pharaoh ever living*!

NOTES

1. I propose to read *ḥws m swḏ3*, taking the two fledglings as mere phonetic complement. There is then a good parallelism with the preceding *k3s ḥnt št3*.

2. The reading of the signs is problematic; cf. Sauneron's discussion, *Esna*, V, 99 (l).

3. Taking *mnw*, "image" (*Wb*. 2,71.3–6) to stand for the human figure as a creation of the god.

4. On the passage see also Sauneron, *BIFAO*, 60 (1960), 37–39.

5. As sustainer of all peoples Khnum is identical with the earth god Tatenen.

6. Ibhat designated a region of Lower Nubia.

7. "First-of-towns" is Elephantine because the Egyptian viewed the earth facing south, hence Elephantine was the first town inside Egypt. In all his cult centers—Elephantine, Iunyt (Esna), Shas-hotep (Hypselis), Herwer, and Semenhor (near Atfih)—Khnum is merged with the other great gods worshiped there by being viewed as their *ba*, i.e., their "soul" or "manifestation."

8. Anubis.

9. Or, the "Eye-Twins," i.e., Shu and Tefnut.

10. Pi-neter was the name of a sanctuary located to the north of the main temple; see Sauneron, *Esna*, V, 316–322 and 334–337.

11. "They" are the various manifestations of Khnum.

12. The bricks on which women sat when giving birth, personified as goddesses.

13. Djed-shepsy, "August Djed Pillar," was a Memphite god who is here viewed as the primeval mound from which rose Khnum as creator god at the start of creation.

14. As above, "Their" and "They" refer to the manifestations of Khnum.

THE LAMENTATIONS OF ISIS AND NEPHTHYS

Pap. Berlin 3008

This text in hieratic script is appended to a hieroglyphic papyrus of the Book of the Dead that belonged to a woman whose name, variously spelled, was Tentruty or Teret. The papyrus dates from the Ptolemaic period. The hieratic text is written in five columns (or pages) of varying size. It consists of lamentations addressed to Osiris by Isis and Nephthys. The text ends with instructions for its use, which show that the lamentations were to be recited by two women impersonating the two goddesses. A rough sketch on the bottom margin of column 5 shows the two women seated on the ground, each holding a vase and an offering loaf.

The text belongs basically to the ritual of the Osiris mysteries as performed in the temples. But by being included in a Book of the Dead it was adapted to the funerary service of a private person, an adaptation made possible by the traditional association of every dead person with the god Osiris. The text resembles a longer work found in Papyrus Bremner-Rhind (Pap. Brit. Mus. 10188), known as "The Songs of Isis and Nephthys." This work, dating to the fourth century B.C., was clearly designed for performance in the temples of Osiris on certain feast days. Comparison of the two compositions shows that the shorter work, the *Lamentations*, was not an abridgment of the far more elaborate *Songs*, but a different version. R. O. Faulkner published both texts and discussed their relationship.

The two texts should also be seen in conjunction with a group of texts embodying the Osiris ritual, namely, the texts from the temples of Edfu, Dendera, and Philae which H. Junker published under the title *Die Stundenwachen in den Osirismysterien*. All three works express the basic ideas that governed the Osiris ritual. They reenact the life, death, and resurrection of the god; they record the lengthy laments over his death; and they dwell on the elaborate protection which the gods give to Osiris, who, though resurrected, vindicated, and worshiped as a cosmic ruler, retains a particular passivity and vulnerability.

Publication: R. O. Faulkner, "The Lamentations of Isis and Nephthys," *Mélanges Maspero I*, 1 (1934), 337–348 and 4 plates.

The related texts (not translated here): R. O. Faulkner, *The Papyrus Bremner-Rhind (Brit. Mus. No. 10188)*, Bibliotheca Aegyptiaca, III (Brussels, 1933), pp. 1–32: "The Songs of Isis and Nephthys," text. *Idem, JEA*, 22 (1936), 121–140, translation.   H. Junker, *Die Stundenwachen in den Osirismysterien*, Akademie der Wissenschaften, Wien, Philosophisch-historische Klasse, Denkschriften, 54/1 (Vienna, 1910).

(1,1) Recitation of blessings made by the Two Sisters in the house of Osiris-Khentamenti, the great god, lord of Abydos, in the fourth month of Inundation, day 25, when the same is done in every place of Osiris, at every feast of his:

To bless his *ba*, steady his body, exalt his *ka*, give breath to the nose of him who lacks breath.[1]

To soothe the heart of Isis and Nephthys, place Horus on his

father's throne, and give life-stability-dominion to the Osiris Tentruty, born of Tekhao, called Persis, the justified.[2]

It benefits the doer as well as the gods. Recitation:

(**2**,1) Isis speaks, she says:
Come to your house, come to your house!
You of On,[3] come to your house,
Your foes are not!

O good musician, come to your house!
Behold me, I am your beloved sister,
You shall not part from me!

O good youth, come to your house!
Long, long have I not seen you!
My heart mourns you, my eyes seek you,
I search for you to see you!

Shall I not see you, shall I not see you,
Good King, shall I not see you?[4]
It is good to see you, good to see you,
You of On, it is good to see you!

Come to your beloved, come to your beloved!
Wennofer, justified, come to your sister!
Come to your wife, come to your wife,
Weary-hearted, come to your house-mistress!

I am your sister by your mother,
(10) You shall not leave me!
Gods and men look for you,
Weep for you together!

While I can see I call to you,
Weeping to the height of heaven!
But you do not hear my voice,
Though I am your sister whom you loved on earth,
You loved none but me, the sister, the sister!

(**3**,1) Nephthys speaks, she says:
O good King, come to your house!
Please your heart, all your foes are not!
Your Two Sisters beside you guard your bier,
Call for you in tears!

Turn around on your bier!
See the women, speak to us!
King our lord, drive all pain from our hearts!

Your court of gods and men beholds you,
Show them your face, King our lord!
Our faces live by seeing your face!

Let your face not shun our faces!
(10) Our hearts are glad to see you, King!
Our hearts are happy to see you!

I am Nephthys, your beloved sister!
Your foe is fallen, he shall not be!
I am with you, your body-guard,
For all eternity!

     (**4**,1) Isis speaks, she says:
Ho you of On, you rise for us daily in heaven!⁵
We cease not to see your rays!
Thoth, your guard, raises your *ba*,
In the day-bark in this your name of "Moon."
I have come to see your beauty in the Horus Eye,
In your name of "Lord-of-the-sixth-day-feast."

Your courtiers beside you shall not leave you,
You conquered heaven by your majesty's might,
In this your name of "Lord-of-the-fifteenth-day-feast."

You rise for us like Re every day,
You shine for us like Atum,
Gods and men live by your sight.

As you rise for us you light the Two Lands,
Lightland is filled with your presence;
Gods and men look to you,
No evil befalls them when you shine.

(10) As you cross the sky your foes are not,
I am your guard every day!
You come to us as child in moon and sun,
We cease not to behold you!

Your sacred image, Orion in heaven,
Rises and sets every day;
I am Sothis who follows him,
I will not depart from him!

(5,1) The noble image issued from you
Nourishes gods and men,
Reptiles and herds live by it.

You flow from your cavern for us in your time,
Pouring out water to your *ba*,
Making offerings to your *ka*,
To nourish gods and men alike.

Ho my lord! There is no god like you!
Heaven has your *ba*, earth your form,
Netherworld is filled with your secrets.
Your wife is your guard,
Your son Horus rules the lands!

    Nephthys speaks, she says:
O good King, come to your house!
Wennofer, justified, come to Djedet,
O lusty bull, come to Anpet![6]
O lover of women,[7] come to Hat-mehyt,
Come to Djedet, the place your *ba* loves!

The *ba*'s of your fathers are your companions,
Your young son Horus, the Sisters' child, is before you;
I am the light that guards you every day,
I will not leave you ever!

O you of On, come to Sais,
"Saite" is your name;
Come to Sais to see your mother Neith,
Good child, you shall not part from her!

Come to her breasts that overflow,
Good brother, you shall not part from her!
O my son, come to Sais!
Osiris Tentruty, called Nyny, born of Persis, justified.[8]

Come to Sais, your city!
Your place is the Palace,[9]
You shall rest forever beside your mother!
She protects your body, repels your foes,
She will guard your body forever!
O good King, come to your house,
Lord of Sais, come to Sais!

    Isis speaks, she says:
Come to your house, come to your house,

Good King, come to your house!
Come, see your son Horus
As King of gods and men!

He has conquered towns and nomes
By the greatness of his glory!
(10) Heaven and earth are in awe of him,
The Bow-land[10] is in dread of him.

Your court of gods and men is his
In the Two Lands, in doing your rites;
Your Two Sisters beside you libate to your *ka*,
Your son Horus presents you offerings
Of bread, beer, oxen, and fowl.

Thoth recites your liturgy,
And calls you with his spells;
The Sons of Horus guard your body,[11]
And daily bless your *ka*.

Your son Horus, champion of your name and your shrine,
Makes oblations to your *ka*;
The gods, with water-jars in their hands,
Pour water to your *ka*.
Come to your courtiers, King our lord!
Do not part from them!

Now when this is recited the place is to be completely secluded, not seen and not heard by anyone except the chief lector-priest and the *setem*-priest. One shall bring two women with beautiful bodies. They shall be made to sit on the ground at the main portal of the Hall of Appearings. On their arms shall be written the names of Isis and Nephthys. Jars of faience filled with water shall be placed in their right hands, offering loaves made in Memphis in their left hands, and their faces shall be bowed. To be done in the third hour of the day, also in the eighth hour of the day. You shall not be slack in reciting this book in the hour of festival.

It is finished.

NOTES

1. Lit., "the one whose throat is constricted."
2. By inserting the name of the owner of the book, the temple ritual of Osiris was made to apply to this deceased person.
3. Osiris is called the "Heliopolitan" because of his association with the sun-god Re of Heliopolis.
4. Probably a phonetic rendering of *in nn iw.i r m3.k*.

5. In this section Osiris is viewed as a cosmic god manifest in both sun and moon. He has a feast on the sixth day of the lunar month and on the fifteenth day when the moon is full. He is also Hapy, the inundating Nile, who nourishes the land.

6. Djedet and Anpet are names of the town of Mendes, and Hatmehyt is the nome of Mendes, the 16th nome of Lower Egypt.

7. Of the various meanings of the root *hni/hnr*, Faulkner, *op. cit.*, p. 344, chose "tomb" and rendered, "thou whom the tomb(?) desired." In view of the preceding "lusty bull," I think it more likely that "harem" or "women of the harem" was meant.

8. Again the name of the deceased woman is inserted here.

9. On the Saite sanctuary called "mansion of the bee" see p. 40, n. 2.

10. Nubia.

11. The "Four Sons of Horus" were the guardians of the Canopic jars in which the embalmed inner organs were buried.

PART TWO

Demotic Texts

THE STORIES OF SETNE KHAMWAS

This is a sequence of two stories built around the personality of Prince Khamwas, the fourth son of King Ramses II. The historical Prince Khamwas had been high priest of Ptah at Memphis, and in that capacity he had been in charge of the Memphite temples and cemeteries. We possess a number of objects inscribed with his name that bear witness to his activities as builder and restorer of sacred monuments. In his lifetime he also acquired fame as a very learned sage. After his death, the popular imagination shaped his memory into that of a powerful magician. And the knowledge of his devotion to the examining and restoring of monuments formed the basis for attributing to him a consuming passion for the study of ancient works. These traits of character, both real and imagined, provided the motivations and motifs of the actions and adventures which the Demotic tales spun around his name.

The principal title by which the historical Khamwas called himself was that of *setem*-priest of Ptah. In the Demotic tales the title is spelled *stme* or *stne* and is used as if it were a personal name. Hence it is customary to call the hero of these Demotic tales Setne Khamwas, and to refer to the two stories about him as Setne I and II, or as I and II Khamwas.

The two stories are preserved on two different papyri; and they are in fact a cycle rather than a sequence. This is so because the second story consists of two distinct tales that have been linked together. Furthermore, there exist text fragments that contain variants and additional episodes.

The first story, *Setne I*, is preserved in the Cairo Museum Papyrus No. 30646. The papyrus originally had six pages, but the first two have been torn away and are lost. A part of the missing beginning, or a variant of it, is preserved on another Cairo Papyrus (No. 30692). This fragment and related fragmentary texts have not been included here. The text of Setne I is written in a careful hand and the writing is of Ptolemaic date. It belongs to the best period of Demotic writing and is free of corruptions and misspellings. An unusual feature of the papyrus is that the pages are numbered, so we know that exactly two pages are missing in the beginning. The third page is damaged at the beginning of each line. The other three pages are in good condition.

The second story, *Setne II*, is written on the *verso* of the British Museum Papyrus No. 604. The writing dates from the Roman period and is careless, abounding in errors and omissions. Here, too, the beginning of the papyrus is lost, but since the pages are not numbered it is not possible to say just how much is missing. Large portions of what is now the first page are also lacking.

Both stories are remarkable for the color and vividness of their narration. In particular, the episode of Setne and Tabubu is a masterpiece of suspenseful storytelling. The central theme of Setne I is the desire of Prince Setne Khamwas to possess a book of magic that had been written by the god Thoth himself. The book had been acquired by force by Naneferkaptah, a prince who had lived long before Setne, who had taken the book with him to his grave, having paid for the possession of the book with his life and the life of his wife and son. When Setne finds the tomb and robs the book, the two princes, both powerful magicians, engage in a contest of skills until Setne is vanquished and returns the book. The tale exemplifies the traditional Egyptian view that magic is a legitimate weapon for man, but the ultimate secrets of life and the world belong only to the gods and may not be acquired by man.

Setne II consists of two distinct tales that are linked through the person of Si-Osire, the son of Setne Khamwas, who is the true hero of both tales and overshadows his father. The centerpiece of the first tale is Setne's visit to the netherworld, to which he is guided by his son Si-Osire. There Setne witnesses the blessed existence of the just who find the reward of their good deeds, and the tortures of the sinners who suffer everlasting punishment.

H. Gressmann's penetrating study, "Vom reichen Mann und armen Lazarus," has made it plausible that the contrasting scenes of the richly buried nobleman who is tortured in the netherworld and the cursorily buried poor man who becomes an honored nobleman in the netherworld were genuinely Egyptian motifs that formed the basis for the parable of Jesus in Luke 16,19–31, and for the related Jewish legends, preserved in many variants in Talmudic and medieval Jewish sources.

The Egyptian conception of the netherworld, as found here in a late form, had also absorbed elements of Greek origin, notably the tortures of Oknos and Tantalos, and the central theme itself, the visit to the netherworld by a living person, which recalls Orpheus descending into Hades and Odysseus conversing with the shades of the dead. The absorption of Greek motifs also underlines the combination of two distinct views of the netherworld: it is both a place in which the life lived on earth continues in a related form, and a place of judgment and retribution. The people whom Setne sees plaiting ropes that are always chewed up by donkeys, and the people who are prevented by pits under their feet from reaching the food suspended above them (Oknos and Tantalos motifs) are not great sinners but rather persons who were luckless in life and receive similar fates in the netherworld.

The presence of Greek motifs in *Setne II* is one of many testimonies to the intermingling of Egyptian and Greek cultures in Greco-Roman Egypt. As the known materials bearing on this phenomenon are more intensively studied, and as new sources come to light, the symbiosis of the two peoples and their cultural syncretism will become ever more tangible.

Setne I: Pap. Cairo 30646

Publication: F. Ll. Griffith, *Stories of the High Priests of Memphis*, Vol. I (Oxford, 1900).   W. Spiegelberg, *Die demotischen Denkmäler*, Vol. II: *Die demotischen Papyrus*, Catalogue général . . . du musée du Caire (Leipzig, 1908), p. 88 and pls. 44–47.   Erichsen, *Lesestücke*, pp. 1–40.

Translation: B. Gunn in B. Lewis, ed., *Land of Enchanters* (London, 1948), pp. 67–83.   Brunner-Traut, *Märchen*, pp. 171–192.   Bresciani, *Letteratura*, pp. 615–626.

Setne II: Pap. British Museum 604 *verso*

Publication: F. Ll. Griffith, *Stories of the High Priests of Memphis*, Vols 1–2 (Oxford, 1900).   Erichsen, *Lesestücke*, pp. 41–49, excerpts.

Translation: Brunner-Traut, *Märchen*, pp. 192–214.   Bresciani, *Letteratura*, pp. 627–641.

Comments to either tale: H. Gressmann, *Vom reichen Mann und armen Lazarus*, Abhandlungen der Berliner Akademie der Wissenschaften, philosophisch-historische Klasse, 1918, No. 7 (Berlin, 1918). M. Pieper, *ZÄS*, 67 (1931), 71–74. K.-T. Zauzich, *Enchoria*, 1 (1971), 83–86. M. Gilula, *Enchoria*, 6 (1976), 125.

On the historical Prince Khamwas: F. Gomaà, *Chaemwese, Sohn Ramses' II. und Hoherpriester von Memphis*, Ägyptologische Abhandlungen, 27 (Wiesbaden, 1973).

References to additional older publications and to the fragments of the Setne cycle not translated here are to be found in the literature cited, and see K.-T. Zauzich, *Enchoria*, 6 (1976), 79–82.

SETNE KHAMWAS AND NANEFERKAPTAH (SETNE I)

The lost beginning may be reconstructed as follows:

Prince Khamwas, son of King Ramses II and high priest of Ptah at Memphis, was a very learned scribe and magician who spent his time in the study of ancient monuments and books. One day he was told of the existence of a book of magic written by the god Thoth himself and kept in the tomb of a prince named Naneferkaptah (Na-nefer-ka-ptah), who had lived in the distant past and was buried somewhere in the vast necropolis of Memphis. After a long search, Prince Khamwas, accompanied by his foster brother Inaros, found the tomb of Naneferkaptah and entered it. He saw the magic book, which radiated a strong light, and tried to seize it. But the spirits of Naneferkaptah and of his wife Ahwere rose up to defend their cherished possession.

Ahwere and her son Merib were not buried in this Memphite tomb but rather in distant Coptos, where they had lost their lives. But the spirit of Ahwere was with her husband at this critical moment, and she now stood before Prince Khamwas and told him how her husband had acquired the magic book and how they had all paid for it with their lives. She begins her story by relating that she and Naneferkaptah had been brother and sister and the only children of a Pharaoh named Mernebptah. They had loved each other very much and had wanted to marry. But Pharaoh wished to marry his son to the daughter of a general and his daughter to the son of a general. In her anguish Ahwere had asked the steward of Pharaoh's palace to plead with Pharaoh in her behalf. The steward had done so and Pharaoh had become silent and distressed. To the steward's question, why he was distressed, Pharaoh answered:

(Here begins the story on page 3 of the papyrus)

"It is you who distress me. If it so happens that I have only two children, is it right to marry the one to the other? I will marry Naneferkaptah to the daughter of a general, and I will marry Ahwere to the son of another general, so that our family may increase!"

When the time came for the banquet to be set before Pharaoh, they came for me and took me to the banquet. But my heart was very sad and I did not have my former looks. Pharaoh said to me: "Ahwere, was it you who sent to me with those foolish words, 'Let me marry [Naneferkaptah, my] elder [brother]'?"

I said to him: "Let me marry the son of a general, and let him marry the daughter of another general, so that our family may increase!" I laughed and Pharaoh laughed.[1]

(5) [When the steward of the palace came] Pharaoh [said to him]: "Steward, let Ahwere be taken to the house of Naneferkaptah tonight, and let all sorts of beautiful things be taken with her."

I was taken as a wife to the house of Naneferkaptah [that night, and Pharaoh] sent me a present of silver and gold, and all Pharaoh's household sent me presents. Naneferkaptah made holiday with me, and he entertained all Pharaoh's household. He slept with me that night and found me [pleasing. He slept with] me again and again, and we loved each other.

When my time of purification came I made no more purification.[2] It was reported to Pharaoh, and his heart was very happy. Pharaoh had many things taken [out of the treasury] and sent me presents of silver, gold, and royal linen, all very beautiful. When my time of bearing came, I bore this boy who is before you, who was named Merib. He was entered in the register of the House of Life.[3]

[It so happened that] my brother Naneferkaptah [had no] occupation on earth but walking on the desert of Memphis, reading the writings that were in the tombs of the Pharaohs and on the stelae of the scribes of the House of Life[4] and the writings that were on (10) [the other monuments, for his zeal] concerning writings was very great.

After this there was a procession in honor of Ptah, and Naneferkaptah went into the temple to worship. As he was walking behind the procession, reading the writings on the shrines of the gods, [an old priest saw] him and laughed. Naneferkaptah said to him: "Why are you laughing at me?" He said: "I am not laughing at you. I am laughing because you are reading writings that have no [importance for anyone]. If you desire to read writings, come to me and I will have you taken to the place where that book is that Thoth wrote with his own hand, when he came down following the other gods. Two spells are written in it. When you [recite the first spell you will] charm the sky, the earth, the netherworld, the mountains, and the waters. You will discover what all the birds of the sky and all the reptiles are saying. You will see the fish of the deep [though there are twenty-one divine cubits of water] over [them].[5] When you recite the second spell, it will happen that, whether you are in the netherworld or in your form on earth, you will see Pre appearing in the sky with his Ennead, and the Moon in its form of rising."

(15) [Naneferkaptah said to him]: "As he (the king) lives, tell me a good thing that you desire, so that I may do it for you, and you send me to the place where this book is!"

The priest said to Naneferkaptah: "If you wish to be sent [to the place where this book is] you must give me a hundred pieces[6] of silver for my burial, and you must endow me with two priestly stipends tax free."

Naneferkaptah called a servant and had the hundred pieces of silver given to the priest. He added the two stipends and had [the priest] endowed with them [tax free].

The priest said to Naneferkaptah: "The book in question is in the middle of the water of Coptos in a box of iron. In the box of iron is a box of [copper. In the box of copper is] a box of juniper wood. In the box of juniper wood is a box of ivory and ebony. In the box of ivory and ebony is a [box of silver. In the box of silver] is a box of gold, and in it is the book. [There are six miles of][7] serpents, scorpions, and all kinds of reptiles around the box in which the book is, and there is (20) [an eternal serpent around] this same box."

When the priest had thus spoken to Naneferkaptah, he did not know where on earth he was. He came out of the temple, he told [me everything that had happened to him]. He [said] to me: "I will go to Coptos, I will bring this book, hastening back to the north again." But I chided the priest, saying: "May Neith curse you for having told him these [dreadful things! You have brought] me combat, you have brought me strife. The region of Thebes, I now find it [abhorrent]." I did what I could with Naneferkaptah to prevent him from going to Coptos; he did not listen to me. He went to [Pharaoh and told] Pharaoh everything that the priest had said to him.

Pharaoh said to him: "What is that [you want]?" He said to him: "Let the ship of Pharaoh be given to me with its equipment. I will take Ahwere [and her boy Merib] to the south with me, I will bring this book without delay."

The ship of Pharaoh was given [him] with its equipment. We boarded it, we set sail, we arrived (25) [at Coptos]. It [was announced] to the priests of Isis of Coptos and the chief priest of Isis. They came down to meet us, hastening to meet Naneferkaptah, and their wives came down to meet me. [We went up from the shore and went into] the temple of Isis and Harpocrates. Naneferkaptah sent for an ox, a goose, and wine. He made burnt offering and libation before Isis of Coptos and Harpocrates. We were taken to a very beautiful house [filled with all good things].

Naneferkaptah spent four days making holiday with the priests of

Isis of Coptos, and the wives of the priests of Isis made holiday with me. When the morning of our fifth day came, Naneferkaptah had [much] pure [wax brought] to him. He made a boat filled with its rowers and sailors. He recited a spell to them, he made them live, he gave them breath, he put them on the water. He filled the ship of Pharaoh with sand, [he tied it to the other boat]. He [went] on board, and I sat above the water of Coptos, saying: "I shall learn what happens to him."

He said to the rowers: "Row me to the place where that book (30) is!" [They rowed him by night] as by day. In three days he reached it. He cast sand before him, and a gap formed in the river. He found six miles of serpents, scorpions, and all kinds of reptiles around [the place where the book was]. He found an eternal serpent around this same box. He recited a spell to the six miles of serpents, scorpions, and all kinds of reptiles that were around the box, and did not let them come up. [He went to the place where] the eternal serpent was. He fought it and killed it. It came to life again and resumed its shape. He fought it again, a second time, and killed it; it came to life again. He [fought it again, a third] time, cut it in two pieces, and put sand between one piece and the other. [It died] and no longer resumed its shape.

Naneferkaptah went to the place where the box was. [He found it was a box of] iron. He opened it and found a box of copper. He opened it and found a box of juniper wood. He opened it and found a box of ivory and ebony. (35) [He opened it and found a box of] silver. He opened it and found a box of gold. He opened it and found the book in it. He brought the book up out of the box of gold.

He recited a spell from it; [he charmed the sky, the earth, the netherworld, the] mountains, the waters. He discovered what all the birds of the sky and the fish of the deep and the beasts of the desert were saying. He recited another spell; he saw [Pre appearing in the sky with his Ennead], and the Moon rising, and the stars in their forms. He saw the fish of the deep, though there were twenty-one divine cubits of water over them. He recited a spell to the [water; he made it resume its form].

[He went on] board, he said to the rowers: "Row me back to the place [I came] from." They rowed him by night as by day. He reached me at the place where I was; [he found me sitting] above the water of Coptos, not having drunk nor eaten, not having done anything on earth, and looking like a person who has reached the Good House.[8]

I said to Naneferkaptah: (40) ["Welcome back! Let me] see this book for which we have taken these [great] pains!" He put the book into my hand. I recited one spell from it; I charmed the sky, (4,1) the earth, the netherworld, the mountains, the waters. I discovered what all the birds of the sky and the fish of the deep and the beasts were saying. I recited another spell; I saw Pre appearing in the sky with his Ennead. I saw the Moon rising, and all the stars of the sky in their forms. I saw the fish of the deep, though there were twenty-one divine cubits of water over them.

As I could not write—I mean, compared with Naneferkaptah,[9] my brother, who was a good scribe and very wise man—he had a sheet of new papyrus brought to him. He wrote on it every word that was in the book before him. He soaked it[10] in beer, he dissolved it in water. When he knew it had dissolved, he drank it and knew what had been in it.

(5) We returned to Coptos the same day and made holiday before Isis of Coptos and Harpocrates. We went on board, we traveled north, we reached a point six miles north of Coptos.

Now Thoth had found out everything that had happened to Naneferkaptah regarding the book, and Thoth hastened to report it to Pre, saying: "Learn of my right and my case against Naneferkaptah, the son of Pharaoh Mernebptah! He went to my storehouse; he plundered it; he seized my box with my document. He killed my guardian who was watching over it!" He was told: "He is yours[11] together with every person belonging to him." They sent a divine power from heaven, saying: "Do not allow Naneferkaptah and any person belonging to him to get to Memphis safely!"

At a certain moment the boy Merib came out from under the awning of Pharaoh's ship, fell into the water, and drowned.[12] All the people on board cried out. Naneferkaptah came out from his tent, recited a spell to him, and made him rise up, though there were (10) twenty-one divine cubits of water over him. He recited a spell to him and made him relate to him everything that had happened to him, and the nature of the accusation that Thoth had made before Pre.

We returned to Coptos with him. We had him taken to the Good House. We had him tended, we had him embalmed like a prince and important person. We laid him to rest in his coffin in the desert of Coptos. Naneferkaptah, my brother, said: "Let us go north, let us not delay, lest Pharaoh hear the things that have happened to us and his heart become sad because of them." We went on board, we went north without delay.

Six miles north of Coptos, at the place where the boy Merib had fallen into the river, I came out from under the awning of Pharaoh's ship, fell into the river, and drowned. All the people on board cried out and told Naneferkaptah. He came out from the tent of Pharaoh's ship, recited a spell to me, and made me rise up, though there were twenty-one divine cubits (15) of water over me. He had me brought up, recited a spell to me, and made me relate to him everything that had happened to me, and the nature of the accusation that Thoth had made before Pre.

He returned to Coptos with me. He had me taken to the Good House. He had me tended, he had me embalmed in the manner of a prince and very important person. He laid me to rest in the tomb in which the boy Merib was resting. He went on board, he went north without delay.

Six miles north of Coptos, at the place where we had fallen into the river, he spoke to his heart saying: "Could I go to Coptos and dwell there also? If I go to Memphis now and Pharaoh asks me about his children, what shall I say to him? Can I say to him, 'I took your children to the region of Thebes; I killed them and stayed alive, and I have come to Memphis yet alive'?"

He sent for a scarf of royal linen belonging to him, and made it into a bandage; he bound the book, placed it on his body, (20) and made it fast. Naneferkaptah came out from under the awning of Pharaoh's ship, fell into the water, and drowned. All the people on board cried out, saying: "Great woe, sad woe! Will he return, the good scribe, the learned man whose like has not been?"

Pharaoh's ship sailed north, no man on earth knowing where Naneferkaptah was. They reached Memphis and sent word to Pharaoh. Pharaoh came down to meet Pharaoh's ship; he wore mourning and all the people of Memphis wore mourning, including the priests of Ptah, the chief priest of Ptah, the council, and all Pharaoh's household. Then they saw Naneferkaptah holding on to the rudders of Pharaoh's ship through his craft of a good scribe. They brought him up and saw the book on his body.

Pharaoh said: "Let this book that is on his body be hidden." Then said the council of Pharaoh and the priests of Ptah and the chief priest of Ptah to Pharaoh: "Our great lord—O may he have the lifetime of Pre—Naneferkaptah was a good scribe and a very learned man!" Pharaoh had (25) them give him entry into the Good House on the sixteenth day, wrapping on the thirty-fifth, burial on the seventieth day. And they laid him to rest in his coffin in his resting place.

These are the evil things that befell us on account of this book of which you say, "Let it be given to me." You have no claim to it, whereas our lives on earth were taken on account of it!

Setne takes the book

Setne said to Ahwere: "Let me have this book that I see between you and Naneferkaptah, or else I will take it by force!" Naneferkaptah rose from the bier and said: "Are you Setne, to whom this woman has told these dire things and you have not accepted them? The said book, will you be able to seize it through the power of a good scribe, or through skill in playing draughts with me? Let the two of us play draughts for it!" Said Setne, "I am ready."

They put before them the game board with its pieces, and they both played. Naneferkaptah won one game from Setne. He recited a spell to him, struck his head with the game-box that was before him, and made him sink into the ground as far as his legs. He did the same with the second game. He won it (30) from Setne, and made him sink into the ground as far as his phallus. He did the same with the third game, and made him sink into the ground as far as his ears. After this Setne was in great straits at the hands of Naneferkaptah.

Setne called to his foster-brother Inaros, saying: "Hasten up to the earth and tell Pharaoh everything that has happened to me; and bring the amulets of my father Ptah and my books of sorcery." He hastened up to the earth and told Pharaoh everything that had happened to Setne. Pharaoh said: "Take him the amulets of his father Ptah and his books of sorcery." Inaros hastened down into the tomb. He put the amulets on the body of Setne, and he jumped up in that very moment. Setne stretched out his hand for the book and seized it. Then, as Setne came up from the tomb, light went before him, darkness went behind him, and Ahwere wept after him, saying: "Hail, O darkness! Farewell, O light! Everything that was (35) in the tomb has departed!" Naneferkaptah said to Ahwere: "Let your heart not grieve. I will make him bring this book back here, with a forked stick in his hand and a lighted brazier on his head!"[13]

Setne came up from the tomb and made it fast behind him, as it had been. Setne went before Pharaoh and related to him the things that had happened to him on account of the book. Pharaoh said to Setne: "Take this book back to the tomb of Naneferkaptah like a wise man, or else he will make you take it back with a forked stick in your hand and a lighted brazier on your head." Setne did not listen to him. Then Setne had no occupation on earth but to unroll the book and read from it to everyone.

Setne and Tabubu

After this it happened one day that Setne was strolling in the forecourt of the temple of Ptah. Then he saw [a woman] who was very beautiful, there being no other woman like her in appearance. She was beautiful and wore many golden jewels, and maid servants walked behind her as well as two men servants belonging to her household. (5,1) The moment Setne saw her, he did not know where on earth he was. He called his man servant, saying: "Hasten to the place where this woman is, and find out what her position is." The man servant hastened to the place where the woman was. He called to the maid servant who was following her and asked her, saying, "What woman is this?" She told him: "It is Tabubu, the daughter of the prophet of Bastet, mistress of Ankhtawi. She has come here to worship Ptah, the great god."

The servant returned to Setne and related to him every word she had said to him. Setne said to the servant: "Go, say to the maid, 'It is Setne Khamwas, the son of Pharaoh Usermare, who has sent me to say, "I will give you ten pieces of gold—spend an hour with me. Or do (5) you have a complaint of wrongdoing? I will have it settled for you. I will have you taken to a hidden place where no one on earth shall find you." ' "

The servant returned to the place where Tabubu was. He called her maid and told her. She cried out as if what he said was an insult. Tabubu said to the servant: "Stop talking to this foolish maid; come and speak with me." The servant hastened to where Tabubu was and said to her: "I will give you ten pieces of gold; spend an hour with Setne Khamwas, the son of Pharaoh Usermare. If you have a complaint of wrongdoing, he will have it settled for you. He will take you to a hidden place where no one on earth shall find you."

Tabubu said: "Go, tell Setne, 'I am of priestly rank, I am not a low person. If you desire to do what you wish with me, you must come to Bubastis, to my house. It is furnished with everything, and you shall do what you wish with me, without anyone on earth (10) finding me and without my acting like a low woman of the street.' "

The servant returned to Setne and told him everything she had said to him. He said, "That suits (me)!" Everyone around Setne was indignant.

Setne had a boat brought to him. He went on board and hastened to Bubastis. When he came to the west of the suburb he found a very lofty house that had a wall around it, a garden on its north, and a seat[14] at its door. Setne asked, "Whose house is this?" They told him, "It is the house of Tabubu." Setne went inside the wall. While he turned his face to the storehouse in the garden they announced him to Tabubu. She came down, took Setne's hand, and said to him: "By the welfare of the house of the prophet of Bastet, mistress of Ankhtawi, which you have reached, it will please me greatly if you will take the trouble to come up with me."

Setne walked up (15) the stairs of the house with Tabubu. He found the upper story of the house swept and adorned, its floor adorned with real lapis-lazuli and real turquoise. Many couches were in it, spread with royal linen, and many golden cups were on the table. A golden cup was filled with wine and put into Setne's hand. She said to him, "May it please you to eat something. He said to her, "I could not do that."

Incense was put on the brazier; ointment was brought to him of the kind provided for Pharaoh. Setne made holiday with Tabubu, never having seen anyone like her.

Setne said to Tabubu: "Let us accomplish what we have come here for." She said to him: "You will return to your house in which you live. I am of priestly rank; I am not a low person. If you desire to do what you wish with me you must make for me a deed of maintenance and (20) of compensation in money for everything, all goods belonging to you."[15] He said to her: "Send for the schoolteacher." He was brought at once. He made for her a deed of maintenance and of compensation in money for everything, all goods belonging to him.

At this moment one come to announce to Setne, "Your children are below." He said, "Let them be brought up." Tabubu rose and put on a garment of royal linen. Setna saw all her limbs through it, and his desire became even greater than it had been before. Setne said: "Tabubu, let me accomplish what I have come here for!" She said to him: "You will return to your house in which you live. I am of priestly rank; I am not a low person. If you desire to do what you wish with me, you must make your children subscribe to my deed. Do not leave them to contend with my children over your property." He had his children brought and made them subscribe to the deed.

Setne said to Tabubu: "Let me accomplish (25) what I have come for!" She said to him: "You will return to your house in which you live. I am of priestly rank; I am not a low person. If you desire to do what you wish with me, you must have your children killed. Do not leave them to contend with my children over your property." Setne said: "Let the abomination that came into your head be done to them." She had his children killed before him. She had them thrown down from the window to the dogs and cats. They ate their flesh, and he heard them as he drank with Tabubu.

Setne said to Tabubu: "Let us accomplish what we have come here for! All the things that you have said, I have done them all for you." She said to him: "Come now to this storehouse."[16] Setne went to the storehouse. He lay down on a couch of ivory and ebony, his wish about to be fulfilled.[17] Tabubu lay down beside Setne. He stretched out his hand to touch her, and she opened her mouth (30) wide[18] in a loud cry. Setne awoke in a state of great heat, his phallus in a . . . ,[19] and there were no clothes on him at all.

At this moment Setne saw a noble person borne in a litter, with many men running beside him, and he had the likeness of Pharaoh. Setne was about to rise but could not rise for shame because he had no clothes on. Pharaoh said: "Setne, what is this state that you are in?" He said: "It is Naneferkaptah who has done it all to me!" Pharaoh said: "Go to Memphis; your children want you; they stand in their rank before Pharaoh." Setne said to Pharaoh: "My great lord—O may he have the lifetime of Pre—how can I go to Memphis with no clothes on me at all?" Pharaoh called to a servant who was standing by and made him give clothes to Setne. Pharaoh said: "Setne, go to Memphis; (35) your children are alive; they stand in their rank before Pharaoh."

Setne returns the book

When Setne came to Memphis he embraced his children, for he found them alive. Pharaoh said to Setne: "Was it a state of drunkenness you were in before?" Setne related everything that had happened with Tabubu and Naneferkaptah. Pharaoh said: "Setne, I did what I could with you before, saying, 'They will kill you if you do not take this book back to the place you took it from.' You have not listened to me until now. Take this book back to Naneferkaptah, with a forked stick in your hand and a lighted brazier on your head."

When Setne came out from before Pharaoh, there was a forked stick in his hand and a lighted brazier on his head. He went down into the tomb in which Naneferkaptah was. Ahwere said to him: "Setne, it is the great god Ptah who has brought you back safely." (6,1) Naneferkaptah laughed, saying, "It is what I told you before." Setne greeted Naneferkaptah, and he found one could say that Pre was in the whole tomb. Ahwere and Naneferkaptah greeted Setne warmly.

Setne said: "Naneferkaptah, is there any matter which is shameful?"[20] Naneferkaptah said: "Setne, you know that Ahwere and her son Merib are in Coptos; here in this tomb they are through the craft of a good scribe.[21] Let it be asked of you to undertake the task of going to Coptos and [bringing them] (5) here."

When Setne had come up from the tomb, he went before Pharaoh and related to Pharaoh everything that Naneferkaptah had said to him. Pharaoh said: "Setne, go to Coptos, bring Ahwere and her son Merib." He said to Pharaoh: "Let the ship of Pharaoh and its equipment be given to me."

The ship of Pharaoh and its equipment were given to him. He went on board, he set sail, he reached Coptos without delay. It was announced to the priests of Isis of Coptos, and the chief priest of Isis. They came down to meet him, they conducted him to the shore.

He went up from it, he went into the temple of Isis of Coptos and Harpocrates. He sent for an ox, a goose, and wine, and made burnt offering and libation before Isis of Coptos and Harpocrates. He went to the desert of Coptos with the priests of Isis and the chief priest of Isis. They spent three days and three nights searching in all the tombs on the desert of Coptos, turning over the stelae of the scribes of the

House of Life, and reading the inscriptions on them. They did not find the resting place (10) in which Ahwere and her son were.

When Naneferkaptah found that they did not find the resting place of Ahwere and her son Merib, he rose up as an old man, a very aged priest, and came to meet Setne. When Setne saw him he said to the old man: "You have the appearance of a man of great age. Do you know the resting place in which Ahwere and her son Merib are?" The old man said to Setne: "My great-grandfather said to my grandfather, 'The resting place of Ahwere and her son Merib is at the south corner of the house of the [chief of police].'"

Setne said to the old man: "Perhaps there is some wrong that the chief of police did to you, on account of which you are trying to have his house torn down?" The old man said to Setne: "Have a watch set over me, and let (15) the house of the chief of police be demolished. If they do not find Ahwere and her son Merib under the south corner of his house, let punishment be done to me."

They set a watch over the old man, and they found the resting place of Ahwere and her son Merib under the south corner of the house of the chief of police. Setne let the two noble persons enter into Pharaoh's ship. He had the house of the chief of police built as it had been before. Naneferkaptah let Setne learn the fact that it was he who had come to Coptos, to let them find the resting place in which Ahwere and her son Merib were. Setne went on board Pharaoh's ship. He went north and without delay he reached Memphis with all the people who were with him. When it was announced before Pharaoh, he came down to meet the ship of Pharaoh. He let the noble persons enter into the tomb in which Naneferkaptah was. He had it closed over (20) them all together.

Colophon

This is the complete text, a tale of Setne Khamwas and Naneferkaptah, and his wife Ahwere and her son Merib. It was copied by – – – – – in year 15, first month of winter.

NOTES

1. By her pert quotation of the king's own words Ahwere won the king over, so that he permitted her to marry her brother.

2. I.e., her menstruation period had failed to come.

3. If that is the correct rendering it implies that members of the royal house were registered in the House of Life.

4. I.e., the inscriptions composed by the scribes of the House of Life.

5. Restored in accordance with the recurrence of the sentence in line 3/37. The correct understanding of the passage is from K.-T. Zauzich,

Enchoria, 1 (1971), 83–86. The "divine cubit" appears to have been identical with the "royal cubit" of 0,525 m; see E. Lüddeckens, "Demotische Texte," *Papyrologia Coloniensia,* 2 (1968), 19–20.

6. Lit., "hundred *deben*," the *deben* being a weight of 91 grams.

7. I.e., the measure *3r* = *iter*; on the length of the *iter* see p. 95.

8. The house of embalming; i.e., she looked like a dead person.

9. Lit., "I was speaking with regard to Naneferkaptah."

10. The new copy.

11. Lit., "He is before you."

12. Lit., "He became one praised of Re."

13. These must have been symbols of repentance.

14. *Ns3.t*: Gunn, "terrace"; Brunner-Traut, "reception hall"; *Glossar,* p. 228, "seat, bench." See also Černý, *Copt. Dic.,* p. 110.

15. I.e., he was to make over to her everything he owned.

16. The same building that had been mentioned before in line 5,13. Apparently the meaning here is not an ordinary storehouse but rather a secluded chamber.

17. Lit., "his wish receiving gold."

18. Lit., "to the ground."

19. The meaning of *šhy3* is not known.

20. I.e., "Is there anything wrong that I could set right for you?"

21. On this sentence see K.-T. Zauzich, *Enchoria,* 1 (1971), 86, and M. Gilula, *Enchoria,* 6 (1976), 125.

SETNE KHAMWAS AND SI-OSIRE (SETNE II)

The beginning is lost and cannot be reconstructed. But it is clear that immediately before the present beginning it had been told that Setne and his wife Mehusekhe had been praying to the gods for a son.

(**1**,1) – – – – – [One night] she dreamed that one spoke to her, [saying: "Are] you Mehusekhe, [the wife] of Setne, who is lying [ᒥhereᒧ in the templeᒧ] so as to receive healing? – – – [When tomorrow has come] go to [the place where your husband] Setne ᒥbathesᒧ. You will find a melon vine grown there. [ᒥBreak off a branchᒧ] with its gourds and grind it. [Make it into] a remedy, put it [in water and drink it]. – – – [you will receive the fluid of conception] from him that [night]."

Mehusekhe awoke [from] the dream in which she had seen these things. She acted in accordance with (5) [everything she had been told in the dream. She lay down by] the side of her husband [Setne]. She received [the fluid of] conception from him. When [her time of purification came she had] the sign [of a woman who has conceived. It was announced to Setne, and] his heart was very happy on account of it. He [hung] an amulet [on her] and recited a spell to her.

One night Setne slept [and dreamed that one spoke] to him, saying: "Mehusekhe, your wife, has received [the fluid of conception from you]. The boy that shall be born [shall be named] Si-Osire. Many are [the wonders that he shall do in Egypt." Setne awoke] from the dream in which he had seen these things, [and his heart was] very [happy].

[Mehusekhe] made [her months of pregnancy] − − −. [When her time of bearing came] she bore a male child. When Setne was informed of it [he named him] Si-Osire, in accordance with what had been said in the dream. − − − (10) − − − , they cradled [him] and nursed him.

When the boy [Si-Osire was one year old] people said of him, "He is two years old." When he was two [years] old, they said, "He is three years old." [Setne did not spend an hour] without looking at the boy Si-Osire, for his love [of him] was very great.

He grew big and strong; he was put in school. [After a short time he surpassed] the scribe who had been given him for instruction. The boy Si-Osire began to recite writings with the scribes of the House of Life in [ˈthe temple of Ptahˈ. All who heard him thought him] the wonder of the land. Setne wished very much [to have him] taken to the banquet before Pharaoh, − − − and to present him to all − − −.

[On a certain day it happened that] Setne was being purified for the banquet − − − [in his house] (15) − − − and the boy Si-Osire [was to go to the] banquet [with him. At that moment] Setne heard the sound of wailing − − −. He looked [down from the window] of his house [and saw the coffin of a rich man] being carried out to the cemetery with [very loud] wailing − − − , and great were the honors − − − . [In another moment] as he was looking down, he saw [the body of a poor man being carried out of Memphis] wrapped (only) in a mat − − − without anyone walking [behind him].

Setne [said]: "By [Ptah, the great god, how much happier is the rich man who is honored] with the sound of [wailing] than the poor man who is carried to the cemetery − − − − − −."

(20) [Si-Osire said to his father: "May it go with you in the netherworld] as it will go with this poor man in the netherworld! [May it not go with you as it will go with this rich man] in the netherworld!"

[When Setne heard the words of Si-Osire his] heart [became] very [sad. He said: "Do I] hear the voice [of my son]?" [The boy Si-Osire answered him: "If you wish I will show you the poor man who was not mourned, and the rich man for whom all the wailing was done]."

(25) [Setne asked him, "How could you do this?" Si-Osire took his father by the hand; he conducted] Setne to a place [in the western desert] − − − − − −.

(30) − − − − − −.[1] [They entered the fourth hall, and Setne saw] people who were [plaiting ropes, while donkeys were chewing them up].

(**2**,1) There were others whose provisions of water and bread were hung above them, and while they scrambled to bring them down, other people were digging pits at their feet, to prevent them from getting at them.

They entered the fifth hall, and Setne saw the noble spirits standing in their ranks. But those who were accused of crimes were standing at the door pleading, and the pivot of the door of the fifth hall was fixed in the right eye of a man who was pleading and lamenting loudly.

They entered the sixth hall, and Setne saw the gods of the [tribunal] of the inhabitants of the netherworld standing in their ranks, while the servants of the netherworld stood making accusations.

They entered the seventh hall, and Setne saw the mysterious form of Osiris, the great god, (5) seated on his throne of fine gold, crowned with the *atef*-crown. Anubis, the great god, was on his left, the great god Thoth was on his right, and the gods of the tribunal of the inhabitants of the netherworld stood on his left and right. The balance stood in the center before them, and they weighed the good deeds against the misdeeds, Thoth, the great god, writing, while Anubis gave the information to his colleague.

He who would be found to have more misdeeds than good deeds [is handed over] to the Devourer, who belongs to the lord of the netherworld. His *ba* is destroyed together with his body, and he is not allowed to breathe ever again.

He who would be found to have more good deeds than misdeeds is taken in among the gods of the tribunal of the lord of the netherworld, while his *ba* goes to the sky together with the august spirits.

He who would be found to have good deeds equal to his misdeeds is taken in among the excellent spirits who serve Sokar-Osiris.[2]

Then Setne saw a rich man clothed in a garment of royal linen, standing near the spot where Osiris was, and he was of very high rank. Setne was astounded by the things he saw in the netherworld.

Si-Osire walked out in front of him and said: "My father Setne, did you not see (10) that rich man clothed in a garment of royal linen, standing near the spot where Osiris is? He is the poor man whom you saw being carried out from Memphis with no one walking behind him and wrapped in a mat. They brought him to the netherworld. They weighed his misdeeds against the good deeds he had done on earth. They found his good deeds more numerous than his misdeeds in relation to his lifespan, which Thoth had assigned him in writing, and in relation to his luck on earth. It was ordered by Osiris to give the burial equipment of that rich man, whom you saw being carried out from Memphis with great honors, to this poor man, and to place him among the noble spirits, as a man of god who serves Sokar-Osiris and stands near the spot where Osiris is.

"That rich man whom you saw: they took him to the netherworld. They weighed his misdeeds against his good deeds. They found his misdeeds more numerous than the good deeds he had done on earth. It was ordered to imprison him in the netherworld. He is [the man whom you saw] with the pivot of the door of the netherworld fixed in his right eye, so that it opens and shuts on his eye, and his mouth is open in great lamentation. By Osiris, the great god, lord of the netherworld,when I said to you on earth, (15) '[May it go] with you as it will go with this poor man; may it not go with you as it will go with this rich man,' I knew what would happen to him!"

Setne said: "My son Si-Osire, many are the marvels that I have seen in the netherworld. Now let me learn [what is happening] to those people who are plaiting ropes while donkeys chew them up; and those others whose provisions of water and bread are hung above them, and while they scramble to bring them down, others dig pits at their feet, to prevent them from getting at them."

Si-Osire said: "In truth, my father Setne, those people whom you saw plaiting ropes while donkeys were chewing them up, they are the kind of people on earth who are under a curse of the god. They labor night and day for their livelihood, while their women rob them behind their backs, and they find no bread to eat. When they came to the netherworld in their turn, their misdeeds were found to be more numerous than their good deeds. It was ordered that what had happened to them on earth should happen to them in the netherworld. So too with those people whom you saw, whose provisions of water and bread were hung above them, and while they scrambled to bring them down, (20) others dug pits at their feet, to prevent them from getting at them. They are the kind of people on earth who have their life[3] before them while the god digs a pit under their feet, to prevent them from finding it. When they came to the netherworld in their turn, what had happened to them on earth was made to happen to them in the netherworld also, while their *ba*'s were received in the netherworld.

"Take it to your heart, my father Setne: He who is beneficent on earth, to him one is beneficent in the netherworld. And he who is evil, to him one is evil. It is so decreed [and will remain so] for ever. The things that you have seen in the netherworld at Memphis, they happen in the forty-two nomes [in which are the judges] of Osiris, the great god. − − − − − −."

When Si-Osire had ended the words spoken to his father, he came down from the desert of Memphis, [his father Setne] embracing him, his hand being in his hand. Setne asked [him]: "My son Si-Osire, is it a different way we are going down (25) than the way we went up?" But Si-Osire did not answer Setne at all.

Setne marveled [at the] things he had experienced, saying: "He will be able [to become] one of the august spirits, a man of god, [and I shall] go with him, saying, 'This is my son!' " Setne recited [a spell from the] book of exorcising spirits, while he was still full of wonder at [the things] he had seen in the netherworld. And those things weighed very heavily [on him] because he could not reveal (them) to any [man on earth].

[When the] boy Si-Osire [reached] twelve years of age, it came to pass that there was no [scribe and learned man] in Memphis [who could compare] with him in reciting spells and performing magic.

The Nubian sorcerer

[After these things] it happened one day that Pharaoh User[mare went] to the court of the palace of Memphis, [and the council] of nobles, generals, and grandees of Egypt [stood in their] ranks in the court. [Then one came to announce: "There is a communication being made by a chieftain of Nubia [which is bound] to his body in a document." When he had been announced (30) [before] Pharaoh, he was brought to the court. He saluted [and said: "Is there anyone who will] read this document [that I have brought] to Egypt before Pharaoh, without breaking its seal, one who will read the writing that is in it without opening it? If [there is no good scribe and learned man in] Egypt who can read it without opening it, I shall take the shame of Egypt to the land of Nubia, my country."

[When] Pharaoh [and the nobles] heard these words [they did not know where on earth] they were. They said: "By Ptah, does a good scribe and learned man have the power to read writings of which he sees only [their] outside, and could one read a document [without opening it]?" Pharaoh [said]: "Summon to me Setne Khamwas, my son!" They ran, they brought him at once. (3,1) He bowed to the ground, he saluted [Pharaoh; he straightened up], stood on his feet and spoke the worshipful greeting of Pharaoh.

Pharaoh said to him: "My [son] Setne, have you heard the words that this chieftain [of Nubia] spoke before me, saying, 'Is there a good scribe and learned man in Egypt who can read this document that is in my hand, without breaking its seal, and shall learn what is written in it without opening it?' "

When Setne heard these words he did not know where [on earth] he was. He said: "My great lord, who is he who could read writing without opening it? But let me be given ten days' time, that I may see what I can (5) do to prevent the shame of Egypt from being taken to the land of Nubia, the country of gum eaters." Said Pharaoh: "They are granted to my son Setne."

They gave rooms to relax in to the Nubian and they prepared muck[4] for him in the Nubian manner. Pharaoh rose from the court with a very sad heart. He lay down without drinking and eating. Setne went to his house without knowing where on earth he was going. He wrapped himself in his garments from head to foot and lay down without knowing where on earth he was.

When his wife Mehusekhe was told of it she came to the place where Setne was. She put her hand inside his clothes; she found no warmth as he lay in his clothes. She said to him: "My brother Setne, there is no warmth in the breast, no ⌈stirring⌉ in the flesh. There is sorrow and grief in the heart." (10) He said to her: "Leave me, my sister Mehusekhe. The matter over which my heart grieves is not a thing fit to be revealed to a woman."

The boy Si-Osire came in, stood over his father Setne, and said to him: "My father Setne, why are you lying down with a grieving heart? Tell me the things that are concealed in your heart, that I may make them cease." He said: "Leave me, my son Si-Osire, you are too young for the things that are in my heart; you are not old enough [to have them told] to you." Said Si-Osire: "Tell them to me; I shall relieve your heart of them!"

Setne said: "My son Si-Osire, a chieftain of Nubia has come down to Egypt with a document fastened to his body, saying, 'Is there anyone who will read it without opening it? If there is no good scribe and learned man in Egypt (15) who can read it, I shall take the shame of Egypt to the land of Nubia, my country.' I lay down because my heart grieves on account of it, my son Si-Osire."

The moment Si-Osire heard these words he laughed for a long time. Setne said to him: "Why do you laugh?" He said: "I laugh because you are lying down with a grieving heart on account of such a small matter! Rise up, my father Setne! I can read the document brought to Egypt without opening it, and I shall learn what is written in it without breaking its seal!"

The moment Setne heard these words he rose up at once and said: "What is the proof for the words you have said, my son Si-Osire?" He said to him: "My father Setne, go to the ground-floor rooms of your house. Every book that you shall take (20) out of the chest, I shall tell you what book it is. I shall read it without seeing it, staying above your ground-floor rooms."

Setne rose and stood on his feet. He did everything exactly as Si-Osire had told him. Si-Osire read all the books that his father Setne lifted up before him without opening them. Setne came up from the ground-floor rooms of his house in the greatest joy. He hastened to the place where Pharaoh was. He related to him all the words that the boy Si-Osire had spoken to him, and his heart was exceedingly happy on account of it. At the same time Pharaoh cleansed himself for a banquet with Setne and had Si-Osire brought to him to the banquet. They drank and made holiday.

On the morning of the next day (25) Pharaoh appeared in the court among his grandees. Pharaoh sent for the chieftain of Nubia. He was brought to the court with the document fastened to his body. When he stood in the center of the court, the boy Si-Osire came to the center, stood with the chieftain of Nubia, and addressed him, saying: "Ho you fiend of Nubia whom Amun, his god, may smite! You who came down to Egypt, the beautiful garden of Osiris, the footrest of Re-Harakhti, the beautiful horizon of Shay,[5] saying, 'I will take [its] shame to the land of Nubia,' may the wrath of Amun, your god, smite you! The words that I shall pronounce are the ones that are written in the document. Do not tell lies about them before Pharaoh, your lord!"

When the chieftain (30) of Nubia saw the boy Si-Osire, as he stood in the court, he bowed his head and said: "All words that you shall say, I will not tell lies about them."

The contents of the document

Here begin the stories that Si-Osire related before Pharaoh and his nobles, with the people of Egypt listening to his voice. He said: What is written in the letter of the chieftain of Nubia, who stands here in the center, is the following:

It came to pass one day in the time of Pharaoh Menkh-Pre-Sia-mun,[6] who was (4,1) beneficent king of the whole land, [with Egypt] overflowing with all good things in his time, for he was generous in giving expenditure and work in the great temples of Egypt—that day it happened that the ruler of the land of Nubia was ⌜resting⌝ [in a pavilion] in the woodlands of Amun, when he heard the voices of three chieftains of Nubia [in the] backroom.

One of them was talking in a loud voice and said among other things: "Were it not that Amun might find fault with me, and the lord of Egypt might [punish me], I would cast my sorceries upon Egypt (5) and would make the people of Egypt spend three days and three nights seeing no light, only darkness."

Another of them said among other things: "Were it not that Amun might accuse me, and the lord of Egypt might punish me, I would cast my sorceries upon Egypt, and would have Pharaoh brought from Egypt to the land of Nubia, and would have him beaten with 500 blows of the stick in public before the Ruler, and would have him returned to Egypt, all within six hours."

⟨The third said: "Were it not that Amun might accuse me, and the lord of Egypt might punish me, I would cast my sorceries upon Egypt, and would cause the land to be barren for three years⟩."

When the ruler of Nubia had heard the words spoken by the three chieftains of Nubia, he had them brought before him and said to them: "Who of you is he who said, 'I would cast (10) my sorceries upon Egypt and not let them see the light in three days and three nights'?" They said, "It is Horus-son-of-the-Sow."

He said: "Who is he who said, 'I would cast my sorceries upon Egypt, and would bring Pharaoh to the land of Nubia, and would have him beaten with 500 blows of the stick in public before the Ruler, and would have him returned to Egypt, all within six hours'?" They said, "It is Horus-son-of-the-Nubian-woman."

He said: "Who is he who said, 'I would cast my sorceries upon Egypt, and would cause the land to be barren for three years'?" They said, "It is Horus-son-of-the-Princess."

The ruler said ⟨to Horus-son-of-the-Nubian-woman⟩: "Carry out your feat of (15) sorcery! By Amun, the bull of Meroe, my god, if your hand succeeds, I will do for you many good things!"

Horus-son-of-the-Nubian-woman made a litter of wax with four bearers. He recited a spell to them, he gave them breath, he made them live. He commanded them, saying: "You are to go to Egypt, you are to bring Pharaoh of Egypt up to the place where the Ruler is. He shall be beaten with 500 blows of the stick in public before the Ruler, and you shall return him to Egypt, all within six hours." They said, "Certainly, we shall not omit anything."

The sorceries of the Nubian flew down to Egypt by night. They overpowered Pharaoh (20) Menkh-Pre-Siamun. They took him to the land of Nubia, to the place where the ruler was. They beat him with 500 blows of the stick in public before the ruler, and they returned him to Egypt, all within six hours.

These were the events that Si-Osire related in public before Pharaoh and his nobles, while the people of Egypt listened to his voice. He said: "May the wrath of Amun, your god, smite you! These words that I have spoken, are they not the ones that are written in the document that is in your hand?" Said the chieftain of Nubia: "Go on reading. All the words that you have spoken are true." Si-Osire spoke before Pharaoh:

When they had returned Pharaoh (25) Siamun to Egypt, his back smitten with very great beating, he lay down in the private chamber[7] of the palace, his back greatly smitten. On the morning of the next day Pharaoh said to his councillors: "What has occurred in Egypt while I was away from it?" Ashamed of their thoughts, which were, 'Perhaps Pharaoh has lost his mind?', the councillors said: "Your health, your health, Pharaoh our great lord! Isis, the great goddess, will drive away your affliction! What is the meaning of the words you have spoken to us, [O Pharaoh] our great lord? You are lying in the private chamber of the palace and the gods protect you!"

Pharaoh raised himself; (30) he let [the councillors] see his back, smitten with a very great [beating]. He said: "By Ptah, the great god, (5,1) I was taken to the land of Nubia this night. I was beaten with 500 blows of the stick in public before the ruler, and I was returned to Egypt, all within six hours." When they saw the back of Pharaoh smitten with a very great beating, they opened their mouths in loud cries.

Now Menkh-Pre-Siamun had a [magician] who was called Horus-son-of-Paneshe, a very [learned] man. He came to where Pharaoh was, uttered a loud cry and said: "My [great lord], these are the sorceries of the Nubians! By the life of your − − − I will make them enter − − − − − − execution!" Pharaoh said to him: "Make haste for me. Do not let me be taken to the land of Nubia (5) another night!"

The [magician Horus-son-of] Paneshe returned [quickly]; he brought his books and his amulets to [where Pharaoh] was. He recited a spell to him and bound an amulet on him, to prevent the sorceries of the Nubians from gaining power over him. He [went] out from Pharaoh's presence, took his offerings and libations, went on board a boat, and hastened to Khmun. He went to the temple of Khmun, [made his] offerings and his libations before Thoth, the eight-times great,[8] the lord of Khmun, the great god. He made a prayer before him saying: "Turn your face to me, my lord Thoth! Let not the Nubians take the shame of Egypt to the land of Nubia! It is you who [created] magic [spells]. It is you who suspended the sky, who founded the earth and the netherworld, who placed the gods with − − −. Let me know how to save Pharaoh [from the sorceries of the] Nubians!"

Horus-son-of-Paneshe lay down (10) in the temple. That night he dreamed a dream in which the mysterious form of the great god Thoth spoke to him, saying: "Are you Horus-son-of-Paneshe, the [magician] of Pharaoh Menkh-Pre-Siamun? When the morning of tomorrow has come, go into the library of the temple of Khmun. You will find a chamber[9] that is locked and sealed. Open it and you will find a chest in this chamber, and in it a papyrus scroll which I wrote with my own hand. Take it out, make a copy of it, and put it back in its place. Its name is "the book of magic." It has protected me from the enemies, and it will protect Pharaoh and will save him from the sorceries of the Nubians."

Horus-son-of-Paneshe awoke from the dream in which he had seen these things. (15) He understood that what had happened was the

doing of the god. He acted according to every word that had been
said to him in the dream. He hastened to the place where Pharaoh
was; he made for him a written amulet of sorceries.

When the second day came, the sorceries of Horus-son-of-the-
Nubian-woman returned to Egypt by night, to the place where
Pharaoh was. In the same hour they returned to the place where the
ruler was, for they were unable to gain power over Pharaoh, owing to
the amulets with sorceries which the magician Horus-son-of-Paneshe
had bound on him. On the morning of the next day Pharaoh told the
magician Horus-son-of-Paneshe everything he had seen by night,
how the sorceries of the Nubians had turned back because they were
unable to gain power over him.

Horus-son-of-Paneshe had quantities of pure wax brought to him.
He made a litter and four bearers. He recited (20) a spell to them, he
gave them breath, he made them live. He commanded them, saying:
"Go to the land of Nubia this night. Bring the ruler down to Egypt, to
the place where Pharaoh is. He shall be beated with 500 blows of the
stick in public before Pharaoh, and you shall return him to the land of
Nubia, all within six hours." They said, "Certainly, we shall not omit
anything."

The sorceries of Horus-son-of-Paneshe flew with the clouds of the
sky and hastened to the land of Nubia by night. They overpowered
the ruler, they brought him down to Egypt, they beat him with 500
blows of the stick in public before Pharaoh, and they returned him to
the land of Nubia, all within six hours.

These were the events which Si-Osire related in public before
Pharaoh and his (25) nobles, while the people of Egypt listened to his
voice. He said: "May the wrath of Amun, your god, smite you, you
fiend of Nubia! The words that I have spoken, are they not the ones
that are written in this document?" Said the Nubian, his head bowed
down: "Go on reading. All the words that you have spoken are written
in this document." Si-Osire said:

When all this had happened and the ruler had been returned to the
land of Nubia within six hours, they put him down in his place. He lay
down, he rose in the morning, greatly smitten by the blows he had
received in Egypt. He said to his nobles: "I have been beaten with 500
blows of the stick in public before Pharaoh of Egypt, and they
returned me to the land of Nubia again." He showed his back to the
nobles, and they opened their mouths in a loud cry.

The ruler sent for Horus-son-of-the-Nubian-woman; he said: "May
Amun, (30) the bull of Meroe, my god, curse you! It was you who
went to the people of Egypt. Now consider for me what you will do to

save me from the hand of Horus-son-of-Paneshe!" He made his sorceries, he bound them on the ruler, in order to protect him from the sorceries of Horus-son-of-Paneshe.

On the night of the second day, the sorceries of Horus-son-of-Paneshe flew to the land of Nubia. They brought the ruler down to Egypt, they beat him with 500 blows of the stick in public before Pharaoh, and they returned him to the land of Nubia, all within six hours. This happened to the ruler for three days, for the sorceries of the Nubians were unable to protect the ruler from the hand of Horus-son-of-Paneshe.

The ruler was greatly distressed. He sent for Horus-son-of-the-Nubian-woman, he said to him: "Woe you fiend of Nubia! You have caused me to be humiliated by (35) the people of Egypt! You could not save me from their hands! By Amun, the bull of Meroe, my god, if you cannot make me [safe] from the sky-boats of the people of Egypt, I shall make you suffer a harsh death which shall be painful to you!" He said: "My lord the Ruler, let me be sent down to Egypt, that I may see him who does sorcery there, that I may do sorcery against him and let him taste the scorn I have in my heart for him!"

Horus-son-of-the-Nubian-woman was sent off by the ruler. He went to the place where his mother, the Nubian woman, was. ⟨He told her all that had happened to him. She said to him⟩: (6,1) "If you go down to Egypt to do sorcery there, beware of the people of Egypt! You will not be able to contend with them. Do not get caught in their hands, for then you will not return to the land of Nubia ever!"

He said: "There is nothing to the words you have said. I cannot avoid going down to Egypt if I want to cast my sorceries into it." The Nubian woman, his mother, said to him: "If it is so that you will go down to Egypt, set some signs between me and you, so that if you are defeated, I shall come to you and see if I can save you." He said to her: "If it happens that I am defeated, then when you are drinking [and eating], the water will take on the color of blood before you, the food before you the color of meat, (5) and the sky will have the color of blood before you."

When Horus-son-of-the-Nubian-woman had set the signs between him and his mother, he hurried down to Egypt, crammed with sorcery. He traversed the land Amun had made to Memphis, to the place where Pharaoh was, searching for him who was doing sorcery in Egypt.

He came to the court before Pharaoh and said in a loud voice: "Woe to you who makes sorcery against me in the court, in the place where Pharaoh is, with the people of Egypt looking to him! You two scribes of the House of Life, (or) you scribe of the House of Life, who does sorcery against the ruler, bringing him down to Egypt inspite of me!"

When he had said these words, Horus-son-of-Paneshe stood in the court before Pharaoh and said: "Woe you fiend of Nubia! Are you not Horus-son-of-the-Nubian-woman, whom I rescued in the gardens of Pre, when your companion (10) from Nubia who was with you and you were drowning in the water, having fallen down from the mountain in the east of On? Do you not repent of having carried off Pharaoh, your lord, and having beaten his back in the place where the ruler is? Do you now come to Egypt, saying, 'Is he here who does sorcery against me?' By Atum, lord of On, the gods of Egypt have brought you here, to pay you back in their land! Beware, I come to you!"

When Horus-son-of-Paneshe had spoken these words, Horus-son-of-the-Nubian-woman answered him, saying: "Is it he whom I taught the language of wolves who does sorcery against me?"

The chieftain of Nubia then did a feat of sorcery: he made a fire break out in the court. Pharaoh and the nobles of Egypt cried out aloud, saying: "Hasten to us, you magician, Horus-son-of-Paneshe!" Horus-son-of-Paneshe made (15) a magic formula and made the sky pour a southern rain on top of the fire. It was extinguished at once.

The Nubian did another feat of sorcery: he cast a big cloud on the court, so that no man could see his brother or his companion. Horus-son-of-Paneshe recited a spell to the sky and made it vanish and be stilled from the evil wind in which it had been.

Horus-son-of-the-Nubian-woman did another feat of sorcery. He made a great vault of stone, 200 cubits long and 50 cubits wide, above Pharaoh and his nobles, so that Egypt would be separated from its king and the land deprived of its lord. When Pharaoh looked up at the sky and saw a vault of stone above him, he opened his mouth in a great cry, together with the people who were in the court. (20) Horus-son-of-Paneshe recited a magic spell: he created a sky-boat of papyrus and made it carry away the vault of stone. It sailed with it to "Great Lake," the big water of Egypt.

Then the chieftain of Nubia knew that he could not contend with the Egyptian. He did a feat of sorcery so as to become invisible in the court, in order to escape to the land of Nubia, his home. Horus-son-of-Paneshe recited a spell against him, revealed the sorceries of the Nubian, and let him be seen by Pharaoh and the people of Egypt who stood in the court: he had assumed the shape of a wild gander and was about to depart. Horus-son-of-Paneshe recited a spell against him and made him turn on his back, while a fowler stood over him, his sharp knife in his hand, and about to do him harm.

When all this happened, the signs that Horus-son-of-the-Nubian-woman had set (25) between him and his mother all happened before her. She hastened down to Egypt in the guise of a goose. She stood above the palace of Pharaoh, her voice screaming to her son, who was in the guise of a wild gander, while the fowler stood over him. Horus-son-of-Paneshe looked up at the sky; he saw the Nubian woman in the guise in which she was; he knew that she was the Nubian woman. He recited a spell against her and made her turn on her back, with a fowler standing over her, his knife about to give her death.

She changed the guise in which she was, assumed her shape of a Nubian woman, and pleaded thus: "[Do not make an end] of us, Horus-son-of-Paneshe! Forgive us this misdeed! If you will give us a sky-boat, we will not return to Egypt ever again!" Horus-son-of-Paneshe made an oath by Pharaoh and the gods (30) of Egypt, saying: "I shall not [let go of] my feat of sorcery until you make an oath to me, not to come back to Egypt for any purpose!" The Nubian woman raised her hand, not to come down to Egypt ever again. Horus-son-of-the-Nubian-woman swore an oath, saying: "I shall not come down to Egypt for 1,500 years!"

Horus-son-of-Paneshe let go of his feat of sorcery. He gave a sky-boat to Horus-son-of-the-Nubian-woman and the Nubian woman, his mother, and they flew to the land of Nubia, their home.

Si-Osire reveals himself

These were the events that Si-Osire related before Pharaoh, with the people of Egypt listening to his voice, while Setne, his father, saw everything, and the head of the chieftain of Nubia was bowed down. He said: "By your life, my great lord, this one before you is Horus-son-of-the-Nubian-woman, whose story I have told, and who has not repented of those things he did previously, and has come down to (35) Egypt at the end of 1,500 years to do sorceries here! By Osiris, the great god, lord of the netherworld, with whom I rest, I am Horus-son-of-Paneshe, I who stand before Pharaoh! When I found out in the netherworld that the fiend of Nubia was going to cast his sorceries here, while there was not a good scribe and learned man in Egypt at this time who would be able to contend (7,1) with him, I begged Osiris in the netherworld to let me come up to the earth again, so as to prevent him from taking the shame of Egypt to the land of Nubia. The order was given by Osiris to let me come to the earth.

"I awoke, I flew up, so as to find Setne, the son of Pharaoh, on the desert of On, or the desert of Memphis. I grew as that melon vine, so as to return to the body again and be born in the land, in order to do sorcery against this fiend of Nubia who stands in the court." Horus-son-of-Paneshe did a feat of sorcery, while being in the shape of Si-Osire, against the chieftain of Nubia. He made a fire around him; it consumed him in the midst of the court, (5) while Pharaoh saw it, together with his nobles and the people of Egypt.

Si-Osire vanished as a shadow from the presence of Pharaoh and Setne, his father, without their seeing him. Pharaoh marveled greatly, together with his grandees, at the things they had seen in the court. They said: "There is not a good scribe and learned man like Horus-son-of-Paneshe! Never, never will there be his like again! Setne opened his mouth in a great cry, because Si-Osire had vanished as a shadow without his seeing him.

Pharaoh rose from the court, his heart excited by the things he had seen. Pharaoh commanded to make preparations on behalf of Setne, so as to receive him, because of Si-Osire, his son, so as to soothe his heart. When night came Setne went [to] his house with a very sad heart. Mehusekhe lay down at his side, (10) and she received the fluid of conception from him that night. At the right time she bore a male child, who was named User-Mont-Hor.

Setne never failed to make burnt offerings and libations to the spirit of Horus-son-of-Paneshe at all times.

Colophon

This is the end of the book, written — — — — — —.

NOTES

1. In the lines now lost it was told that they entered the netherworld and saw seven halls.

2. I.e., these people remain in the netherworld and may not go up to the sky.

3. Perhaps "livelihood," rather than "life," was intended.

4. A coarse word designed to express the Egyptian contempt for Nubian food.

5. The god who personifies fate.

6. A garbled throne name. It is not clear which king the Demotic author had in mind.

7. *Knh.t* must mean something else besides "shrine, chapel." Here it is probably a "private chamber" or "bedroom." See also *Instruction of Ankhsheshonq*, 2/19 (p. 162, below), and the suggested meaning "dark (place)" in Černý, *Copt. Dic.*, p. 60, based on E. Hornung's remarks on *knh*, "grow dark, make dark" in *ZÄS*, 86 (1961), 113–114.

8. So, according to Griffith's restoration.

9. Again the word is *knh.t*.

PRINCE PEDIKHONS AND QUEEN SERPOT

From Vienna Demotic Papyrus 6165

The text translated here is an episode in the tale called *Egyptians and Amazons*, a tale belonging to the group of texts known as the Story-Cycle of King Petubastis. Incompletely preserved in many fragmentary demotic papyri of Greco-Roman date, the Story-Cycle of Petubastis is a sequence of tales woven around the persons of certain rulers, notably

King Pedibast of Tanis, Prince Inaros of Heliopolis, their kinsmen Pemu and Pedikhons, and others.

The central themes of the cycle are contests and combats between the various heroes and their adversaries, the combats being preceded by lengthy challenges and speeches. The tales seem to be rooted in the historical situation of the Post-Imperial Epoch, when Egypt was ruled by numerous petty princes who fought each other for power and prestige. But as literary topics, the duels between heroes and their elaborate challenges probably owe more to a knowledge of the Homeric epics and other works of Greek literature. Moreover, certain themes are clearly inspired by Greek models, notably the tale *Egyptians and Amazons*, which echoes the story of Achilles and Penthesilea.

Six distinct stories are presently known to belong to the Petubastis cycle, all of them unfortunately in a very fragmentary state. They are: (1) *Inaros and the Griffin,* (2) *The Contest for the Benefice of Amun,* (3) *The Contest for the Breastplate of Inaros,* (4) *Egyptians and Amazons,* (5) *Naneferkasokar and the Babylonians,* and (6) a fragment mentioning Pemu and two other heroes.

The papyrus containing *Egyptians and Amazons* is in tatters, with less than half of the text preserved and without the beginning. In its present form it starts with the arrival of Prince Pedikhons in the land of Khor, the term Khor being an old designation of Syria which here also denotes Assyria. A region within the land of Khor is ruled by Amazons under their Queen Serpot. Prince Pedikhons has invaded the land of the Amazons and is encamped near their principal fortress. The episode translated below begins with Queen Serpot's war council and her decision to send her younger sister Ashteshyt, dressed as a man, to spy out the Egyptian camp with its army, consisting of Egyptian and Assyrian troops. After Ashteshyt has accomplished her mission, Serpot decides to take the offensive. She marshals her troops, exhorts them, attacks, and inflicts heavy losses on the Egyptian and Assyrian troops. Prince Pedikhons has watched the fighting without taking part. At night he tells his troops that on the morrow he will fight Queen Serpot in single combat. On the next day he challenges the queen and they fight the entire day. At sunset they agree on an armistice and engage in a conversation which becomes increasingly friendly; and when at last they look at each other closely they fall in love. This is the end of the episode translated here.

Publication: A. Volten, *Ägypter und Amazonen, MPON,* n.s., 6 (Vienna, 1962).

Comments: A. Volten, *Akten des 8. Internationalen Kongresses für Papyrologie, MPON,* n.s., 5 (Vienna, 1956), 147–152, relation to Greek literature.   Kitchen, *Third Intermediate,* Excursus G, pp. 455–461, historical background of the Petubastis cycle and list of the six stories.   A. Spalinger, *JARCE,* 13 (1976), 140–147, historical background.

(**2**,8) Serpot, the Queen[1] of the land of the women, sat – – – of her tent, [with the leaders][2] of the land of the women standing to the left and right of her.[3] She raised her face [and looked at her troops] who were not numerous, being (10) – – – the fortress of the land of the women. She said: "Give me help,[4] O Isis, my [mistress], great goddess, and Osiris, great god! Do you not see as I do how the army has made camp – – –?"

(12) − − − she called Ashteshyt, her younger sister, and said: "Do not delay [to go to the place] where those millions of troops [are encamped], so as to learn the situation inside the camp. Take [men's clothing] − − − the manner (14) − − − . . . the army. Learn every matter and every purpose for [which] the troops have come. [Learn the name of] the chief at their head and the [circumstances under] which they have come."

Ashteshyt, the younger sister of Serpot, the queen of [the land of the women], went out. She changed (16) [her mode of dress] and went out among the army. They did not notice her going about − − − − − −, nor that she was a woman. [She learned] the nature of everything that went on in the camp. She learned that it was the Egyptian [Prince] Pedikhons (18) [who was] at their head. She sought out how he had come alone to the fortress [of the land of the women] − − − − − −. She learned [the nature] of everything, without anyone on earth recognizing her.

She returned to the place − − − where Serpot was. (20) She [told] her the nature of everything she had seen and the [facts about Prince] Pedikhons − − −, without anything being changed in it. As soon as Serpot, [the queen of the land of] the women, had heard these things (22) [she said: "Give] me help, O Isis, great goddess, and Osiris, great god, (and) great gods − − − − − − [the] evil [serpent] of an Egyptian . . . Lo, for many days we have heard of his deeds! [He has gone to war] against the king − − − (24) the land of Khor.[5] He has fought with one chief one day and has battled with another [the next day, a chief] whose gods [did not] know how to receive him. We will know how to receive him, we will, we will! The right plan is that we shall forestall them! [It is better to forestall] them than to let them (26) forestall us. I shall marshal the army on the battlefield [against the army] of the Egyptian. [Let] the trumpet [sound], let the horn sound in the land of the women with [all] its regions, [and let it be] said, 'Make your (28) [preparation] for combat with a foreign people which stands outside.' Do not [delay] − − − − − −."

A short [time] after this, the army of all the women from the regions of the land of [the women was assembled]. They came (30) [to the] fortress − − − the great ⌈tomb⌉[6] of the land of the women, with their army − − − battle[field]. Serpot − − − through the army; she inspected the women [equipped with their] armor and their weapons (32) [of attack]; − − − − − − those who were mounted on − − −, [those who were mounted on] − − −, and those who harnessed − − − − − −, bearing armor − − − − − − [hel]mets with bulls' faces. (34) − − − − − − the opponents − − − who hurry toward their − − − − − − breastplates, while they arrayed and marshaled, creating fear and standing (36) − − − − − − their manner of doing battle.

Serpot made her preparation − − − − − she inspected their man-
ner of setting up camp, and her heart was happy (38) − − − − − −.
[She said]: "May you not have the evil eye![7] The army[8] is beautiful.
The recruits − − − − −. Osiris, the great god, our good bull, our good
Mnevis, he will not − − − − − −."

(40) − − − − − [They said: "Serpot, our Queen] is with us; she will
not abandon us. − − − − − − what is fitting − − − with the Queen (42)
− − − − − −. [We shall show] Pedikhons how we come among the
− − − − − −." [Serpot said]: " − − − [when I] see you. You shall seize
them (44) − − − − − −. Do not be distressed − − − − − −. [Isis], the
great goddess, arrays the army of the (46) [women]. − − − − − −, he
can not sit." Serpot − − − − − − that camp. Serpot said: (48)"− − − − − −
who are at the gate of the fortress − − − − − − the leaders outside the
camp (50) − − − − − − [no one] at all go out of their camp − − − − − −
the . . . of fighting (52) − − − − − −." They acted according to every
word that (**3**,1) Serpot had commanded. − − − − − −

They went to the place where [Prince Pedikhons was] − − − − − − (3)
of the fight against the − − − − −. Prince Pedikhons sent − − − − − −.
[They called out] (5) curses and taunts, the speech of [warriors]
− − − − − − from the first to the last. − − − − − −. [Serpot went] (7) out
into the army of the − − − − − − a multitude. She destroyed − − − − − −
(9) suddenly against them. Those who wished − − − − − − she slaugh-
tered − − −. [The slaughter of a bird of prey] (11) among the birds
[was what Serpot did among] − − − − − −. [The raging] of Apopis was
what Serpot did − − − − − − (13) grasped their hands − − − − − − with
her, in their eyes − − − − − − (15) that day.

Pedikhons − − − − − −, he uttered a loud cry − − − − − − (17) the
dust − − − − − − of the Assyrians − − − − − −. [They said]: "− − − − − −
(19) against us − − − − − − with us, and we − − − − − −. (21) − − − − − −
them − − − − − −." [Pedikhons said]: "I have not striven − − − − − −.
[Tomorrow will] be (23) beautiful, after the bitterness [of today].
− − − − − − to the [battle]field today − − − − − − to the battle[field] in
order to − − − − − −. . . . the land of the women without − − − − − −
(25) shall happen . . . − − − the land of the women. You shall find
glory, the glory of − − − − − − his comrade. − − − − − − you shall do
tomorrow. The army of [the women] − − − − − − (27) a harsh death
which shall be painful to [them]."[9]

The Assyrians went to their tents − − − − − − very much. Prince
Pedikhons went to his tent. He drank like a hero and ate − − − − − −
(29) ⌐in⌐ the ways of warfare − − − on his eye. When the morning of
the next day came [Prince] Pedikhons [donned] his armor and took up
his weapons − − − of a warrior − − − [from the first (31) [to the] last. He
took . . . − − − a scimitar − − − of a warrior − − − − − − of fighting, his

head bent to the shafts of his lances. He gave − − − − − − (33) doing battle. He was like a roaring lion, like a bull bursting with strength, − − − − − − announcing attack.

It was reported and announced at the fortress, at the place where Serpot was, [saying: "There has come] (35) a single Egyptian to the battlefield today." She said: "Give me help, my mistress [Isis, great goddess]! Save me from the slaughter of this evil serpent of an Egyptian!" There stepped [up to her] (37) Ashteshyt, her younger sister, and said: "You did much fighting yesterday. [Now let me go] to the battlefield to fight with this Egyptian today!" [Serpot said]: (39) "That does not suit me!¹⁰ It is the cowardly manner of the Assyrians − − − − − − begin on the battlefield today. You know their [manner, you have fought] (41) against them. By Isis, the great goddess, the mistress of the land of the women, it is I who shall don [armor and go] to the battlefield against the evil serpent of an Egyptian today!"

She − − − − − − (43) left her ⟨without⟩ another word. They brought her armor and weapons to [her].¹¹ [She] donned her armor, she took up the warrior's weapons − − − − − − (45) according to her custom. They opened the bolts before her, she went out, she announced combat − − − − − − Pedikhons. Each was ready to meet the other.

They spread the − − − − − − (47) out before them. They beat the engraved work of their ornate shields¹² − − −. [They called out curses and] taunts, the speech of warriors. They took death to themselves as neighbor, as being greater than life. − − − − − − (49) duel, their blows were beautiful, their strokes deceitful, − − − − − −. They rushed to the [slaughter] like vultures − − − − − −, (4,1) they attacked like panthers, they made − − − like − − − − − − Sobk. The ground resounded − − − from − − − − − −. (3) They made feints, they struck, they jumped. [Neither gave way] to the other, his opponent. − − − − − −. Neither gave way to the other, [his opponent]. − − − − − − (5) [the] time of [light] of the morning until the [setting of the sun] in the evening.

[Serpot, the queen of the] land of the women, called to Prince Pedikhons [saying]: "My brother, you fighter of E[gypt] − − − − − − (7) [the sun] has gone down; it will rise over us again tomorrow." Prince [Pedikhons] said: "− − − − − −. One does not fight in the dark."

Serpot, [the queen of the land of the women], said to him: (9) "[My brother Pedikhons, the sun] has gone down and rests. − − − rest − − − − − −." . . . [Said] (11) Serpot: "− − − − − − my mistress, the Queen, Isis the great, the mother of the [gods] − − − − − − my brother [Pedikhons] − − − − − − fight tonight!" − − − − − − (13) stood − − − − − −. [Serpot said: "My brother Pedikhons, why have you come] here to the regions of [the land of the women]?" − − − − − − fate of combat − − − − − (15) − − − − − if you wish − − − − − between us (17) − − − − − between us − − − − − −." She laughed − − − − − (19) − − − − − in the regions − − − − − (21) − − − − − we do not − − − − − (23) − − − − − great − − − − − among us − − − − − Serpot − − − − − brought them into (25) − − − − − the prince − − − − − hard stone.

[As soon as Serpot, the queen of the land of the women, looked at him] she did not know where on earth [she was, owing to] the great love that had entered (27) [into her] − − −. [As soon as] Prince [Pedikhons] himself [looked] at her [he did not know] where on earth he was − − − − −. [He said] to her: "My sister Serpot − − − − −

NOTES

1. The word is "Pharaoh" with the feminine ending.
2. All the restorations are guesswork.
3. The signs look more like *i3by wnm* than like Volten's reading *tp-r3*, "door."
4. Or, "Give me protection"; the phrase occurs several times in *P. Krall*, where the sign for *nḥt* has a more conventional form.
5. "Khor" here is Syria as well as Assyria; see Volten, *op. cit.*, p. 7.
6. Owing to the small lacuna after "fortress," the connection between the "fortress" and the *ht3* which Volten rendered "tomb" is not clear. If this is the word *hyt*, "pit," the meaning "tomb" seems possible but not certain.
7. The same phrase occurs in *P. Krall* 2/9 and 17/18.
8. The noun *ḥtby.t* was apparently used both for "combat" and "combat force, army." The latter meaning appears suitable here and it prevails in *P. Krall*.
9. The same expression as in *Setne II*, 5/36.
10. The same idiom, here in the negative, as in *Setne I*, 5/10.
11. Compare *P. Krall* 12/24.
12. Read *ipy.t st.t*, "engraved work," and see *Glossar*, p. 472.2. The meaning is they beat the ornamental metal work on the surface of their shields so as to make it resound. Similarly in *P. Krall* 23/7: *gl'n sty n ipy*, "shield of engraved work."

THE LION IN SEARCH OF MAN

From Leiden Demotic Papyrus I 384

The long Demotic story known as *The Myth of the Eye of the Sun* (Leiden Dem. Pap. I 384) tells how Tefnut, the daughter and "eye" of the sun-god Re, who after quarreling with her father had left Egypt and settled in Nubia, was persuaded to return to Egypt. The sun-god had sent Thoth, the counsellor and mediator among the gods, to appease the angry goddess and bring her back. Tefnut at first resisted the blandishments of Thoth, and there ensued lengthy debates in the course of which Thoth told her several animal fables, each designed to teach a moral lesson. Eventually, the goddess relented and, on the journey back to Egypt, Thoth continued to entertain her with fables. Thus the main story serves as a narrative frame for the fables, of which the fable of *The Lion in search of Man* is translated here.

Animal fables may have been current in Egypt since the New Kingdom, for we possess a number of illustrated papyri and ostraca of New Kingdom date which depict animals acting in human situations, such as festivities, labors, and combats. But no fable texts have come down to us from before the Greco-Roman period.

The fable of *The Lion in Search of Man* is especially remarkable, because here the Egyptian stepped out of himself, looked at man, and found him evil. The final episode of the fable, the encounter of lion and mouse, occurs in a shorter version among the Fables of Aesop.

The fable of *The Lion in Search of Man* occupies pages 17/9—18/34 of the Leiden papyrus.

Publication of the whole myth: W. Spiegelberg, *Der ägyptische Mythus vom Sonnenauge (Der Papyrus der Tierfabeln "Kufi") nach dem Leidener Demotischen Papyrus I 384* (Strassburg, 1917).

Fragments of a Greek translation of the myth: S. West, "The Greek Version of the Legend of Tefnut," *JEA*, 55 (1969), 161—183.

Related studies: H. Junker, *Der Auszug der Hathor-Tefnut aus Nubien*, *APAW*, Phil.-hist. Klasse, Anhang, 1911, No. 3 (Berlin, 1911). K. Sethe, *Zur altägyptischen Sage vom Sonnenauge das in der Fremde war*, Untersuchungen, V/3 (Leipzig, 1912), reprint, Hildesheim, 1964.

The Lion in Search of Man: Spiegelberg, *op. cit.*, pp. 43—47, text and translation. Erichsen, *Lesestücke*, pp. 59—67 and 69—72, text. Brunner-Traut, *Märchen*, pp. 133—136, translation.

On Egyptian animal fables: E. Brunner-Traut, "Altägyptische Tiergeschichte und Fabel: Gestalt und Strahlkraft," *Saeculum*, 10 (1959), 124—185.

(**17**,9) There was a [lion on the] mountain who was mighty in strength and was good at hunting. [The small game of the] mountains knew fear of him and (11) terror of him. One day it happened that he met a panther whose fur was stripped, whose skin was torn, who was half dead and half alive [because of his] wounds. (13) The lion said: "How did you get into this condition? Who scraped your fur and stripped your skin?" The panther [said to him]: "It was man." (15) The lion said to him: "Man, what is that?" The panther said to him: "There is no one more cunning than man. May you not fall into the hand of man!"[1] The lion became enraged against man. He ran away from (17) the panther in order to search for [man].

The lion encountered a team yoked − − − − − − . . . so that one [⌈bit⌉] was in the mouth of the horse, the other ⌈bit⌉ [in the] mouth of the donkey. (19) The lion said to them: "Who is he who has done this to you?" They said: "It is man, our master." He said to them: "Is man stronger than you?" They said: "Our lord, there is no one more cunning than man. May you not fall into (21) the hand of man!" The lion became enraged against man; he ran away from them.

The same happened to him with an ox and a cow, whose horns were clipped, whose noses (23) were pierced, and whose heads were roped. He questioned them; they told him the same.

The same happened with a bear whose claws had been removed and whose (25) teeth had been pulled. He asked him, saying: "Is man stronger than you?" He said: "That is the truth. I had a servant who prepared my food. He said to me: 'Truly, (27) your claws stick out² from your flesh; you cannot pick up food with them. Your teeth protrude; they do not let the food reach (29) your mouth. Release me, and I will cause you to pick up twice as much food!' When I released him, he removed my claws and my teeth. I have no food and no strength (31) without them! He strewed sand in my eyes and ran away from me." The lion became enraged against man. He ran away from the bear in order to search for man.

(33) He met a lion who was [tied to] a tree of the desert, the trunk being closed over his paw, and he was very distressed because he could not run away. The lion (18,1) said to him: "How did you get into this evil condition? Who is he who did this to you?" The lion said to him: "It is man! Beware, do not trust him! Man is bad. Do not fall (3) into the hand of man! I had said to him: 'What work do you do?' He said to me: 'My work is giving old age. I can make for you an amulet, so that you will never die. Come, (5) I will cut a tree for you and place it on your body as an amulet, so that you will never die.' I went with him. He came to this tree of the mountain, sawed it, and said to me: 'Stretch out (7) your paw.' I put my paw between the trunk; he shut its mouth on it.³ When he had ascertained of me that my paw was fastened, so that I could not run after him, he strewed (9) sand into my eyes and ran away from me."

Then the lion laughed and said: "Man, if you should fall into my hand, I shall give you the pain that you inflicted on (11) my companions on the mountain!"

Then, as the lion was walking in search of man, there strayed into his paw a little mouse, small in size, (13) tiny in shape. When he was about to crush him, the mouse said to him: "Do not [crush] me, my lord the lion! If you eat me you will not be sated. (15) If you release me you will not hunger for me either. If you give me my breath (of life) as a gift, I shall give you your own breath (of life) as a gift. If you spare me from your destruction, I shall make you (17) escape from your misfortune." The lion laughed at the mouse and said: "What is it that you could [do] in fact?⁴ Is there anyone on earth who would attack me?" (19) But he swore an oath before him, saying: "I shall make you escape from your misfortune on your bad day!" Now although the lion considered the words of the mouse as a joke, (21) he reflected, "If I eat him I shall indeed not be sated," and he released him.

Now it happened that there was a huntsman with a net who set traps (23) and had dug a pit before the lion. The lion fell into the pit and fell into the hand of man. He was placed in the net, he was bound with (25) dry (leather) straps, he was tied with raw straps. Now as he lay suffering on the mountain, in the seventh hour of the night, Fate[5] wished to make his joke[6] come true, (27) because of the boastful words that the lion had spoken, and made the little mouse stand before the lion. He said to him: "Do you recognize me? I am the little mouse (29) to whom you gave his breath (of life) as a gift. I have come in order to repay you for it today, and to rescue you from your misfortune, since you are suffering. It is beautiful to do good (31) to him who does it in turn." Then the mouse set his mouth to the fetters of the lion. He cut the dry straps; he gnawed through all the raw straps (33) with which he had been bound, and released the lion from his fetters. The mouse hid himself in his mane, and he went off with him to the mountain on that day.

NOTES

1. The phrase *ir 3w‘3(.t)* occurs six times, and in all but the last occurrence it is construed with *n tr.t*. While the meaning "suffer at the hand of man" would also be possible here and in the next instance (17/20−21), it is unlikely in the third instance (18/2−3) and impossible in the fourth (18/10). Without "at the hand of," it means "to suffer" (18/30); cf. *Glossar*, p. 22, and Černý, *Copt. Dic.*, p. 141.

2. This is the required meaning but it is not clear what word is written; perhaps *ky*, "high," in the sense of "long"?

3. I.e., the man sawed the tree trunk lengthwise, held the cleft open with a wedge, and when the lion had inserted his paw he removed the wedge, and the cleft snapped shut.

4. Lit., "in the end."

5. The god Shay, the personified fate.

6. The promise of the mouse which the lion had treated as a joke.

THE INSTRUCTION OF ANKHSHESHONQ

P. British Museum 10508

Acquired by the British Museum in 1896, the papyrus was in a damaged condition and its provenance is unknown. It consists of twenty-eight columns (or pages) with large parts missing from pages 1 and 2. From pages 24 onward holes and considerable rubbing of the surface have made much of the lines illegible. In addition, the top edge of the papyrus is damaged throughout its whole length, so that all first lines are missing. The handwriting is of late Ptolemaic date, while the composition itself may be earlier; no firm dating has yet been achieved.

Like earlier *Instructions*, the text has an introductory narrative which purports to describe the circumstances that led to the composition of the maxims, and, like its prototypes, the introduction is a literary device and a fiction. The inventor of this introduction must have striven for originality, for he placed the composition of the maxims into the setting of a foiled plot against the life of a Pharaoh.

Ankhsheshonq, a priest of Re at Heliopolis, has come to visit his boyhood friend Harsiese at Memphis, where the latter has recently obtained the position of chief royal physician. Ankhsheshonq has a personal problem for which he seeks the help of his friend. Harsiese invites him to stay with him for a long time and confides in him that he and other courtiers are plotting to kill Pharaoh. Ankhsheshonq tries unsuccessfully to dissuade his friend from the plot. Their conversation is overheard by a servant who reports it to the king. Harsiese and the other plotters are executed, and Ankhsheshonq is sent to prison for having failed to inform the king. Languishing in prison he composes the Instruction for the benefit of his youngest son.

The maxims that follow the introduction differ considerably from earlier Instructions. Whereas the older Instructions were composed of interconnected groups of sentences that taught moral lessons through drawing vignettes of life, the Instruction of Ankhsheshonq and other Demotic Instructions as well consist of single, self-contained prose sentences, each occupying one line on the page. Several successive sentences may, but need not, deal with the same topic; and no attempt is made to bring all statements on one topic into one sequence. Thus the content is diverse and miscellaneous.

The particular flavor of the Instruction of Ankhsheshonq comes from its combination of pragmatism and humor. The moralizing is down-to-earth and utilitarian rather than lofty and idealistic, so much so that sometimes expediency takes the place of moral principle. The sayings are either phrased as commands or as generalized observations, and many of them, especially of the latter type, may have been proverbs. But unless they are repeated more than once in this text or elsewhere, we cannot be sure that they were proverbs. Like all Instructions, this one must have been composed, or compiled, by a member of the scribal class, and the sayings are addressed to everybody, especially to the average man. P. Walcot's attempt to find significant resemblances between the Instruction of Ankhsheshonq and Hesiod's *Works and Days* is unconvincing.

The text presents numerous difficulties. Glanville's first edition must be studied in conjunction with Stricker's annotated Dutch translation which contains many improvements. In particular, Stricker adopted a number of textual readings differing from Glanville's, almost all of which I have accepted. They are identified in my notes.

Publication: S. R. K. Glanville, *Catalogue of Demotic Papyri in the British Museum*, Vol. II, *The Instructions of 'Onchsheshonqy* (*British Museum Papyrus 10508*) (London, 1955).

Translation: B. H. Stricker, "De Wijsheid van Anchsjesjonq," *OMRO*, 39 (1958), 56–79, annotated Dutch translation. *Idem*, Vooraziatisch-Egyptisch Genootschap Ex Oriente Lux, *Jaarbericht*, 15 (1958), 11–38, same translation without notes.   Bresciani, *Letteratura*, pp. 563–584.

Comments: A. Volten, *OLZ*, 52, No. 3/4 (1957), cols. 126–128. H. S. Smith, *JEA*, 44 (1958), 121–122. B. Gemser in *Congress Volume, Oxford 1959*, Supplements to Vetus Testamentum, 7 (Leiden, 1960), 102–128. R. A. Parker, *RdÉ*, 13 (1961), 133–135. P. Walcot, *JNES*, 21 (1962), 215–219. J. H. Johnson, *Serapis*, 2 (1970), 22–28.

(1,9) . . . − − − − − −. Pharaoh asked him many [things] and (10) he answered them all. − − − − − − . . . (11) of the chief physician; and the chief physician did nothing without consulting (12) Harsiese son of Ramose about it. A few days later it happened that the chief physician went (13) to his fathers.[1] Harsiese son of Ramose was made chief physician, and he was given everything that belonged to the chief physician (14) entirely, and his brothers were made priests without fee. And Pharaoh did nothing without (15) consulting Harsiese son of Ramose about it.

After this it happened one (16) day that Ankhsheshonq son of Tjainufi − − − was in great trouble. He thought (17) to himself, saying: "What I should like to do is to go to Mem[phis] and stay with (18) Harsiese son of Ramose. I have been told he has been made chief physician [and has been given everything] that belonged to the chief physician (19) entirely, and his brothers have been made priests without fee. Perhaps the god will put it [in his heart] to do for me what is right."

He went away (20) from Heliopolis without [informing] any man on earth of his going. He found a ship which was sailing (2,x) − − − − − − (2,1) − − − − − −. (2) "− − − − − − [stay] here in Memphis with me. (3) − − − − − − your people three times a month."[2] (4) [Ankhsheshonq son of Tjainufi stayed with] Harsiese son of Ramose; and he (5) − − − − − − to Heliopolis (to) his people three times a month.

(6) − − − − − − consulting about an evil ⌜destiny⌝[3] (7) − − − − − − Harsiese son of Ramose, the chief physician, consulted (8) − − − − − − Ankhsheshonq son of Tjainufi about it. Then said (9) Ankh[sheshonq son of Tjainufi] to him: " − − − may your life prosper![4] Pharaoh is the image of Pre! (10) − − − − − −[5] agree to the misfortune of Pharaoh? Pharaoh has done for you many good things, [more than to] all [the courtiers of] the palace. You were brought to the palace when you (12) had nothing in the world. He appointed you chief physician. He let you be given everything that belonged to the chief physician entirely. (13) He had your brothers made priests without fee. Is what you are doing in return to have him killed?" Said he: "Let go (14) of me, Ankhsheshonq son of Tjainufi. There is nothing to the words you have said. The councillors,[6] the generals, (15) the grandees of the palace are all agreed to do it."

Now it happened that everything (16) Harsiese son of Ramose was saying to Ankhsheshonq son of Tjainufi, and that Ankhsheshonq said to him (17) in reply—there was a man of the household ⌈inside⌉[7] a [place] where he heard the voices of the two men who was called Wahibre-(18)makhy son of Ptahertais. It was the turn of this same man[8] to lie down that night in the vestibule (19) of the private chamber[9] where Pharaoh was. When [night] came he lay down in the vestibule of the (20) private chamber where Pharaoh was.

In the 8th hour of the night (21) Pharaoh awoke, uncovered his face, and called out, saying, "Who is outside?" Wahibre-makhy (22) son of Ptahertais answered him. Pharaoh said to him: "Woe − − −, woe at the hand of Pre and the gods who are (3,x) − − − − − (3,1) − − − − − −.[10] (2) − − − − − − when he had [⌈said⌉] − − − − − −, he said: "Shall I (3) be saved, shall I be saved, Wahibre-makhy son of Ptahertais, shall I be saved?" He said: "You will be saved by the hand of Pre and (4) the gods who are with him, and great Neith, the mother, the great goddess, shall place the peoples of the whole (5) earth beneath the feet of Pharaoh." He related to Pharaoh everything he had overheard (6) Harsiese son of [Ra]mose saying to Ankhsheshonq son of Tjainufi and what Ankhsheshonq had said to him (7) in reply, without altering a single word. Pharaoh was unable to sleep till morning.

When (8) the morning of the next day had come, Pharaoh took his seat in the hall of the palace in Memphis. (9) The magistrates stood in their station and the generals in their ranks. Pharaoh looked to the station (10) of Harsiese son of Ramose. Pharaoh said to him: "Harsiese son of Ramose, you were brought to the palace (11) when you had nothing in the world. I appointed you chief physician and let you be given everything that belonged to the chief physician (12) entirely; and I had your brothers made priests without fee. What have you done, conspiring against me to have me killed?"

(13) He said to Pharaoh: "My great lord! On the day on which Pre commanded to do good to me he put Pharaoh's good fortune (14) in my heart. On the day on which Pre commanded to do harm to me he put Pharaoh's misfortune (15) in my heart."

Pharaoh said to him: "The words, since they were said to us,[11] did you say them to any man at all?" He said: "I said them (16) to Ankhsheshonq son of Tjainufi, a priest of Pre who is here in Memphis with me." Pharaoh said to him: "Ankh(17)sheshonq son of Tjainufi, what is he to you?" He said: "His father was the friend of my father. His heart (18) was much ⌈attached⌉ to him."

(19) Pharaoh said: "Let (20) Ankhsheshonq son of Tjainufi be brought!" They ran for ⟨Ankhsheshonq son⟩ of Tjainufi; they ran and returned bringing him (21) before Pharaoh at once.

Pharaoh said to him: "Ankhsheshonq son of Tjainufi, did you eat my bread and hear evil against me without coming to inform me of it, saying, 'They are conspiring against you to kill you'?" (**4**,x) − − − − − (**4**,1) − − − − − − 'Is what you are doing in return, to have him killed?'[12] By your face, my great lord, I did all I could with him, but he did not give me (3) an answer. I knew that these matters would not be hidden from Pharaoh."

As soon as he had said this, Pharaoh (4) had an altar of earth built at the door of the palace. He had Harsiese son of Ramose placed in (5) the fire[13] together with all his people and every man who had conspired in Pharaoh's doom. Pharaoh had (6) Ankhsheshonq son of Tjainufi taken to the houses of detention of Daphnae.[14] A personal servant, a staff-(7)bearer, a man of Pharaoh's household, was assigned to him, and his food was brought from the palace (8) daily.

After this there occurred the accession-day of Pharaoh. Pharaoh released everyone who was (9) (in) the prisons at Daphnae except Ankhsheshonq son of Tjainufi.[15] His heart sank (10) on account of it. He said to the staff-bearer who was assigned to him: "Let a favor be done to me by you. Let (11) a palette and a scroll be brought to me. For I have a boy whom I have not yet been able to instruct. (12) I shall write an Instruction for him and have it taken to Heliopolis to instruct him with it." The staff-bearer said: "I will (13) report it before Pharaoh first." The staff-bearer reported (14) it before Pharaoh first. Pharaoh commanded, saying: "Let a palette be taken to him; do not let a scroll be taken (15) to him." They took a palette to him; they did not take a scroll to him. He wrote on the sherds of jars the matters which he could (16) teach his son in writing.

(17) This is the Instruction which the divine father Ankhsheshonq, whose mother was − − −, wrote for his son on the sherds (18) of the jars that were brought in to him containing mixed wine, while he was imprisoned in the house of detention of Daphnae. He (19) said:

Mistreatment and misery, my great lord Pre! Imprisonment, mistreatment[16] is what is done to me in return for not having killed a man! This is what you despise,[17] my great lord Pre! Is this not how Pre is angry with a land? Oh (21) you people who shall find these potsherds, hear from me how Pre is angry with a land!

(**5**,x) − − − − −
(**5**,1) [When Pre is angry] with a land he causes − − − − − −.
(2)   [When] Pre is angry with a land its ruler neglects the law.
(3)   When Pre is angry with a land he makes law cease in it.
(4)   When Pre is angry with a land he makes sanctity[18] cease in it.
(5)   When Pre is angry with a land he makes justice cease in it.

(6)   When Pre is angry with a land he makes value scarce in it.[19]

(7)   When Pre is angry with a land he does not let one be trusting in it.

(8)   When Pre is angry with a land he does not let one ⌜receive ransom⌝ [in] it.

(9)   When Pre is angry with a land he makes great its humble people and humbles its great people.

(10) When Pre is angry with a land he sets the fools over the wise.

(11) When Pre is angry with a land he orders its ruler to mistreat its people.

(12) When Pre is angry with a land he appoints its scribe to rule it.

(13) When Pre is angry with a land he appoints its washerman as chief of police.[20]

(14) Here follow the words that Ankhsheshonq son of Tjainufi wrote on (15) the sherds of the jars that were brought in to him containing mixed wine, so as to give them (16) as an Instruction to his son, and which were reported before Pharaoh and (17) his great men daily. Ankhsheshonq son of Tjainufi had realized (18) the fact that he was to linger in prison since they had not released him, (19) and he wrote on the sherds of the jars the matters that he could teach his son in writing.

(**6**,x) — — — — — —

(**6**,1) S[erve your] god, that he may guard you.

(2)   Serve your brothers, that you may have good repute.

(3)   Serve a wise man, that he may serve you.

(4)   Serve him who serves you.

(5)   Serve any man, that you may find profit.

(6)   Serve your father and mother, that you may go and prosper.

(7)   Examine every matter, that you may understand it.

(8)   Be gentle and patient,[21] then your heart will be beautiful.

(9)   It is in maturity[22] that instruction succeeds.

(10) Do not rely on the property of another, saying, "I will live on it"; acquire your own.

(11) Do not abuse[23] when you fare well, lest you fare badly.

(12) Do not send a low woman[24] on a business of yours; she will go after her own.

(13) Do not send a wise man in a small matter when a big matter is waiting.

(14) Do not send a fool in a big matter when there is a wise man whom you can send.

(15) Do not send into town when you may find trouble in it.

(16) Do not long for your home when you do an errand.

(17) Do not long for your home to drink beer in it in midday.

(18) Do not pamper your body, lest you become weak.
(19) Do not pamper yourself when you are young, lest you be weak when you are old.
(20) Do not hate a man to his face when you know nothing of him.
(21) Do not fret so long as you own something.
(22) Do not worry so long as you own something.
(23) Do not fret at all.
(24) Do not fret about your occupation.

(**7**,x) – – – – – –
(**7**,1) – – – – – –.
(2) Force [your son], do not let your servant force him.
(3) Do not spare your son work when you can make him do it.
(4) Do not instruct a fool, lest he hate you.
(5) Do not instruct him who will not listen to you.
(6) Do not rely on a fool.
(7) Do not rely on the property of an idiot.
(8) Do not hide and then let yourself be found.[25]
(9) Do not hide when you have no food.
(10) He who hides when he has no food is in the place of one who seeks it.
(11) Do not go away and then come back of your own accord.
(12) Do not run away after you have been beaten, lest your punishment be doubled.
(13) Do not insult your superior.
(14) Do not neglect to serve your god.
(15) Do not neglect to serve your master.
(16) Do not neglect to serve him who can serve you.
(17) Do not neglect to acquire a manservant and a maidservant when you are able to do so.
(18) A servant who is not beaten is full of curses in his heart.
(19) A small man with great wrath makes much stench.
(20) A great man with small wrath gets much praise.
(21) Do not say "young man" to one who is old.
(22) Do not belittle an old man in your heart.
(23) Do not speak hastily, lest you give offense.
(24) Do not say right away what comes out of your heart.[26]

(**8**,x) – – – – – –
(**8**,1) – – – – – –.
(2) Learning and foolishness belong to the people of your town; respect the people of your town.
(3) Do not say "I am learned"; set yourself to become wise.
(4) Do not do a thing that you have not first examined.
(5) Examining makes your good fortune.

(6) If you examine three wise man about a matter it is perfect; the outcome lies with the great god.[27]

(7) Do well by your body in your days of well-being.[28]

(8) There is no one who does not die.

(9) Do not withdraw from a scribe who is being taken to the house of detention.

(10) If you withdraw from him they will take him to his house of eternity.

(11) Do not go to court against your superior when you do not have protection [against] him.

(12) Do not take to yourself a woman whose husband is alive, lest he become your enemy.

(13) In strait times or happy times wealth grows because of spreading it.

(14) May your fate not be the fate of one who begs and is given.

(15) When you work the land do not pamper your body.

(16) Do not say "Here is my brother's acre"; look to your own.

(17) The wealth of a town is a lord who does justice.

(18) The wealth of a temple is the priest.

(19) The wealth of a field is the time when it is worked.

(20) The wealth of a storehouse is in stocking it.

(21) The wealth of a treasury is in (being in) a single hand.[29]

(22) The wealth of property is a wise woman.

(23) The wealth of a wise man is his speech.

(**9**,x) − − − − − −

(**9**,1) The wealth − − − − − −.

(2) The wealth of an army is its [leader].

(3) The wealth of a town is not taking sides.

(4) The wealth of a craftsman is his equipment.

(5) Do not scorn a document that has a claim on you.

(6) Do not scorn a remedy that you can use.

(7) Do not scorn Pharaoh's business.

(8) Do not scorn a matter that concerns a cow.

(9) He who scorns matters too often will die of it.

(10) Do not quarrel[30] over a matter in which you are wrong.

(11) Do not say "My land thrives"; do not cease to inspect it.

(12) Do not dwell in a house with your in-laws.

(13) Do not be a neighbor to your master.

(14) Do not say "I have plowed the field but there has been no payment." Plow again, it is good to plow.

(15) More joyous is the face of him who rests above the field than of him who spends the day in town.[31]

(16) Do not say "It is summer"; there is winter too.

(17) He who does not gather wood in summer will not be warm in winter.

(18) Do not dwell in a house in which you get no income.[32]

(19) Do not entrust your wealth to a ⌐house of profit.⌐

(20) Do not put your wealth into a house only.

(21) Do not put your wealth in a town ⌐to which you must send.⌐ [33]

(22) Wealth takes hold of its owner.

(23) The owner of a cow gets to run.

(24) Do not spend before you have set up your storehouse.

(25) Spend according to the size of your means.

(**10**,x) — — — — — —

(**10**,1) Do not say — — — — — —.

(2) Do not say "I am good at writing" — — — — — —.

(3) A scribe (in) a shipyard, a craftsman (in) a . . .

(4) When the crocodile shows itself its reputation[34] is measured.

(5) A crocodile does not die of worry,[35] it does of hunger.

(6) "What they do insults me," says the fool when one instructs him.

(7) You may trip over your foot in the house of a great man; you should not trip over your tongue.

(8) If you are thrown out of the house of your master, be his doorkeeper.

(9) If your master is sitting by the river, do not (10) immerse your hands in front of him.

(11) May my brother be a groom! When he mounts I would boast.[36]

(12) May my companion say ⌐"Thoth knows not."⌐

(13) May he not die for whom I would rend my clothing![37]

(14) May the "elder brother" of the town be the one to whom it is entrusted!

(15) May the kindly brother of the family be the one who acts as "elder brother" for it!

(16) May I have something and my brother have something, that I may eat my own without abstaining![38]

(17) May the floodwater never fail to come!

(18) May the field never fail to flourish!

(19) May the poor plot of land be the one that grows fodder in abundance!

(20) May the cow receive her bull!

(21) May the son do honor to his father!

(22) May it be a master's son who becomes master!

(23) May my mother be my hairdresser, so as to do for me what is pleasant!

(24) May the moon follow the sun and not fail to rise!

(25) May existence always follow death!

(11,x) — — — — — —

(11,1) May I — — — — — —.

(2)   May I stretch out my hand to my — — — . . .

(3)   May I get to know my neighbor, that I may give him my goods.

(4)   May I get to know my brother, that I may open my heart to him.

(5)   Do not be a hindrance[39] often, lest you be cursed.

(6)   Do not get drunk often, lest you go mad.

(7)   Take a wife when you are twenty years old, that you may have a son while you are young.

(8)   Do not kill a snake and then leave its tail.

(9)   Do not hurl a lance if you cannot hold its aim.[40]

(10) He who sends spittle[41] up to the sky will have it fall on him.

(11) A man's character is his family.

(12) A man's character is his ⌈destiny.⌉[42]

(13) A man's character is on his face.

(14) A man's character is one of his limbs.

(15) The fisherman ⌈throws on board⌉ without knowing that it is the god who sends to every house.

(16) Do not stay on the road till evening, saying "I am sure of the houses." You do not know the hearts of their inhabitants.

(17) A magistrate who steals, his son will be poor.

(18) Do not ⌈tie your donkey's foot to the palm tree⌉ lest he shake it.

(19) Do not laugh at your son in front of his mother, lest you learn the size of his father.

(20) It is not of a bull that a bull is born.

(21) Do not say "The enemy of the god is alive today"; look to the end.

(22) Say "Good fate" at the end of[43] old age.

(23) Put your affairs in the hand of the god.

(12,x) — — — — — —

(12,1) Do not — — — — — —.

(2)   Do not — — — — — — suffer.

(3)   Man does not know the days of his misfortune.

(4)   Do not entrust your people[44] to one who has not experienced distress.

(5)   Do not delay to get yourself a tomb on the mountain; you do not know the length of your life.

(6)   Do not do evil to a man and so cause another to do it to you.

(7)   Do not be discouraged[45] in a matter in which you can ask (advice).

(8)   Happy is the heart of him who has made a judgment before a wise man.

(9)   A wise master who asks (advice), his house stands forever.

(10) Disdain ruins a great man.

(11) A great crime . . . . . . is what one despises.

(12) The work of a fool does not succeed in a house where a wise man is.

(13) Let your wife see your wealth; do not trust her with it.

(14) Do not trust her with her provisions for one year.

(15) As long as my brother does not abstain[46] from stealing, I do not abstain from restraining him.

(16) Do not retaliate; do not let one retaliate against you.

(17) Let your benefaction reach him who has need of it.

(18) Do not be stingy; wealth is no security.

(19) Even a kind master will kill to have peace.

(20) The prudent killer does not get killed.

(21) Do not undertake a matter if you cannot carry it out.

(22) Do not speak harshly to a man if you cannot make him yield by it.

(23) Loud is the voice of him who acts (or, has acted) because he has been commanded.

(24) Do not say something when it is not the time for it.

(**13**,x) − − − − − −

(**13**,1) − − − − − −

(2) A wise man seeks [a friend; a fool] seeks an enemy.

(3) He to whom a good deed was done in the past cannot repay it.[47]

(4) . . . . . .

(5) Do not give your son to the wet nurse and so cause her to set aside her own.

(6) The friend of a fool is a fool; the friend of a wise man is a wise man.

(7) The friend of an idiot is an idiot.

(8) The mother makes a child, the way makes a companion.[48]

(9) Every man acquires property; it is a wise man who knows how to protect it.

(10) Do not hand over your property to your younger brother and thereby make him act as your elder brother.

(11) Do not prefer one of your children to another; you do not know which one of them will be kind to you.

(12) If you find your wife with her lover get yourself a bride to suit you.

(13) Do not get a maidservant for your wife if you do not have a man-servant.

(14) Do not speak in two voices.

(15) Speak truth to all men; let it cleave to your speech.

(16) Do not open your heart to your wife; what you have said to her goes to the street.

(17) Do not open your heart to your wife or to your servant.

(18) Open it to your mother; she is a woman of ⌜discretion.⌝

(19) A woman knows her own business.

(20) Instructing a woman is like having a sack of sand whose side is split open.

(21) Her savings are stolen goods.

(22) What she does with her husband today she does with another man tomorrow.

(23) Do not sit down beside your superior.

(24) Do not take a youth for your companion.

(**14**,x) − − − − − −

(**14**,1) − − − − − −.

(2) He will make him give − − − while the condemnation of the god is yet after him.

(3) Do not have a thief for a companion [lest] he cause you to be killed.

(4) Even a small concern has a man in its grip.[49]

(5) Shut up a house and it will perish as a result.

(6) He who is patient[50] in a bad situation will not be harmed by it.

(7) He who steals from the property of another will not profit by it.

(8) If you become the companion of a wise man whose heart you do not know, do not open your heart to him.

(9) If you do good to a hundred[51] men and one of them acknowledges it, no part of it is lost.

(10) Make burnt offering and libation before the god; let the fear of him be great in your heart.

(11) A thief steals by night; he is found by day.

(12) Do not make many words.

(13) A house is open to him who has goods in his hand.

(14) He who is bitten of the bite of a snake is afraid of a coil of rope.

(15) The man who looks in front of him does not stumble and fall.

(16) Do not abandon a woman of your household when she has not conceived a child.

(17) Good fortune[52] turns away destruction by a great god.

(18) Honor your (fellow)man . . . . . .

(19) Do not let your servant lack his food and clothing.

(20) Do not cast glances at another's property lest you become poor.[53]

(21) Do not trespass on the territory of another.

(22) Do not put a house on farmland.

(23) Do not cause a man to sue you.

(**15**,x) − − − − − −

(**15**,1) Do not − − − − − −.

(2) Do not − − − something which your − − − − − −.

(3)   There is no − − − reaches the sky.

(4)   There is no − − − without crying.

(5)   Do not say "− − − a good deed to this man but he did not acknowledge it to me."

(6)   There is no good deed except a good deed which you have done for him who has need of it.

(7)   If you have reached your prime and gained much property let your brothers be great with you.

(8)   Need, if its condition becomes known in the street, is reckoned a disgrace.

(9)   When a youth who has been taught thinks, thinking of wrong is what he does.

(10) When a man has earned his first money he spends it on drinking and eating.[54]

(11) When a man smells of myrrh his wife is a cat before him.

(12) When a man is suffering his wife is a lioness before him.

(13) Do not be afraid to do that in which you are right.

(14) Do not commit theft; you will be found out.

(15) Do not let your son marry a woman from another town, lest he be taken from you.

(16) Muteness is better than a hasty tongue.

(17) Sitting still is better than doing a mean errand.[55]

(18) Do not say "I undertook the matter," if you did not undertake it.

(19) Being evil[56] will not provide for you.

(20) Gluttony will not give you food.

(21) If you are sent to get chaff[57] and you find wheat, do not buy [it].

(22) If you trade in straw when it is wanted, you should not go around with wheat.

(23) Do not do to a man what you dislike, so as to cause another to do it to you.

(24) Do not consort with a man who is discouraged and who may say "I am discouraged right now."[58]

(25) A hundred men are slain through one moment of discouragement.

(**16**,x) − − − − − −

(**16**,1) Do not − − − [lest you be] poor forever.

(2)   Do not − − − − − −.

(3)   Do not let your schoolboy son go to the door of the storehouse in a lean year.

(4)   Do not go to your brother when you are in distress; go to your friend.

(5)   Do not drink water in the house of a merchant; he will charge you for it.

(6)   Do not deliver a servant into the hand of his master.

(7) Do not say "My master dislikes me, I will not serve him."
(8) Zealous service removes dislike.
(9) Borrow money at interest and put it in farmland.
(10) Borrow money at interest and take a wife.
(11) Borrow money at interest and celebrate your birthday.
(12) Do not borrow money at interest in order to live well on it.
(13) Do not swear falsely when you are in distress, lest you become worse off than you are.
(14) Do not ask advice from the god and then neglect what he said.
(15) Do not laugh at a cat.
(16) Do not speak of Pharaoh's business when drinking beer.
(17) Do not make a judgment in which you are wrong.
(18) Do not be fainthearted in a bad situation.
(19) Do not conceal yourself from a stranger who comes from outside.
(20) If there is nothing in your hand there may be something in his.
(21) Do not lend money at interest without obtaining a security.
(22) Do not be too trusting lest you become poor.
(23) Do not dislike one who says to you "I am your brother."
(24) If my share in my father's house is small it will not increase.[59]
(25) Do not disdain a small document, a small fire, a small soldier.[60]

(**17**,x) – – – – –
(**17**,1) – – – – – –.
(2) – – – – – ......
(3) [Do not] insult a woman whose husband is your subordinate.
(4) [Do not ⌈scorn⌉] to do the work by which you can live.
(5) Do not acquire goods if you do not have a storehouse.
(6) Do not accept a gift if you are not going to make a contract.
(7) Do not say "My illness has passed, I will not use medication."
(8) Do not go away (from work) often, lest you become disliked.
(9) Do not cast a weary glance at the door bolt.[61]
(10) Do not hasten when you speak before your master.
(11) Do not run too hard lest you must halt.
(12) Do not often clean yourself with water only.
(13) Water ⌈grinds⌉[62] the stone.
(14) Do not walk the road without a stick in your hand.
(15) Do not ... a man before his opponent at the trial.[63]
(16) Do not walk alone at night.
(17) Do not scorn your master before an inferior.
(18) If you have grown up with a man and are faring well with him, do not abandon him when he fares badly.
(19) Let him attain his house of eternity.
(20) He who comes after him will support you.

(21) A woman who is loved, when one abandons her she is (truly) abandoned.

(22) Inspect your house at all times and you will find its thief.

(23) Teach your son to write, plow, fowl and trap against a year of low Nile, so that he will reap the profit of what he has done.[64]

(24) Gather dung, gather clay, but do not make an occupation out of scavenging.[65]

(25) Do not talk much before your master.

(26) Be gentle and your reputation[66] will increase in the hearts of all men.

(**18**,x) $-----$

(**18**,1) $-----$.

(2) [If] a gardener becomes a fisherman his [trees] perish.[67]

(3) If you have acquired $---$ give one part of them for protection.

(4) [If you] work the land do not practice deception.

(5) Better an honorable failure than a half success.

(6) If you are powerful throw your documents into the river; if you are week throw them also.

(7) If an inferior says "I will kill you," he will surely kill you.

(8) If a superior says "I will kill you," lay your head on his doorstep.

(9) Give a hundred silver pieces to a prudent woman; do not accept two hundred from a foolish one.

(10) He who battles together with the people of his town will rejoice with them.

(11) The children of the fool wander in the street, those of the wise man ⌈stand before him.⌉[68]

(12) He who hides from his master will get a hundred masters.

(13) A man who has no town, his character is his family.

(14) A man who has no property, his wife is his partner.

(15) Do not rejoice in your wife's beauty; her heart is set on her lover.

(16) Do not say "I have this wealth, I will not serve god nor will I serve man."

(17) Wealth comes to an end; serving the god is what creates (it).

(18) Do not send to someone whom you do not know at all.

(19) He who loves his house so as to dwell in it warms it to its beams.

(20) He who hates it builds it and ⌈mortgages⌉[69] it.

(21) Do not be despondent when you are ill; your landing is not made yet.[70]

(22) Do not say "I shall give this property to this man" if you are not going to give it to him.

(23) Take a superior to your house, take an inferior to your boat.

(24) When Hapy comes he sets limits for everyone.

(25) When the fish is brought up from the water ⌜it sends⌝[71] him who would eat it!

(**19**,x) – – – – –
(**19**,1) – – – – –.
(2) If you say – – – – –.
(3) Sweeter is the water of him who has given it than the wine of him [⌜who has received⌝] it.
(4) If a cow is stolen from the field one – – – its owner to the town.
(5) If your enemy seeks you do not hide from him.
(6) If a bird[72] flies to the place of another it will lose a feather.
(7) There is no son of Pharaoh at night.
(8) If a fool follows his heart he acts wisely.
(9) A man does not love what he hates.[73]
(10) Do a good deed and throw it in the water; when it dries you will find it.
(11) When two brothers quarrel do not come between them.
(12) He who comes between two brothers when they quarrel will be placed between them when they are reconciled.
(13) If the daughter of the strong man is the one who eats, her rival is the daughter of the . . .
(14) If the son of the master were to act as master, the people would not worship before the god.
(15) Do not be impatient[74] when you are suffering, so that you pray for death.
(16) He who is alive, his herb grows.[75]
(17) There is none wretched except him who has died (or, is dying).[76]
(18) With a thousand servants in the merchant's house the merchant is one of them.
(19) If your master speaks wise words to you, you should fear him.
(20) A wise man is one who knows what goes on before him.
(21) Give your words with your goods, and it will make two gifts.
(22) Beer matures only on its mash.
(23) Wine matures as long as one does not open it.
(24) A remedy is effective only through the hand of its physician.
(25) If you are given bread for being stupid you may despise instruction.

(**20**,x) – – – – –
(**20**,1) – – – – –.
(2) . . . – – – – –.
(3) . . . – – – – –.
(4) End by planting any tree, begin by planting a sycamore.
(5) The warp does not stray away from the woof.

(6) All good fortune is from the hand of the god.
(7) A single[77] plowing does not produce . . .
(8) A single ⌐measuring¬ is not adequate.
(9) The hissing of the snake is more effective than the braying of the donkey.
(10) There is a running to which sitting is preferable.
(11) There is a sitting to which standing is preferable.
(12) Do not dwell in a house which is decaying; death does not say "I am coming."
(13) A snake that is eating has no venom.
(14) A window with a large opening gives more heat than coolness.
(15) All kinds of cattle[78] are welcome in a house; a thief is not welcome.
(16) Coming close to a fool is to flee him.
(17) If you harness a big team you may lie down in its shade.
(18) Honor the old men in your heart, and you will be honored in the hearts of all men.
(19) A woman lets herself be loved according to the character of her husband.
(20) A man does not eat what is under his eyes.
(21) Even if filled with soap, a storehouse yields a profit.
(22) The waste of a house is not dwelling in it.
(23) The waste of a woman is not knowing her.
(24) The waste of a donkey is carrying bricks.
(25) The waste of a boat is carrying straw.

(**21**,x) − − − − − −
(**21**,1) There is no − − − − − −.
(2) There is no − − − − − −.
(3) There is no − − − − − −.
(4) There is no tooth that rots yet stays in place.
(5) There is no Nubian who leaves his skin.[79]
(6) There is no friend who goes by alone.
(7) There is no wise man who comes to grief.
(8) There is no fool who finds profit.
(9) There is none who insults his superior who is not in turn insulted.
(10) There is none who abandons his traveling companion whom the god does not hold to account for it.
(11) There is none who deceives who is not deceived.
(12) There is none who sins yet goes and prospers.
(13) Do not hasten to reach a magistrate and then draw back from him.[80]
(14) He who is ashamed to sleep with his wife will not have children.
(15) Do not be greedy, lest you be scolded.[81]
(16) Do not be stingy, lest you be hated.

(17) Do not steal copper or cloth from the house of your master.

(18) Do not violate a married woman.

(19) He who violates a married woman on the bed will have his wife violated on the ground.

(20) Better a statue of stone than a foolish son.

(21) Better no brother than one who is evil.

(22) Better death than want.

(23) If you are thirsty at night let your mother give you to drink.

(24) Do not stay in a town in which you have no one.

(25) If you stay in a town in which you have no one, your character is your family.[82]

(**22**,x) − − − − − −

(**22**,1) − − − − − −

(2)   Do not − − − − − −

(3)   Do not start [a fire if you] can[not put] it [out].

(4)   Give your daughter in marriage to a goldsmith (or, gold dealer); [do not] give − − − [to] his daughter.

(5)   He who shakes the stone will have it fall on his foot.

(6)   He who makes love to a woman of the street will have his purse cut open on its side.[83]

(7)   One does not load a beam on a donkey.

(8)   If a woman loves a crocodile she takes on its character.

(9)   A woman at night, praise in midday.

(10) Do not slander a woman who is beloved.

(11) Do not praise a woman who is disliked.

(12) A fool wanting to go with a wise man is a goose wanting to go with its slaughter knife.

(13) A fool in a house is like fine clothes in a wine cellar.

(14) A decaying house does not get hold of a stranger.

(15) A crocodile does not get hold of a townsman.

(16) When you are hungry eat what you despise; when you are sated despise it.

(17) He who has not got his eye on the river should pay attention to the water jugs.

(18) If you come to say something to your master count on your fingers till ten.[84]

(19) Give one loaf to your laborer, receive two from (the work of) his arms.

(20) Give one loaf to the one who labors, give two to the one who gives orders.

(21) Do not insult a common man.[85]

(22) When insult occurs beating occurs.

(23) When beating occurs killing occurs.

(24) Killing does not occur without the god knowing.

(25) Nothing occurs except what the god ordains.

(**23**,x) – – – – – –

(**23**,1) – – – – – –.

(2) – – – – – –.

(3) – – – – – –.

(4) Silence conceals foolishness.

(5) One uses sunlight – – – – – –.

(6) Do not make love to a married woman.

(7) He who makes love to a married woman is killed on her doorstep.

(8) It is better to dwell in your own small house than to dwell in the large house of another.

(9) Better is small wealth which is kept together than large wealth which is dispersed.

(10) A slip of the tongue in the royal palace is a slip of the helm at sea.

(11) A bull does not bellow at a calf; a great stable is not destroyed.

(12) The way of the god is before all men (but) the fool cannot find it.

(13) "Am I going to live?" says the dying.[86]

(14) Every hand is stretched out to the god (but) he accepts (only) the hand of his beloved.

(15) A cat that loves fruit hates him who eats it.

(16) "Your word is my word" says the weakling.

(17) Do not be active in all sorts of business and slack in your own.

(18) He who is not slack, his father will be active for him.

(19) The builders build houses, the musicians inaugurate them.[87]

(20) The frogs praise Hapy, the mice eat the emmer.

(21) The oxen harvest the barley and emmer, the donkeys eat it.

(22) Do not ⌈grovel⌉[88] before a great man.

(23) Do not drink the water of a well and then throw the pitcher into it.

(24) Belly of woman, heart of horse.[89]

(**24**,x) – – – – – –

(**24**,1) – – – – – –.

(2) – – – – – –.

(3) – – – – – –.

(4) If much wealth accrues to you – – – – – –.

(5) – – – ... – – – you die.

(6) Do not marry an ailing woman.[90]

(7) If a donkey goes with a horse it adopts its pace.

(8) If a crocodile loves a donkey it puts on a wig.[91]

(9) One uses a horse to go after a – – –; one does not take a donkey to attain it.

(10) Man is even more eager to copulate than a donkey; his purse is what restrains him.[92]

(11) One gives bread to the inspector for inspecting; if he does not inspect one cuts it off.

(12) Yesterday's drunkenness does not quench today's thirst.

(13) Better to − − − hunger than to die of want.

(14) Do not be ashamed to do your − − − without blaming it.

(15) If you quarrel with your − − − do not tell him you are patient.[93]

(16) If a town comes to . . . − − − − − −.

(17) If a town comes to ruin − − − − − −.

(18) He who does not carry his father's wheat will carry chaff[94] ⌈to⌉ their storehouses.

(19) Do not take charge of a matter if you cannot take charge to its end.

(20) A woman is a stone quarry; the . . . exploits her.

(21) A good woman of noble character is food[95] that comes in time of hunger.

(22) My son is useless if I do not . . . − − −.

(23) My servant is useless if he does not do my work.

(24) My brother is useless if he does not take care of me.

(**25**,x) − − − − − −

(**25**,1) − − − − − −.

(2)   − − − − − −.

(3)   − − − − − −.

(4)   More nu[merous are the] − − − of the god − − − than the appearances of Pre in the great hall.

(5)   If [a woman is at peace] with her husband it is the influences of the god.

(6)   Do not sell your house and your income for the sake of one day and then be poor forever.

(7)   Do not remove a common man[96] from the property of Pharaoh, lest he destroy you and your family.

(8)   Do not take − − − of a woman to your heart.

(9)   She is a harmful woman who does not leave a tree undamaged.

(10) Learn how to send (a report) to the palace of Pharaoh.

(11) Learn how to sit in the presence of Pharaoh.

(12) Learn the constitution[97] of the sky.

(13) Learn the constitution of the earth.

(14) May the heart of a wife be the heart of her husband, that they may be free of strife.

(15) Choose a prudent husband for your daughter; do not choose for her a rich husband.

(16) Spend one year eating what you possess, so that you spend three years − − − the bank.

(17) Do not marry an impious woman, lest she give your children an impious upbringing.

(18) If a woman is at peace with her husband they will never fare badly.

(19) If a woman whispers about her husband [they will never] fare well.

(20) If a woman does not desire the property of her husband she has another man [in her] heart.

(21) A low woman[98] does not have a life.

(22) A bad woman does not have a husband.

(23) The wife of a fool . . . − − − − − −.

(24) − − − − − −.

(**26**,x) − − − − − −

(**26**,1) − − − − − −.

(2)   − − − − − −.

(3) [There is] − − − [for ⌜throwing⌝] a man out.

(4) There is a stick for bringing him in.

(5) There is imprisonment for giving life.

(6) There is release for killing.

(7) There is he who saves and does not profit.

(8) All are in the hand of the fate and the god.[99]

(9) All sickness is troublesome; the wise man knows how to be sick.[100]

(10) A deed happens to its doer.[101]

(11) The god looks into the heart.

(12) [It is] in battle that [a man] finds a brother.

(13) It is on the road that a man finds a companion.

(14) The plans of the god are one thing, the thoughts of [men] are another.[102]

(15) The plans of the fishermen are one thing, − − − − − −.

(16) If a merchant finds a merchant − − − − − −.

(17) There is one who plows yet does not [reap].

(18) There is he who reaps[103] yet does not [⌜eat⌝].

(19) He whose . . . − − − − − −.

(20) He who bears . . . − − − − − −.

(21) He who digs a pit − − − − − −.[104]

(22) I love my friend − − − − − −.

(23) There is no great protection − − − − − −.

(**27**,x) − − − − − −

(**27**,1) − − − − − −.

(2) $------$.

(3)   A fool who does not know $------$.

(4)   Do not cause another to be well off $---$ you are badly off yourself.

(5)   If $-----$ to the ground.

(6) $------$.

(7)   If a wife is of nobler birth than her husband he should give way to her.

(8) $-----$ say to him "Do not," he says "I will."

(9)   If one orders you $------$ your flesh . . .

(10) Another's instruction does not enter the heart of a fool; what is in his heart is in his heart.

(11) Do not say $------$.

(12) $-----$ because of the god.

(13) A man who reviles the people of his town is wretched forever.

(14) Do not dwell in a house cursed by the god,[105] lest his destruction turn against you.

(15) Do not $------$.

(16) If one leaves a wise man $---$ he perishes.

(17) If I make $------$ I find my right.

(18) If I fear $------$.

(19) If you do not $------$ . . .

(20) Do not $------$ your enemy $---$.

(21) If you $------$ the god.

(22) Do not call $---$ if he is [not] with you.

(23) $------$.

(**28**,x) $------$

(**28**,1) $------$.

(2)   Do not say "I am [rich] in goods" $------$ one greater than you.

(3)   Speak kindly [to your] servants $------$.

(4)   Do not have a merchant for a friend; [he] lives for taking a slice.[106]

(5)   Do not let $---$ linger $---$ without inquiring after her.

(6) $------$ . . .

(7)   Do not often speak wrathfully[107] to a common man, lest you be scorned.

(8)   Do not often speak $---$ to a common man, lest he be ruined . . .

(9)   Do not $------$ find out what you are doing.

(10) Do not weary of calling to the god; he has his hour for hearing the scribe.

(11) Written.

NOTES

1. I.e., he died.

2. In the missing lines it will have been told that Harsiese invited Ankhsheshonq to stay with him for a long time and advised him to communicate three times a month with his family in Heliopolis.

3. The word *3brt*, not known from other texts, recurs in line 11/12 where the meaning "destiny" would be very suitable. The missing lines will have told how Harsiese got involved in the conspiracy against Pharaoh.

4. Read *p3y.k t3w my wd.f* as proposed by Stricker.

5. The missing words will have been something like "How can you, Harsiese," and so on.

6. Read *knb.t* rather than *s3w.t,* also in lines 3/9, 11/17, and 21/13 (Stricker).

7. I read *hr tbn*; see *Glossar,* p. 624.2.

8. The words *rn p3 rmt rn.f* form the beginning of the sentence.

9. On *knh.t,* which I take to be "private chamber," see my n. 7 on p. 151.

10. Pharaoh had a bad dream in which his life was threatened.

11. Read *n.n* (Stricker).

12. Ankhsheshonq defends himself by quoting the words with which he had tried to dissuade Harsiese.

13. Read *p3 'h,* without *hmt* (Stricker).

14. In *JEA,* 54 (1968), 212 n. 1, H. S. Smith identified the place-name as Daphnae.

15. Smith (ibid., pp. 209−214) showed that *h'-nsw* was the term for the accession of Pharaoh and also for its anniversary, and he discussed the practice of amnesty.

16. On *hbr,* "abuse, mistreat, torment," which recurs in 6/11, see *Glossar,* p. 273, and *Instruction of Papyrus Insinger* where it is used six times.

17. *Bty.t,* "abomination, contempt," recurs in 19/25 and 22/16, and the verb in 12/11 and 22/16. It is the old word *bw.t* (*Wb.* 1,453) and it is distinct from *btw,* "crime," derived from *bt3* (*Wb.* 1,483); see G. R. Hughes, *JEA,* 54 (1968), 181.

18. Or, "priesthood."

19. Compare *P. Insinger* 31/13.

20. The reading *tp-mr-mš'* was proposed by G. R. Hughes in G. Mattha and G. R. Hughes, *The Demotic Legal Code of Hermopolis West* (Cairo, 1975), p. 68.

21. Lit., "Be small of wrath, wide of heart." "Small of wrath" recurs in 7/20 and 17/26, and "wide of heart" in 14/6 and 24/15. Both terms are common in *P. Insinger,* where "wide of heart" clearly means "patient."

22. Stricker identified *t3y-3my.t* with Bohairic *ti-maiē,* "grow in size, increase"; see also Černý, *Copt. Dic.,* p. 77. This identification throws light on the original meaning of *3my.t*: it is "shape, form, kind," hence came to mean "character" and "behavior." Its Egyptian antecedent is probably *im, im3,* "shape, form" (*Wb.* 1,78.1 and 80.10) rather than *imy,* "inside" (*Wb.* 1,72). The evolution of meaning is identical with that of Greek *tropos.*

23. On *hbr* see n. 16, above.

24. Read *nḏs.t,* also in 25/21 (Stricker).

25. I.e., do not act inconsistently. The same point is made in a number of sayings, e.g., 7/11, 11/8–9, 16/14, 23/17.

26. This is the Egyptian way of saying "Do not say the first thing that comes into your head."

27. Read *n pḥ.w ntr ʿ3* (Stricker); lit., "in the end the great god."

28. Read *n3y.k* (Stricker).

29. Read *wʿ.t* (Stricker).

30. Read *ḥnt* (Stricker).

31. Read *ḥtp r ḥry,* "rests above" (Stricker). I am rendering the participle *iir* as the present tense; see nn. 76 and 86, below.

32. Adopting Stricker's rendering of *n3.w nkt* as "income."

33. I.e., "in a town which is far from you"?

34. *Šfʿ.t,* "reputation, respect," as in 17/26.

35. The word that Glanville read *3tl* is in fact *3rl.* The horizontal line of the alleged *t* belongs to the determinative. The shortness of the *r* before *l* is common in words containing the pair *rl* (also short first *l* in the pair *ll*). The word *3rl* is surely Coptic *alôl,* "be worried," for which Černý, *Copt. Dic.,* p. 5, supplies a very plausible Late-Egyptian antecedent in *3rr,* "frustration (?)" of P. Brit. Mus. 10083,25. Note the identical determinatives in *3rl* and *3rr.* The meaning "worry" may not be quite accurate but the reading is certain.

36. Read *iw.i ʿbʿ* (Stricker).

37. Read *ḥbs* (Stricker).

38. I take this to be the word *ḏm,* "be still" of *Glossar,* p. 678. It recurs in 12/15, and as *ḏmʿ* in *P. Insinger* 25/24.

39. For *šḫt = sḫt,* "hinder," see *Glossar,* pp. 458 and 461, and *syḫt* in *P. Insinger* 26/9.

40. I.e., be consistent; see n. 25, above.

41. Read *tf3* (Stricker).

42. On *3brṭ* see n. 3, above.

43. Read *n pḥ.w* and compare *P. Insinger* 19/20.

44. Read *mšʿ* (Stricker).

45. The context here and in 15/24–25 shows that *šʿt-h3.t,* "trimmed of heart," can be a temporary condition; hence it is likely to mean "discouraged" rather than "heartless."

46. On *ḏm* see n. 38, above.

47. On *ty šp* meaning "repay" see Stricker and *Mythus* 15/12.

48. A pun on *mw.t,* "mother," and *my.t,* "way, teaching."

49. Lit., "A man who has a small matter, it is that which grips him."

50. On "wide of heart" = "patient" see n. 21, above.

51. Read "100," also in 15/25 (Stricker).

52. I do not think that *ʿš-shn nfr* means a "good deed." The text consistently uses *mt.t nfr.t* for "good deed," while *ʿš-shn nfr* means "good fortune," in contrast with *ʿš-shn bin,*" which is "misfortune, doom," see 2/10, 3/13–14, 8/5 and 20/6. *Wt.t,* "destruction," recurs in 27/14, and see *Glossar,* p. 106. The meaning of the saying might be that a state of good fortune is a charm that can protect against an ill-disposed god.

53. For *šfʿ,* "poor," see Westendorf, *Kopt. Hw.,* p. 562.6.

54. Lit., "the drinking of it, the eating of it is the spending of it." On *ṯ3y,* "spend," see *Glossar,* p. 668.

55. Read *hb sř* (Stricker).

56. I read *bin3.t* and take it to be the infinitive of *bin*.

57. This is *š·*, "chaff," which recurs in 24/18; see Coptic *ešo, šo* in Černý, *Copt. Dic.*, p. 40 and Westendorf, *Kopt. Hw.*, p. 43.

58. Read *n3-šʿt*, and at the end of the line *t3 nty mtw.i* (Stricker). On "discouraged" see n. 45.

59. Read *tny.t* instead of *mw.t* and *bn* instead of *tn* (Stricker). I take it to mean that if a son's inheritance is small because he has brothers and sisters he should be content.

60. Read *gl-sř* (Stricker).

61. So, following Volten, *OLZ*, 52 (1957), 127.

62. Stricker, *ht*, "grinds," Glanville, *ht*, "flows down."

63. The meaning of *šk* has not been established. *Wpy.t* is spelled as in 12/8 and 16/17 and hence is the word for "trial, judgment," not the word *wpy.t*, "rejoicing," which occurs in 18/10. *'Iry n wpy.t* is likely to be the "opponent at a trial"; cf. *iry n dd* in *Glossar*, p. 38.

64. The last words are written below the line.

65. On *sksk*, "scavenge," see Černý, *Copt. Dic.*, p. 150.

66. On "small of wrath" = "gentle" see n. 21; on *šfʿ.t*, "reputation," n. 34.

67. Read [*i.ir*] *k3m ir wh iw n3y.f* [*šny.w*] *hf* (Stricker).

68. See Glanville's n. 224.

69. The meaning of *gr·* is not clear; cf. *Glossar*, pp. 583 and 589.

70. *Thr* in the sense of "be ill," as in 17/7, provides the right sense in connection with *mn*, "landing," i.e., "death." See also 19/15–16.

71. It is not clear what sense should be assigned to *wt*.

72. Read *ipt*, "goose, bird," also in 22/12 (Stricker).

73. Or, "whom he hates"? Meaning?

74. Lit., "small of heart."

75. I.e., "a healing herb"; cf. Volten, *op. cit.*, p. 127.

76. This is one of several cases in which it seems to me that the participle *iir* may signify the present tense; see also 9/15, 12/23, 19/3, and 23/13 with n. 86. *P. Insinger* has numerous instances of the participle *iir* in what seems to be the present tense. I have discussed the matter in a forthcoming article.

77. Read *wʿ.t* here and in the next line (Stricker).

78. Read *tp n i3w.t* (Stricker).

79. Read *hny.t*, "skin." Stricker suggested it meant animal skin worn as clothing; Černý, *Copt. Dic.*, p. 287, proposed "leather thongs." But the saying in Jeremiah xiii:23, "Can the Nubian change his skin?" suggests a sense akin to the biblical passage.

80. Taking *3nt* to be the verb *inty*, "draw back, hinder" of *Wb.* 1,102.2–7 (Stricker); it recurs in 24/10.

81. On *štm*, "scold, quarrel" see Stricker and *Wb.* 4,557.13.

82. Compare 11/11 and 18/13. The repetition is a good indication that the saying was a proverb. A similar saying is *P. Insinger* 25/16.

83. Read *iw t3y.f 3sw.t šʿt n ʿt.s* (Stricker).

84. Stricker read *ip hr tr.t.k š3· 100*, which I have adopted except for the numeral which I read as *10*. Compare the writing of *100* in 14/9 and 15/25.

85. *Rmt ʿš3*, the "mass man," is the "common man"; see also 25/7, 28/7–8, and *Glossar*, p. 72.

86. This sentence has been rendered " 'Am I alive?' asks the dead man," or, " 'Shall I live?' asks he who has died." But is it plausible that in a wholly pragmatic Instruction a dead man is made to speak? It seems to me that the participle *iir* could have the meaning of a gnomic present; see n. 76. It goes without saying that as the question of a dying person, the phrase "Am I going to live?" records observed reality.

87. Read *i.kt.w*, "builders," and *t3y-'yk*, "inaugurate" (Stricker).

88. Compare the different renderings of Glanville, Stricker, and Volten. I venture the suggestion that *ty 3byn* might mean "act the poor man," or, "behave humbly, grovel," in contrast with *ir 3byn*, "become poor," in 16/22.

89. Does this mean, just as a horse thinks of food so a woman is by nature greedy?

90. On *thr* see n. 70, though a meaning like "sad" would also suit here.

91. Read *hrk*, "wig" (Stricker).

92. On *3nt* see n. 80.

93. For the phrase *m-ir dd n.f 'w h3.t.k* compare *P. Insinger* 10/15.

94. *Š'*, "chaff," as in 15/21.

95. Read *tfw* (Stricker).

96. Read *rmt 'š3* and see n. 85.

97. Read *snt* (Stricker).

98. On *nds.t* see n. 24.

99. Or, "the fate of the god." This series of paradoxes, and the conclusion that such paradoxical conditions are the work of fate recall the extensive use of similar paradoxes in *P. Insinger.*

100. Read *šn* (Stricker).

101. Or, to bring out the second tense, "It is to its doer that a deed happens." Here too the participle *iir* makes good sense if taken as a gnomic present.

102. This is the proverb, "Man proposes, God disposes," known from *Amenemope* 19/16–17. On *wt*, "differ," see *Glossar*, p. 104.

103. Read *'wy* (Stricker).

104. As Stricker noted, this is the biblical proverb, "He who digs a pit for another will fall into it." (Proverbs xxvi:27).

105. Read *n p3 '.wy* [*nty*] *shwr* (Stricker).

106. I am guessing that *t3y š't* is literally "take a slice" in the sense of "profiteer."

107. Read *t3y.k b3.t* (Stricker).

THE INSTRUCTION OF PAPYRUS INSINGER

In 1895, when J. H. Insinger purchased on behalf of the Rijksmuseum in Leiden the Demotic papyrus which was to bear his name, the 613-cm-long papyrus lacked a considerable portion of its beginning, amounting to about eight columns (or pages). We are thus deprived of its introduction and of the first five and a half of its chapters. The handwriting dates from the first century A.D., while the composition itself may go back to the latter part of the Ptolemaic period.

Four fragmentary papyri in the Carlsberg collection in Copenhagen, and some smaller fragments in other collections, contain variant versions of the text. Hence we know that this Instruction was a popular work transmitted in numerous copies, the transmission entailing deliberate changes as well as errors. The version that we have before us in the copy of P. Insinger is in fact replete with omissions, transpositions, misunderstandings, and other kinds of errors.

Textual corruption in the transmission of the text was fostered by the fact that, like the Instruction of Ankhsheshonq, the Instruction of Papyrus Insinger consists of individual single-sentence maxims, each occupying one line on the page. But in contrast with the very miscellaneous character of Ankhsheshonq, the author-compiler of P. Insinger arranged the individual maxims into groups according to content, affixed suitable descriptive headings, and thus created chapters which he labeled "teachings" and to which he gave numbers. Furthermore, it looks as if many of the maxims were the author's own formulations, for the Instruction as a whole has a distinctive and coherent point of view.

In some respects the Instruction of P. Insinger is unique, especially in the use of paradoxical formulations which appear at the end of each chapter. Where fully preserved and not garbled in transmission, the paradoxical chapter endings consist of seven sentences made up of two pairs of of paradoxes followed by two final conclusions and a refrain. The whole sequence is designed to qualify the teaching of the chapter by pointing out that through the agency of fate and fortune the god may bring about conditions which are contrary to the expectation embodied in the moral teaching. For example, the eighth chapter warns against gluttony, recommends frugality, and heaps scorn on the glutton and the reckless spender. Yet the chapter ends by observing that he who lives wisely and frugally may nevertheless become poor, and he who lives recklessly may yet be wealthy, such reversals being the work of fate and fortune sent by the god.

In the teaching of P. Insinger morality and piety have been completely fused and they are exemplified in the character of the "wise man" who is capable of enduring reversals of fortune and remains confident of vindication. His counterpart is the "fool" or "impious man" whose disregard of the divine commands makes him commit crimes which, inevitably, result in his punishment. Like all earlier Egyptian sages the author of P. Insinger believed in an all-embracing divine order which governed nature and human existence. To this basic and traditional view he added his specific notion of fate and fortune as agents of change which are part of the divine order though they confound man's understanding.

In its present incomplete state, P. Insinger begins with a page of which only a few words remain, and its second page has a number of lacunae. Thereafter, all pages are complete and, including the fragmentary page 1, amount to a total of thirty-five pages. Volten's important study and partial translation has done much to advance the understanding of this very difficult text beyond the level of is first editions by Boeser and Lexa. But not all of his emendations are plausible, and many of his translations of individual passages require modification. Those of Volten's emendations that I have adopted are indicated in the notes.

Publication: W. Pleyte and P. A. A. Boeser, *Suten-Xeft, le livre royal; papyrus démotique Insinger*, Monuments égyptiens du Musée d'Antiquités des Pays-Bas à Leide, 34 (Leiden, 1899). *Suten-Xeft, le livre royal; édition en phototypie*, Supplément à la 34e livraison des Monuments égyptiens du Musée d'Antiquités des Pays-Bas à Leide (Leiden, 1905).

P. A. A. Boeser, "Transkription und Übersetzung des Papyrus Insinger," *Internationales Archiv für Ethnographie,* Vol. 26 (1925) = *OMRO,* n. s., 3/1 (Leiden, 1922).   F. Lexa, *Papyrus Insinger: Les enseignements moraux d'un scribe égyptien du premier siècle après J.-C. Texte démotique avec transcription, traduction française, commentaire, vocabulaire et introduction grammaticale et littéraire.* 2 vols. (Paris, 1926).

Study: A. Volten, *Kopenhagener Texte zum Demotischen Weisheitsbuch,* Analecta Aegytiaca, 1 (Copenhagen, 1940).   *Idem, Das Demotische Weisheitsbuch,* Analecta Aegytiaca, II (Copenhagen, 1941), partial transcription, translation, and study. Hereafter cited as Volten, *Weisheitsbuch* I and II.   R. J. Williams, *The Morphology and Syntax of Papyrus Insinger,* Ph.D. dissertation, University of Chicago, 1948.

Translation only: P. A. A. Boeser, "Demotic Papyrus from Roman Imperial Time," *Egyptian Religion,* 3 (1935), 27–63.   F. W. von Bissing, *Altägyptische Lebensweisheit* (Zurich, 1955), pp. 91–120.   Bresciani, *Letteratura,* pp. 585–610.

Comments: W. Spiegelberg, *OLZ,* 19 (1916), 70–72; and *idem, OLZ,* 31 (1928), 1025–1037.   P. A. A. Boeser, *Acta Orientalia,* 1 (1923), 148–157.   H. Junker, *OLZ,* 28 (1925), 371–375.   F. Lexa, *Archiv Orientalni,* 1 (1929), 111–146.   P. A. A. Boeser, *Egyptian Religion,* 2 (1934), 1–5.   A. Volten in *Miscellanea Gregoriana,* pp. 376–379.   H. Kees, *OLZ,* 46 (1943), 16–19.   R. J. Williams, *JEA,* 38 (1952), 62–64.   G. Botti and A. Volten, *Acta Orientalia,* 25 (1960), 29–42.   A. Volten in *Les sagesses du proche orient ancien,* colloque de Strasbourg 17–19 mai 1962 (Paris, 1962), pp. 80–85.   M. Gilula, *JAOS,* 92 (1972), 460–465.   K.-T. Zauzich, *Enchoria,* 5 (1975), 119–122.

[THE SIXTH INSTRUCTION]

(**2**,1) Good food in his time and his ——————.[1]

(2)   Good sleep in the time of feebleness ————— because of it.

(3)   ⌜Weigh his wish with good nature;⌝[2] do not ——— what he ⌜commands.⌝

(4)   Do not eat your fill of what you love at [the moment when] he desires it.

(5)   Do not outdo him in dress in the street, so that one looks [at you more than at him].

(6)   Do not . . . ——— . . . ———.

(7)   Do not sin against him in the days of life, for then you are headed [for] death.

(8)   Doing good to him who looks to it is better than gold and fine linen.

(9)   Do not forget the burial, do not be ⌜tardy⌝[3] about the [honors] which the god has commanded.

(10)   Though the burial is in the hand of the god a wise man concerns himself with it.

(11)   The grace of the god for the man of god is his burial and his resting place.

(12) The renewal of life before the dying⁴ is leaving his name on earth [behind] him.

(13) [The] name and the burial and the time of feebleness . . . – – –
. . .

(14) [There is he] who employs his life for the honor of his father
– – – – – –.

(15) [There is he] who acquires blame through cursing his – – – – – –
character.

(16) [He is not] merciful who is beneficent to a son.

(17) Nor is he evil who lets hunger – – – nourished him.

(18) Retaliation and – – – of the fool are caused by his own judgment.

(19) The [good] fate of the good man is given him by his own heart.

(20) The fate [and] the fortune that come, it is the god who sends them. [Total]: 52.

(21)   [THE SEVENTH INSTRUCTION]

(22) [The teaching] to be measured⁵ in everything, so as to do nothing but what is [fitting].

(23) – – – – – – the wise man of character without a portion of – – –.

(24) – – – – – –in the heart of the people [ᴦgivesˡ] protection ᴦandᴵ respect.

(25) – – – – – – listening without blame – – – – – –.

(3,1) Do not rage against him who reprimands you because he reprimands you in public.

(2) Do not let yourself be called "the bad man" because of merciless evildoing.

(3) Do not let yourself be called "the rude one" because of ignorant shamelessness.

(4) Do not ⟨let⟩ yourself be called "fool" because of your thoughtless gluttony.

(5) Do not let yourself be called "who collects by abuse"⁶ because of violence.

(6) Do not let yourself be called "the prattler" because your tongue is everywhere.

(7) Do not let yourself be called "idiot" because of silence when it is time to speak.

(8) Do not let ⟨yourself⟩ be called "stupid" because of the weariness which your words cause.

(9) Do not do what you desire with a woman by cajoling her.

(10) Do not speak arrogantly when counseling in public.

(11) Do not speak rudely when a superior hears your speech.

(12) Do not lead the way insultingly before one who is old.

(13) Do not sit down before a dignitary.

(14) Do not tie yourself to one who is [greater] than you, for then your life will be ruined.

(15) Do not go about much with the fiend because of his name.

(16) Do not consort with [a woman] who consorts with your superior.

(17) If she is beautiful ⌈place yourself away⌉ from her.[7]

(18) Do not forget him who makes haste and him who is strong in his work.

(19) In the hand of the wise man reward and the stick are measured.

(20) Do not be concerned about vengeance; do what is before you.

(21) Better the small (deed) of him who is quick than the large one of him who delays.

(22) Do not make your weight heavy when your balance is weak.

(23) The fool who is vengeful to the wretch is one who falls on the battlefield.

(24) ⌈Do not hurry to fight a master whose stick is quick.⌉[8]

(4,1) [He who] is violent [like] the wind will founder in the storm.

(2) Do not hasten to seek a quarrel with a powerful ruler.

(3) He who thrusts his [chest] at the spear will be struck by it.

(4) Do not speak of royalty and divinity with hostility when you are angry.

(5) The foolish tongue of the stupid man is his knife for cutting off life.

(6) Do not squander the little you have if there is no storehouse behind you.

(7) Do not eat the profit of something before the fate has given it.

(8) Do not be greedy for wealth in a lifetime which you cannot know.

(9) The impious man leaves his savings at death and another takes them.

(10) Do not by yourself adopt a custom which differs from those of the land.

(11) He who raves with the crowd is not called[9] a fool.

(12) Do not say "the chance is good" and forget the fate in it.

(13) The impious man who is proud of himself is harmed by his own heart.

(14) The beam that is longer than its right measure, its excess is cut off.

(15) The wind that is greater than its right measure wrecks the ships.

(16) All things that are good through right measure, their owner does not give offense.

(17) The great god Thoth has set a balance in order to make right measure on earth by it.

(18) He placed the heart hidden in the flesh for the right measure of its owner.

(19) If a learned man is not balanced[10] his learning does not avail.

(20) A fool who does not know balance is not far from trouble.

(21) If a fool is not balanced he cannot live ⌜off⌝ another.

(22) Pride and arrogance are the ruin of their owner.

(23) He who knows his own heart, the fate knows him.

(**5**,1) He who is gentle by virtue of his good character creates his own fate.

(2) He who is wrathful about a mistake is one whose death will be hard.

(3) There is the man wise of heart whose life is hard.

(4) There is he who is content with ⟨his⟩ fate, there is he who is content with his knowledge.

(5) He is not a man wise in character who lives by it (the character).

(6) He is not a fool as such[11] whose life is hard.

(7) The god lays the heart on the scales opposite the weight.

(8) He knows the impious and the pious man by his heart.

(9) There is curse or blessing in the character that was given him (i.e., them).

(10) The commands that the god has commanded to those who are good are in the character.

(11) The fate and the fortune that come, it is the god who sends them. Total: 62.

(12) THE EIGHTH INSTRUCTION. Do not be a glutton, lest you become the companion of poverty.

(13) The fool who does not control himself will be in want[12] through gluttony.

(14) The fool who has power, what happens to him is bad.

(15) It is the god who gives wealth; it is a wise man who guards ⟨it⟩.

(16) The virtue of a wise man is to gather without greed.

(17) The great glory of a wise man is to control himself in his manner of life.

(18) The fool is in bad odor in the street because of gluttony.

(19) It is not only in one way that he becomes miserable.

(20) There is he who ⟨cannot⟩ eat yet in his heart desires much food.

(21) There is he who is weary from yesterday yet has a craving for wine.

(22) [There is] he who dislikes intercourse yet ⟨spends⟩ his surplus on women.

(23) [There is] he who dies in misery on account of gluttony.

(**6**,1) [The] evil that befalls the fool, his belly and his phallus bring it.

(2) [One] hunts on the river after the god (i.e., the crocodile) because of[13] his ⌜frightfulness.⌝

(3)   Death[14] comes to the snake because of its love of biting.

(4)   The one among the cattle that is the first to be sated is the one that is suitable for slaughter.

(5)   [One catches] the bird that flies onto the fish in order to fill its belly.

(6)   The pigeon brings harm on its young[15] because of its belly.

(7)   The swallow comes to grief for its little food.

(8)   The life that controls excess is a life according to a wise man's heart.

(9)   Vegetables and natron are the best foods that can be found.

(10) Wealth ⟨⌜through⌝⟩ saving is the equivalent of labor . . . . . .

(11) Illness befalls a man because the food harms him.

(12) He who eats too much bread will suffer illness.

(13) He who drinks too much wine lies down in a stupor.

(14) All kinds of ailments are in the limbs because of overeating.

(15) He who is moderate in his manner of life, his flesh is not disturbed.

(16) Illness does not burn him who is moderate in food.

(17) Poverty does not take hold of him who controls himself in purchasing.

(18) His belly does not relieve itself in the street because of the food in it.

(19) The fool has neither shame nor fidelity because of his gluttony.

(20) He who is insolent among men becomes the first among women.

(21) He who eats for the sake of his belly is violated by his companions.

(22) He who is gluttonous through lack of shame draws all kind of blame to himself.

(23) He who eats when there is no reserve is one who sleeps while death is before him.

(24) He who spends without an income must pay interest on interest.

(**7**,1) It is an illness without recovery; one reaches death through it.

(2)   It is an imprisonment without a future; one is confined forever.

(3)   An old man without subsistence, that is an undesired life.

(4)   An old man[16] who has provisions is strong for what confronts him.

(5)   ⌜Savings in the house are effective for every need.⌝[17]

(6)   The fool who forgets the morrow will lack food in it.

(7)   The little he has is good (i.e., seems good) if he is sated with plenty of food.

(8)   Hunger is good for him who can be sated so that harm does not befall him.

(9)   Lawful punishment[18] attains the man who is foolish because of his belly.

(10) A shameless glutton draws all kinds of blame to himself.

(11) A wise man is harmed because of a woman he loves.

(12) He who is abstemious with his belly and guarded with his phallus is not blamed at all.

(13) There is one who lives on little so as to save, yet he becomes poor.

(14) There is one who does not know, yet the fate gives (him) wealth.

(15) It is not the wise man who saves who finds a surplus.

(16) Nor is it the one who spends who becomes poor.

(17) The god gives a wealth of supplies without an income.

(18) He also gives poverty in the purse without spending.

(19) The fate and the [fortune] that come, it is the god who sends them. Total: 55.

(20)   THE NINTH INSTRUCTION. The teaching not to be a fool, so that one does not fail to receive you in the house.

(21) Wrongdoing [occurs][19] to the heart of the fool through his love of women.

(22) He does not think of the morrow for the sake of wronging the wife of another.

(23) The fool who looks at a woman is like a fly[20] on blood.

(24) His − − − attains the bedroom, unless the hand of another attains him.

(8,1) the [fool] brings disturbance to − − − because of his phallus.

(2) His love of fornication does harm to his livelihood.

(3) He who knows how to hold his heart has the equivalent of every teaching.

(4) If a woman is beautiful you should show you are superior to her.[21]

(5) A good woman who does not love another man in her family is a wise woman.

(6) The women who follow this teaching are rarely bad.

(7) Their good condition comes about through the god's command.

(8) There is she who fills her house with wealth without there being an income.

(9) There is she who is the praised mistress of the house[22] by virtue of her character.

(10) There is she whom I hold in contempt as an evil woman.[23]

(11) Fear her on account of the fear of Hathor.

(12) The fool who wrongs the mistress of the house,[24] his portion is to be cursed.

(13) He who is worthy before the god will have respect for them.

(14) There is he who forgets a wife when he is young because he loves another woman.

(15) She is not a good woman who is pleasing to another (man).

(16) She is not the fool of the street who misbehaves in it.

(17) He is not a wise man who consorts with them.[25]

(18) The work of Mut and Hathor is what acts among women.

(19) It is in women that good fortune and bad fortune are upon earth.[26]

(20) Fate and fortune go and come when he (the god) commands them. Total: 23.

(21)   THE TENTH INSTRUCTION. The teaching not to weary of instructing your son.

(22) A statue of stone is the foolish son whom his father has not instructed.[27]

(23) It is a son's good and blessed portion to receive instruction and to ask.

(24) No instruction can succeed if there is dislike.[28]

(9,1) The youth [who] is not spoiled by his belly is not blamed.

(2)   He who is abstemious with his phallus, his name does not stink.

(3)   He who is persevering[29] and thoughtful is chosen among the people.

(4)   He who listens to a reprimand protects himself from another.

(5)   The fault in every kind of character comes from not listening.

(6)   Thoth has placed the stick on earth in order to teach the fool by it.

(7)   He gave the sense of shame to the wise man so as to escape all punishment.[30]

(8)   The youth who has respect through shame is not scorned with punishment.

(9)   A son does not die from being punished by his father.

(10) He who loves his spoiled son will spoil himself with him.

(11) The stick and shame protect their owner from the fiend.

(12) The son who is not taught, his ⟨. . .⟩[31] causes astonishment.

(13) The heart of his father does not desire a long life (for him).

(14) The sensible one among the children is worthy of life.

(15) Better the son of another than a son who is an accursed fool.

(16) There is he who has not been taught, yet he knows how to instruct another.

(17) There is he who knows the instruction, yet he does not know how to live by it.

(18) He is not a true son who accepts instruction so as to be taught.

(19) It is the god who gives the heart, gives the son, and gives the good character.

(20) The fate and the fortune that come, it is the god who determines them.[32] Total: 25.

(21)   THE ELEVENTH INSTRUCTION. The teaching how to acquire protection for yourself so that you are not harmed.

(22) To serve by virtue of [his] character is protection for him who seeks protection.

(23) Small wrath, shame, and care make the praise of the wise man.

(**10**,1) [It is the god who] gives protection to the wise man because of (his) service.

(2)   A wise man who has a mortgage gives service for ⌐security.⌐

(3)   A wise man in quietude gives service for a livelihood.

(4)   The fool who does not give service, his goods will belong to another.

(5)   The fool who has no[33] protection sleeps in prison.

(6)   He who has found his asylum is not taken away by force.

(7)   He who spends something on protection sleeps safely in the street.

(8)   He who gives bread (or, a gift) when there is an accusation is vindicated without being questioned.

(9)   He who is partial in benefaction and partial in service causes annoyance.

(10) Do not withhold your name, lest you spoil your reward.

(11) Do not vaunt what you have done as a service, for then you annoy.

(12) Do not approach when it is not the time for it, for then your master will dislike you.

(13) Do not be far, lest one must search for you and you become a stench to him.

(14) Do not multiply complaints about obtaining a reward which you desire.

(15) Do not tell him you were patient at the time of his benefaction.

(16) Do not make free in speaking to him so that he should know you were patient.[34]

(17) Do not slight him in the street, lest his stick[35] admonish you.

(18) Do not say something evil to him when he reproaches your stupidity.

(19) Do not say something good to him out of concern for his enmity.[36]

(20) Do not say anything to him when there is anger in his heart.

(21) Do not sit or stand still in an undertaking which is urgent.

(22) Do not tarry when he gives an order, lest his time be wasted.

(23) Do not [hasten to] do an evil deed because he said something that should not be listened to.

(**11**,1) Do not be forgetful at the time of questioning.[37]

(2)   Do not report at all when something else is in his heart.

(3)   Do not answer when he questions you about an undertaking which you do not know.

(4)   Do not vaunt your livelihood when he knows it.

(5)   Do not let your name come before him in any matter concerning a woman.

(6)   Do not carry a word into the street from a consultation in his house.

(7)   Do not accuse him to another person by blaming his character.

(8)   Do not be ashamed at the time of an accusation when he questions you and examines you.

(9)   ⌐You should serve him when he is near as well as when he is far from you.⌐[38]

(10) Know the condition of his character, do not do what his heart despises.

(11) If he finds fault with you, go and plead with him until he is reconciled to you.

(12) If he gives you a gift, take it to the god and he will let you have it.

(13) There is no true protection except the work of the god.

(14) There is no true servant except the one who serves him.

(15) He is a wall of copper for his lord in the darkness.

(16) He brings punishment to the impious without protection behind him.

(17) There is he who is tormented, and it is his master who questions.

(18) He is not a powerful lord who gives protection to another.

(19) Nor is he a powerless outcast who is tormented.

(20) Before the god the strong and the weak are a joke.

(21) Fate and fortune go and come when he commands them. Total: 47.

(22)   THE TWELFTH INSTRUCTION.

(23) Do not trust one whom you do not know in your heart, lest he cheat you with cunning.

(24) The blind one whom the god blesses, his way is open.

(**12**,1) The lame one whose heart is on the way of the god, his way is smooth.

(2)   The god blesses trust[39] with protection.

(3)   The evil man is evilly punished because of (his) deceit.

(4)   Do not trust a fool because he brings you (something) with a blessing.

(5)   The fool who seeks to deceive, his tongue brings him harm.

(6)   Do not trust another on the way if there are no people near you.

(7) The work of the fiend succeeds against the wise man through cunning.

(8) Do not trust your enemy, lest his heart bring forth cursing.

(9) The fool who is insolent is overpowered by the fiend.

(10) The evil man takes two-thirds and seeks the other third.

(11) Do not trust a fool because of an oath.

(12) Do not trust a fool at any time in an undertaking.

(13) The property of a wise man is lost through being left in the hand of a fool.

(14) One does not discover the heart of a man in its character if one has not sent him (on a mission).

(15) One does not discover the heart of a wise man if one has not tested him in a matter.

(16) One does not discover the heart of an honest man if one has not consulted him in a deliberation.

(17) One does not discover ⟨the heart⟩ of a trustworthy man if one has not sought something from him.

(18) One does not discover the heart of a friend if one has not consulted him in anxiety.

(19) One does not discover the heart of a brother if one has not begged ⟨from him⟩ in want.

(20) One does not discover the heart of a son until the day when one seeks goods from him.

(21) One does not discover the heart of a servant as long as his master ⌈is not attacked.⌉

(22) One does not ever discover the heart of a woman anymore than (one knows) the sky.

(23) When a wise man is tested few discover his perfection.

(24) One who is foolish with his tongue is surely discovered by many.

(25) There is he who trusts the moment, and it goes well with him forever.

(**13**,1) There is he who trusts no one but himself.

(2) He is not a man[40] of heart who is tested in every kind of behavior.

(3) Nor is he a fool who is discovered by examining it (the behavior).

(4) The sense of shame is the gift of god to him in whom one trusts.

(5) He does not apportion it to the evil man nor to the impious one.

(6) Falsehood does not depart from them nor the cunning which he loves (i.e., which they love).

(7) The fate and the fortune that come, it is the god who determines them. Total: 35.

(8)   THE THIRTEENTH INSTRUCTION.

(9) Do not trust a thief, lest you come to grief.

(10) Better a serpent in the house than a fool who frequents it.

(11) He who frequents a fool is drawn into crime.

(12) He who lives with a fool dies in prison.

(13) The friend of a fool sleeps bound to him.

(14) The crimes of a fool harm his own brothers.

(15) A crocodile in fury harms its divine brothers.

(16) A fool who lights a fire goes close to it and burns.

(17) A fool who starts a fight goes close to it and falls.

(18) When a thief commits a theft his companions get a beating.

(19) He who walks with a wise man shares his praise.

(20) He who goes by with a fool makes a stench in the street.

(21) There is he who meets grief because he has met a fool.

(22) There is he who is far from him, yet he gets into crime without knowing it.

(23) He is not one who consorts with a fool who perishes through foolishness.[41]

(**14**,1) He is not a wise man who shows the way to another.

(2) The fate and the fortune that come, it is the god who determines them. Total: 17.

(3)   THE FOURTEENTH INSTRUCTION. Do not let the inferior man rule, lest he make your name that of a fool.

(4) If the food is rightly measured[42] and the work fixed, the servant is humble before its master.

(5) To slay the fool is to draw him away from his evil character.[43]

(6) A fool before whom there is no stick has no concern in his heart.

(7) A fool who has no concern gives concern to him who sends him (on an errand).

(8) The pay due the inferior man, let it be food and the stick.

(9) The inferior man whose face is downcast is one who has been well instructed.

(10) A fool who has no work, his phallus does not let him rest.

(11) If the stick is far from the master, the servant does not listen to him.

(12) The god blesses him who punishes lawfully.

(13) And he is angered if the fool is left to his stupidity.

(14) The ruler is punished for letting the impious man have power.

(15) The god leaves his city during the rule of an evil master.

(16) Law and justice cease in a town when there is no stick.[44]

(17) Grief comes to the people through the disorder caused by the fool.

(18) Evil counsel comes to the fool when there is no control.[45]

(19) The god gives power to the wise man for the sake of command.

(20) A great temple is ruined because its leaders are in discord.

(21) Do not absolve one who commits a crime.[46]

(22) Do not leave the fool or the evil man to the behavior that he likes.

(23) Do not leave the ignorant man or the fool at a work that he does not know.

(**15**,1) Do not let an impious or inferior man command the people.

(2) There is a trace of the inferior man in the character of the godly man.[47]

(3) He is not a great man who is chosen because of character.[48]

(4) Nor is he an inferior man who leaves the way because of foolishness.

(5) The heart and the character and their owner are in the hand of the god.

(6) Fate and fortune go and come when he commands them. Total: 28.

(7)   THE FIFTEENTH INSTRUCTION. Do not be greedy lest your name stink.

(8) A mortgage with greed is coal that burns its owner.

(9) Theft with greed brings a lawful killing.[49]

(10) The god gives wealth to the wise man because of (his) generosity.

(11) The wealth of the generous man is greater than the wealth of the greedy.

(12) Greed puts strife and combat in a house.

(13) Greed removes shame, mercy, and trust from the heart.

(14) Greed causes disturbance in a family.

(15) He who is greedy does not like to give to him who gave to him.

(16) He does not think of the morrow because he lives for the moment.

(17) He does not eat his fill of anything because of (his) stupidity.

(18) Money with greed, its wrong does not end.

(19) Money is the snare the god has placed on the earth for the impious man so that he should worry daily.

(20) But he gives it to his favorite so as to remove worry from his heart.

(21) He who is generous in giving food through it (money) is one to whom the fate gives it.

(22) Wealth goes to him who gives food through it.

(**16**,1) Burnt offering and libation are appropriate for (giving) food.

(2) A funeral is appropriate for giving food in it.

(3) The heart of the god is content when the poor man is sated before him.

(4) If property accrues to you give a portion to the god; that is the portion of the poor.

(5)   If much property accrues to you spend for your town, so that there is no torment in it.

(6)   If it is in your power, invite him who is far as well as him who is near you.

(7)   He who invites him who is far, his name will be great when he is far.

(8)   He who loves his neighbor finds family around him.

(9)   The good repute of the good man conveys a great name from one to another.

(10) (Giving) food without dislike removes all dislike.

(11) The god gives a thousandfold to him who gives to another at a feast.

(12) The god lets one acquire wealth in return for doing good.

(13) He who gives food to the poor, the god takes him to himself in boundless mercy.

(14) The heart of the god is pleased by the giving of food ⟨more than⟩ the heart of the recipient.

(15) He who loves to give food to another will find it before him in every house.

(16) He who hides because of avarice is like a stranger who is hidden.

(17) He who is mean to his people dies without prayers being said for him.

(18) A family of wise men accrues to him who thinks of rewarding it.

(19) The death of the evil man is a feast for the household left behind.

(20) Praise in the street is the exchange for the goods of the storehouse.[50]

(21) Small wealth with blessing is Hapy in his time of ⌜growth.⌝[51]

(22) The goods of the greedy are ashes driven by the wind.

(23) There is he who buries them when they are gathered, and then the earth conceals them.

(**17**,1) He is not greedy and stingy who has a reserve in the storehouse.

(2)   It is the god who gives wealth and poverty[52] according to that which he has decreed.

(3)   The fate and the fortune that come, it is the god who determines them. Total: 42.

(4)   THE SIXTEENTH INSTRUCTION. Do not let your flesh suffer when you have something in the storehouse.

(5)   The heart cannot rise up when there is affliction in it.

(6)   Death and the life of tomorrow, we do not know their ⟨nature⟩.

(7)   Today with its livelihood is what the wise man asks for.

(8)   He who loves to hoard wealth[53] will die robbed of it.

(9)   The good life of him who has become old is provided by ⌜what is in⌝ his hand.

(10) He who is wretched although there is wealth in the storehouse is one who will (have to) beg his share of it.

(11) He who has passed sixty years, everything has passed for him.

(12) If his heart loves wine, he cannot drink to drunkenness.

(13) If he desires food, he cannot eat as he used it.

(14) If his heart desires a woman, her moment does not come.

(15) Wine, women, and food give gladness to the heart.

(16) He who uses them without loud shouting[54] is not reproached in the street.

(17) He who is deprived of one of them becomes the enemy of his body.

(18) The wise man who utilizes provisions, his time will not become poor.

(19) Better is the short time of him who is old than the long life of him who begs (or, has begged).

(20) The life of one who saves (or, has saved) is one that passes (or, has passed) without its having been known.

(21) The life that approaches the peak, two-thirds of it are lost.[55]

(22) He (man) spends ten ⟨years⟩ as a child before he understands death and life.

(23) He spends another ten ⟨years⟩ acquiring the work of instruction by which he will be able to live.

(18,1) He spends another ten years gaining and earning possessions by which to live.

(2)   He spends another ten years up to[56] old age before his heart takes counsel.

(3)   There remain sixty years of the whole life which Thoth has assigned to the man of god.[57]

(4)   One in a million, the god giving his blessing, is he who spends them with fate consenting.

(5)   Neither the impious nor the godly man can alter the lifetime that was assigned him.

(6)   He who is fortunate in his days thinks of death in them.

(7)   He who thinks of it (death) for the sake of gain, the riches will bring about his end.

(8)   The chief demon is the first to punish (him) after the taking of the breath.

(9)   Cedar oil, incense, natron, and salt are ⌜small⌝[58] remedy for healing his wounds.

(10) A merciless inflammation[59] burns his body.

(11) He cannot say "Remove your hand," during the punishment by him who deals out beatings.

(12) The end of the godly man is being buried on the mountain with his burial equipment.

(13) The owner of millions who acquired them by hoarding cannot take them to the mountain in his hand.

(14) One does not give a lifetime to him who hoards (or, has hoarded) in order to leave them (the millions) to another after him.

(15) He who thinks of the god and his power is one who does what he (the god) wishes on earth.

(16) The gift of the god to the man of god is making him patient in his time of mercy.

(17) Great is the affliction of those who left the path at leaving their savings to another.

(18) He who knows what is within the man of god does not hoard riches.

(19) Eat and drink when no brother is hungry, when no father and mother ⌐beseach⌐ you.

(20) Make holiday generously as long as no one begs from you.

(21) Enjoy yourself with whom you wish as long as no fool joins you.

(22) As for a good woman of proven good character, you will not be able to blame her on account of it.[60]

(23) A timely remedy is to prevent illness by having the greatness of the god in your heart.

(**19**,1) There is he who uses his portion for himself in a lifetime without blame.

(2) There is he who hoards riches until death arrives.

(3) He is not the owner of millions in wealth who uses his portion thereof.

(4) He is not a greedy one who is concerned for his next day's food.

(5) Fate and fortune go and come when he (the god) commands them. Total: 51.

(6)   THE SEVENTEENTH INSTRUCTION. Do not let worry flourish lest you become distraught.

(7) If the heart worries about its owner it creates illness for him.

(8) When worry has arisen the heart seeks death itself.

(9) It is the god who gives patience to the wise man in misfortune.

(10) The impious man who forgets the god dies stricken in his heart.

(11) A short day in misfortune is many (days) in the heart of the impatient man.

(12) The support of the godly man in misfortune is the god.

(13) The fool does not call to him in trouble because of (his) impiety.

(14) He who is persevering[61] in hardship, his fate goes and comes on account of it.

(15) The fate together with the god bring happiness after anxiety.[62]

(16) Do not be heartsore in (your) town because you are weak.

(17) He who is weak in (his) town becomes strong in it again.

(18) Do not prefer death to life in misfortune out of despair.

(19) The god returns contentment, the dead do not return.

(20) He creates the good through the fate at the end of[63] old age.

(21) The weak man who has no resentment, his food is not hard.

(22) What is good for a man is not to be vengeful when the fate is hard.

(23) Do not be heartsore about a matter if its course[64] comes to a halt.

(**20**,1) The day of loss is lost ⌈for its very gain.⌉

(2) Do not sail the course of the evil man even when fate favors him.

(3) The impious man does not die in the fortune which he likes.

(4) Do not be heartsore during an imprisonment; the work of the god is great.

(5) The man of god is in prison ⌈for his very gain.⌉

(6) ⌈Death saves from prison because of prayer.⌉

(7) Do not worry your heart with the ⌈bitterness⌉ of one who is dying (or, is dead).

(8) No one turns away from life because of another's dying.

(9) Nor is there anyone who listens because of your praying to the sky.

(10) He who dies (or, has died) in the middle of life, the god knows what he has done.

(11) The god does not forget the punishment for any crime.

(12) What passes by (or, has passed by) of vexations today, let them be yesterday to you.

(13) What comes (or, has come) of hardship, leave yourself in the hand of the god in it.

(14) On day is not like another for him whose heart cares.

(15) One hour is not like another in a lifetime without blame.

(16) It so befell in the beginning when the gods were on earth.

(17) When Pre had weakened before the enemies, they weakened before him in turn.

(18) When Horus had been hidden behind the papyrus, he became ruler of the earth in turn.

(19) Happiness came to Isis out of misfortune after[65] what she had undergone.

(20) Good steering[66] comes out of trouble after grief.

(21) The god turns away fear in the straits when death is near.

(22) He saves the ox after whose branding is the slaughter block.

(23) The fear of the man of god is that which goes just as it came.

(**21**,1) Hardship when there is no fault is not to be feared.

(2) A time in misfortune does not make the man of god give up.

(3) There is he who is persevering about tomorrow without his hand succeeding.

(4) There is he who does not take care and fate cares for him.

(5) He is not the wise man in misfortune who takes his heart for a companion.

(6) The fate and the fortune that come, it is the god who sends them. Total: 48.

(7) THE EIGHTEENTH INSTRUCTION.

(8) The teaching of being patient until you have taken counsel, lest you give offense.

(9) The patience of a wise man is to consult with the god.

(10) Patience without blame results in good steering.

(11) ⌜The enemy of the evil man becomes the first of Thoth in his heart.⌝

(12) Harm attains the fool because he does not take counsel.

(13) He who listens to the judgment of his heart sleeps untroubled.

(14) He who guards his heart and his tongue sleeps without an enemy.

(15) He who reveals a secret matter, his house will burn.

(16) He who repeats it ⟨because of⟩ impatience is one who defiles his tongue.[67]

(17) He who turns away from his anger is one who is far from the anger of the god.

(18) The fool who is impatient, the god is impatiently after him.

(19) When a fool is patient time drags for him.

(20) The patience of a fool is like a flame that flares and then dies.

(21) The patience ⟨of a fool⟩ equals a water that is held back and then its dam gives way.

(22) The patience of a fool is such that when his master sends him he who has sent him must go after him.

(23) Patience and impatience, fate is their master who makes them.

(**22**,1) All their time is examined by the wise man.

(2) Their determination is through the counsel which the god has decreed.

(3) He who finds counsel is not a wise man who takes counsel.

(4) Nor is he whose manner annoys a fool or an idiot.

(5) Taking counsel, thought, and patience are in the hand of the god.

(6) Fate and fortune go and come when he commands them.

(7) THE NINETEENTH INSTRUCTION. The teaching of making your speech calm.

(8) Gentleness in every kind of behavior[68] makes the praise of the wise man.

(9) The power of a fool in command is one that goes to a swift death.

(10) Do not make your voice harsh, do not speak loudly with your tongue.

(11) A loud voice causes harm to the parts of the body just like an illness.

(12) Do not be impatient when you inquire so that you get angry when listening.

(13) Do not reveal what is secret to a wise man for the sake of (his) listening.

(14) His praise is great before the people because he listens.

(15) Water goes into the temple although there is no water before it.

(16) Do not be vengeful to him who is (or, has been) vengeful until his day has come.

(17) He who fares downstream with the ⌜oar rows⌝ when it is time to ⌜row.⌝

(18) Do not reveal what is in your heart to your master when (he is) deliberating.[69]

(19) The counsel that occurs to the fool is as weightless as the wind.

(20) Do not give way often to your tongue to advise when you have not been asked.

(21) He who hastens with his voice when he speaks gives a false answer.

(22) One does not listen to the voice of a ⌜chatterbox⌝[70] in an accusation.

(23) One does not judge according to the complaint of a fool because it is loud.

(**23**,1) One does not torment someone unless he has been found out through (his) pleading.

(2) One does not pity the impious man during punishment because he cries loudly.

(3) One does not praise a donkey carrying a load because it brays.

(4) A fool does not obtain a portion of something because he brings (something).[71]

(5) Better is the portion of him who is silent than the portion of him who says "Give me."

(6) It is better to bless someone than to do harm to one who has insulted you.

(7) If a wise man is not calm his manner is not perfect.

(8) If there is no[72] calm in combat its army does not get a rest.

(9) If there is no calm in a feast its master cannot enjoy himself.

(10) If there is no calm in a temple its gods are the ones who abandon it.

(11) One places a chapel under a god because of its name.⁷³

(12) Praise is given to the wise man because of (his) calm.

(13) Old age is the good (time) in life because of (its) gentleness.

(14) He who makes his behavior harsh goes to a bad death.

(15) There is the evil man who is calm like a crocodile in water.

(16) There is the fool who is calm like heavy lead.

(17) He is not a restless fool who is gripped by unrest.

(18) It is the god who gives calm and unrest through his commands.

(19) The fate and the fortune that come, it is the god who sends them. Total: 36.

(20)　　THE TWENTIETH INSTRUCTION. Do not slight a small thing lest you suffer from it.

(21) Deadly harm⁷⁴ comes to the fool for slighting greatness in his heart.

(22) In turn harm is done to a great man for slighting smallness.

(23) It is the god who gives the heart to the wise man for the sake of having respect.

(24) It is he who leaves the impious man to harm because of (his) brutality.

(25) Do not slight royalty and divinity in order to injure them.

(**24**,1) He who fears harm escapes all harm.⁷⁵

(2) Do not slight a small illness for which there is a remedy; use the remedy.

(3) He to whom an illness returns day after day, his recovery is difficult.

(4) Do not slight a small amulet at a time when it is needed.

(5) An amulet that does no harm protects its owner from it.

(6) Do not slight a small god, lest his retaliation teach you.

(7) The small shrew mouse vents its anger.

(8) The small scarab ⟨is great⟩ through its secret image.

(9) The small dwarf is great because of his name.⁷⁶

(10) The small snake has poison.

(11) The small river has its demon.

(12) The small fire is (to be) feared.

(13) The small document has great benefit.

(14) The small of age (the youth), his name is made in combat.

(15) The small cord binds its ⌐oar.⌐

(16) The small truth, its owner ⌐destroys ⟨by it⟩.⌐

(17) The small falsehood makes trouble for him who commits it.

(18) The little food gives health to its owner.

(19) The small service, if it is steady, removes dislike.

(20) A little saving creates wealth.

(21) A little bread stops killing.

(22) The heart in its smallness sustains its owner.

(23) A small worry breaks[77] the bones.

(24) A small good news makes the heart live.

(25) A little dew makes the field live.

(**25**,1) A little wind carries the boat.

(2) The little bee brings the honey.

(3) The small *škt*[78] carries away the field.

(4) The small locust destroys the grapevine.

(5) A small wrong hastens toward death.

(6) A small benefaction is not hidden from the god.

(7) Many are the small things that are worthy of respect.

(8) Few are the great things that are worthy of admiration.

(9) There is he who fears blame, yet he commits a great crime.

(10) There is he who shouts out of scorn, yet he gives service.

(11) He who guards himself is not a wise and respectful man.

(12) Nor is he to whom harm comes a deceitful fool.

(13) The fate and the fortune that come, it is the god who determines them. Total: 44.

(14)   THE TWENTY-FIRST INSTRUCTION. The teaching not to be mean, lest you be slighted.

(15) The hand that is not greedy, its owner is not reproached.

(16) In a town in which you have no family your heart is your family.[79]

(17) A man's good character makes company around him.

(18) Do not love your belly, know shame in your heart, do not scorn the voice of your heart.

(19) He who scorns one of them makes a stench in the street.

(20) Do not dance in the crowd, do not make face[80] in the multitude.

(21) Do not let your tongue differ from your heart in counsel when you are asked.

(22) A deceitful man does not tell another man what is in his heart.

(23) What he desires does not come about through his counsels.

(24) Do not fear, do not be lazy, do not worry excessively.

(**26**,1) The reward of the fool and the inferior man is the laughter that falls on him (i.e., on them).

(2) Do not demand something that belongs to another out of scorn for him.

(3) Do not scorn an inferior man because he stretches out his hand[81] when it is not the time for it.

(4) The fool makes his questioner hostile by his not listening.

(5) Do not flatter nor be rude in any house because of love of your belly.

(6) He who goes without having been invited is one to whom the house is narrow (i.e., inhospitable).

(7)   When the evil man has well-being he asks for death in it.

(8)   When the wise man suffers, death is an astonishment to him.

(9)   Do not think of hindering[82] a fool or one bereft of judgment.

(10)   He who loves worry does not listen to reproof of what he has done.

(11)   Do not do a work which is scorned if you can live by another.

(12)   Do not be close to one in whose heart there is hatred.

(13)   The fool with his bad character does not cease to hate.

(14)   Do not beg for a gift from an evil brother in the family.

(15)   There is no brother in a family except the brother who is kind-hearted.

(16)   Do not borrow money at interest[83] in order to provide plenty of food with it.

(17)   He who controls himself in his manner of life is not reproached on account of his belly.

(18)   Do not alter your word when spending, do not cheat at the time of sealing (an agreement).

(19)   A wise man who is trusted, his pledge is in one's hand.

(20)   His word in a matter is a pledge without an oath.

(21)   Do not set a due date for someone while another (date) is in your heart.

(22)   What is in the heart of the wise man is what one finds on his tongue.

(23)   Do not draw back from what you have said except from an unlawful wrong.[84]

(24)   The honor of the scribe is having a wise man's honesty in his words.

(27,1)   Do not cheat when you are questioned, there being a witness behind you (i.e., the god).

(2)   Do not steal out of hunger, for you will be investigated.

(3)   Better death in want than life in shamelessness.

(4)   Do not raise your hand, there being one who listens.

(5)   . . . . . .

(6)   He who is silent under wrong is one who escapes from harm.

(7)   Do not desire to take revenge on your master in order to seek justice.

(8)   Do not approach[85] the strong man even when you have protection behind you.

(9)   When a wise man is stripped he gives his clothes and blesses.

(10)   Do not undertake any work and then fail to be satisfied by it.

(11)   Do not render judgment to the people if you have no stick ⟨to make them⟩ listen to you.

(12)   The fool who is in the right is more annoying than he who wronged him.

(13) Do not be brutal to one who is silent, lest his heart beget contention.

(14) The snake on which one steps ejects a strong poison.

(15) The fool who is brutal to another is scorned for (his) brutality.

(16) There is he who is scorned for (his) gentleness, yet he is patient toward another through it.

(17) There is he who is arrogant, and he makes a stench in the street.

(18) He who is chosen among the people is not a wise man.

(19) Nor is he a great man who is respected by another.

(20) It is the god who gives the praise and the blameless character.

(21) The fate and the fortune that come, it is the god who sends them. Total: 57.

(22)   THE TWENTY-SECOND INSTRUCTION.

(23) The teaching not to abandon the place in which you can live.

(**28**,1) Lowly work and lowly food are better than being sated far away.

(2) The occupation of one who is foolish about his belly is to run after a violent death.

(3) When a wise and godly man has an illness close to death he will yet recover from it.

(4) The god who is in the city is the one by whose command are the death and life of his people.

(5) The impious man who goes abroad puts himself in the hand of the fiend.

(6) The godly ⟨man⟩ who is far from his town, his worth is not better known than that of another.

(7) He who dies far from his town is buried[86] only out of pity.

(8) The wise man who is unknown is one who is scorned by the fools.

(9) The town of the fool is hostile to him because of his wandering about.[87]

(10) The impious man who leaves the way of his town, its gods are the ones who hate him.

(11) He who loves wrongful roaming is one who gets lawful punishment.

(12) The crocodiles get their portion of the fools because of (their) roaming.

(13) Such is the way of life of people who roam.

(14) He who goes away saying "I shall come back" is one who returns by the hand of the god.

(15) He who is far while his prayer is far, his gods are far from him.

(16) No blood brother reaches him in (his) anxiety.

(17) He who escapes abroad from an evil is one who gets into it.

(18) Everywhere the stranger is the servant of the inferior man.

(19) He arouses wrath in the crowd though he has done no wrong.

(20) Someone will despise him ⟨though⟩ he does not spite him.

(21) He must listen to insulting cursing and laugh at it as a joke.

(22) He must forget the crime of (being treated as) a woman because he is a stranger.

(23) A rich man who is abroad is one whose purse gets rifled.

(24) When a wise man is far away his heart seeks his town.

(**29**,1) He who worships his god in the morning in his town will live.

(2)   He who pronounces his (the god's) name in misfortune is saved from it.

(3)   The wise man who goes and comes will place the greatness of the god in his heart.

(4)   He who goes and comes while on his (the god's) way returns to him again.

(5)   Wherever the wise man is, the praise of his name is with him.

(6)   The fool ⟨with⟩ his bad character gets into crime through it.

(7)   There is not many a man of the town who knows how to live in it.

(8)   Nor is he a stranger whose life is hard.

(9)   It is the god who shows the way through the teaching of how to live.

(10) It is he who leaves the impious man to go and come without a place to stay.

(11) The fate and the fortune that come, it is the god who sends them. Total: 38.

(12)   THE TWENTY-THIRD INSTRUCTION. Do not burn, lest the god burn you ⟨with⟩ punishment.

(13) The poison of the breathing snake is (in) its mouth; the poison of the inferior man is (in) his heart.

(14) He equals ⟨the snake⟩ which kills; he is merciless like the crocodile.

(15) One cannot remove the poison of the crocodile, the snake, or the evil man.

(16) One cannot find a remedy against the sting of a fool's tongue.

(17) The fool who roams about loves neither peace nor him who brings it.

(18) The impious man does not like to be merciful to him who has done wrong to him.

(19) His eye is insatiable for blood in lawless crime.

(20) He who burns about an evil gets into crime through it.

(21) The burning fire is extinguished[88] by water while the water turns into it.

(22) Natron and salt are destroyed in their work (i.e., their action) because of (their) burning.

(23) Milk is spoiled in a jug . . .

(**30**,1) It is good to be firm because of many[89] foods.

(2)   The evil man whose heart loves evil will find it.

(3)   He who thinks of the good is one who masters it.

(4)   The good action of incense comes from its nature.[90]

(5)   The impatient man[91] gets into trouble through seeking to annoy by it.

(6)   What comes from the earth returns to it again.

(7)   The god gives the lamp and the fat according to the heart.

(8)   He knows his favorite and gives goods to him who gave to him.

(9)   The impious man does not desist from the behavior which he loves.

(10) The godly man does not burn to injure, lest one burn against him.

(11) The evil man who has power does not let harm attain him.

(12) The godly man stays in misfortune until the god is reconciled.

(13) He who knows how to steer his heart is not one who is merciful.

(14) Nor is he who knows the curse of haste one who burns.

(15) All these are in the power of the fate and the god.

(16) The fate and the fortune that come, it is the god who sends them. Total: 28.

(17)   THE TWENTY-FOURTH INSTRUCTION.

(18) The teaching of knowing the greatness of the god, so as to put it in your heart.

(19) Heart and tongue of the wise man, the greatness of their dwelling-place is being that of the god.

(20) When heart and tongue are blameless, steering results from it.[92]

(21) The work of the god is a joke to the heart of the fool.

(22) The life of the fool is a burden to the god himself.

(23) A lifetime is given to the impious man in order to make him encounter retaliation.

(24) Property is given to the evil man in order to deprive him of his breath through it.

(**31**,1) One does not understand the heart of the god until what he has decreed has come.

(2)   When the people raise their hands the god knows it.

(3)   He knows the impious man who thinks of evil.

(4)   He knows the godly man and that he has the greatness of the god in his heart.

(5)   Before the tongue has been questioned the god knows its answers.

(6)   The blow of the lance that comes from afar, the place where it lands is decreed for it.

(7)   The impious man alone suffers a thousandfold.

(8)   The god lets him escape from slaughter after having bound him.

(9)   One says "A wonder of the god" when one is in fear without fault.

(10)   He guards at night against the reptiles of the dark.

(11)   He directs the heart and the tongue by his commands.

(12)   He gives good judgment through the counsel which no one knows.

(13)   He creates abundant value[93] without there being a storehouse behind him.

(14)   It is he who makes the way safe without there being a guard.

(15)   It is he who gives the just law without there being a judgment.

(16)   He lets the great-of-birth[94] be great in his lifetime because of (his) mercy.

(17)   He makes the poor beggar a master because he knows his heart.

(18)   The impious man does not say "There is god" in the fortune which he decrees.

(19)   He who says "It cannot happen" should look to what is hidden.

(20)   How do the sun and moon go and come in the sky?

(21)   Whence go and come water, fire, and wind?

(22)   Through whom do amulet and spell become remedies?

(23)   The hidden work of the god, he makes it known on the earth daily.

(24)   He created light and darkness in which is every creature.

(**32**,1) He created the earth, begetting millions, swallowing (them) up and begetting again.

(2)   He created day, month, and year through the commands of the lord of command.

(3)   He created summer and winter through the rising and setting of Sothis.

(4)   He created food before those who are alive, the wonder of the fields.

(5)   He created the constellation of those that are in the sky, so that those on earth should learn them.

(6)   He created sweet water in it which all the lands desire.

(7)   He created the breath in the egg though there is no access to it.

(8)   He created birth in every womb from the semen which they receive.

(9)   He created sinews and bones out of the same semen.

(10)   He created going and coming in the whole earth through the trembling of the ground.

(11)   He created sleep to end weariness, waking for looking after food.

(12)   He created remedies to end illness, wine to end affliction.

(13) He created the dream to show the way to the dreamer in his blindness.

(14) He created life and death before him for the torment of the impious man.

(15) He created wealth for truthfulness, poverty for falsehood.

(16) He created work for the stupid man, food for the common man.

(17) He created the succession of generations so as to make them live.

(18) He lets the destiny of those on earth be hidden from them so as to be unknown.

(19) He lets the food of the servant be different from that of the master.[95]

(20) He lets a woman of the royal harem have another husband.

(21) He lets the stranger who has come from outside live like the citizen.

(22) There is no fellowman[96] who knows the fortune that is before him.

(23) There is he who follows his counsel, yet he finds a slaying in it.

(24) There is the wrong which the fool commits, yet he has success with it.[97]

(**33**,1) He who is at the head of the crowd is not one who runs.

(2) Nor is he who falls on the way one who kills.

(3) Fate and retaliation turn around and bring about what he (the god) commands.

(4) Fate does not look ahead, retaliation does not come wrongfully.[98]

(5) Great is the counsel of the god in putting one thing after another.

(6) The fate and the fortune that come, it is the god who sends them.

(6)   THE TWENTY-FIFTH INSTRUCTION.

(7) The teaching to guard against retaliation, lest a portion of it reach you.

(8) Violent vengefulness against the god brings a violent death.

(9) Vengefulness which is powerful brings retaliation in turn.

(10) The god does not forget, retaliation does not rest.

(11) The impious man does not fear it, retaliation does not become sated with him.

(12) But gentleness toward the weak is in the way of the godly man.

(13) He who is arrogant in the town is one who is (i.e., will be) weak on his ground.

(14) He who is loud-mouthed in the temple is one who is[99] (i.e., will be) silent in it because of weakness.

(15) He who leaves the weak in torment is one who complains (i.e., will complain) when he is no longer protected.

(16) He who takes food by force is one who begs (i.e., will beg) for it because of hunger.

(17) He who hastens to make an oath is one whose death will hasten.

(18) He who uncovers the affairs of another is one who will be uncovered.

(19) He who violates a man by force, his offspring will soon be buried.

(20) He who does harm for harm, his old age will be harmed.

(21) He who lets his heart be wakeful about retaliation will not find it.

(22) When you are sated with strength, leave a little of it to the street.

(23) When you live as one who has power, let the wrath of your heart be small.

(24) When you walk along the street, leave the way to him who is old.

(**34**,1) When you look at the weak man, fear the fate because of weakness.

(2) When you look at retaliation, fear retaliation because of crime.

(3) Retaliation is exalted because of its name and belittled because of impatience.

(4) Its punishment is heavier than the punishment of Sakhmet when she rages.

(5) . . . . . .

(6) When it (retaliation) comes into a house, fate will seek to escape from it.

(7) When it comes into a family, it leaves the brothers as enemies.

(8) When it comes into a town, it leaves strife among its people.

(9) When it comes into a nome, it lets the evil man have power.

(10) When it comes into the temples, it lets the fools be strong.

(11) When it comes to the impious man, it makes another man fear him.

(12) When it comes to the wise man, it makes (him) foolish, bad, and stupid.

(13) There is no counsel and consideration in a wise man (who is) in a state of retaliation.[100]

(14) No work quickens for the quick without fate.

(15) No man holds a mortgage or a pledge if he is under a curse.

(16) There is no worry or harm at a time when the god is content.

(17) Retaliation does not cease to harm the destroyer.

(18) Fortune, blessing, and power are by his (the god's) command.

(19) He metes out punishment for sin, he gives reward for benefaction.

(20) He creates hunger after satedness, satedness in turn after hunger.

(21) Men cannot avoid the god or retaliation when he decrees (it) for them.

(22) He who burns to (do) every harm, the god will burn him with harm.

(23) He who lets pass a small fault dissolves dislike and is content.

(**35**,1) Violence, poverty, insult, and unkindness are never, never at rest.

(2) I have not burned to do evil . . ., my heart, the god knows [it].

(3) I have not taken vengeance on another; another has not suffered on my account.

(4) The sin which I have committed unwittingly, I beg [forgiveness for it].

(5) I call to the god to have mercy on me and give me ⌈sweetness⌉ ⎯ ⎯ ⎯.

(6) He removes the worry about prosperity, without there being a reserve.

(7) He gives a lifetime without despair and a [good] burial.

(8) He relies on your heart on its way in its time ⎯ ⎯ ⎯.

(9) Apis and Mnevis abide at the window of Pharaoh forever.

(10) They will do good to him who will listen to these (words) and to him who will say ⎯ ⎯ ⎯.

(11) The heart of the wise man, its reward is the eye of the god . . . ⎯ ⎯ ⎯.

(12) The heart of the impious man who does not know . . . ⎯ ⎯ ⎯.

(13) The end of the instruction. May his *ba* flourish forever:

(14) Phebhor son of Djedherpaan. His *ba* will serve Osiris-Sokar,

(15) the great god, the lord of Abydos. May his *ba* and his body be young for all eternity.

NOTES

1. What is now page 2 contains the second half of the sixth instruction; it deals with behavior toward parents.

2. Lit., "Measure his heart in good character."

3. P. Insinger has many examples of the term "wide-of-heart" meaning "patient," and some examples of "great-of-heart" meaning "proud, arrogant," both "wide" and "great" being spelled ʿ*w*. In this instance "patient" appears preferable if its connotations extended to "tardy." The meaning "proud, arrogant" occurs in 3/10 and 4/13.

4. Or, "for the heart of the dying (or, the dead)." On my suggestion that *p3 iïr mwt* might mean "the dying" as well as "the dead" see p. 184, n. 86.

5. Following Volten, *Weisheitsbuch* II,9−10 and 126 in emending *dnt* to *dnf*, in accordance with the variant of P. Carlsberg II,1.2.

6. Collection of debts seems to be meant; on *hbr*, "abuse, mistreat, torment" see p. 181, n. 16.

7. Lit., "place your name at length from her," with "name" in the sense of "self, person." Cf. the different rendering of Volten, *Weisheitsbuch* II, 159.

8. So, if one adopts the emendations proposed by Volten, *Weisheitsbuch* II, 13–14, based on the variant of P. Carlsberg II,1.17.

9. So, with the emendation made by Volten, *Weisheitsbuch* II,15 in accordance with the variant of P. Carlsberg II,2.1.

10. Adopting the emendation of *rḫ* to *mḫy*, here and in the next two lines, proposed by Volten, *Weisheitsbuch* II,40, in accordance with the probable reading of the variant in P. Carlsberg II,2.10. Without the emendation the three sentences are nonsensical.

11. Lit., "to his face."

12. Adopting the emendation of *šm* to *ir wš*, made by Volten, *Weisheitsbuch* II,16 in accordance with the variant of P. Carlsberg II,2.19.

13. Emending *nty* to *r-tb3* as proposed by Volten, *Weisheitsbuch* II,18.

14. Is this *wḏ3*, "well-being," a euphemism for death? Cf. *Glossar*, p. 108.

15. Adopting the emendation to *n3y.s šr.w*, made by Volten, *Weisheitsbuch* II,20 in accordance with the variant of P. Carlsberg II,3.5.

16. Emending *mḥl* to *ḫl-'3* as proposed by Volten, *Weisheitsbuch* II, 23–24.

17. So, if one adopts the emendations made by Volten, *Weisheitsbuch* II,27.

18. Taking *grṭ*, "knife" in the sense of "punishment," cf. *Glossar*, p. 587.

19. Emending *bw* to *ḥr*, as done by Volten, *Weisheitsbuch* II, 26, in ac- accordance with the variant of P. Carlsberg II,3.24.

20. Emending *iwf* to *'f'*, as done by Volten, *Weisheitsbuch* II, 46, in ac- cordance with the variant of P. Carlsberg II,4.1.

21. The preceding lines make it clear that *ḥry*, "being superior," here means self-mastery.

22. This is P. Insinger's way of writing *pr*, as was recognized by Volten, *Weisheitsbuch* II,35 and 83.

23. So, if one does not emend; but see Volten, *Weisheitsbuch* II,176 and 49.

24. Emending *nb* to *nb.t pr*, as proposed by Volten, *Weisheitsbuch* II, 27–28.

25. The pair of introductory paradoxes is missing, and line 17 is out of place. It is one of the many instances in which the paradoxes have been garbled.

26. So, according to G. R. Hughes, *JEA*, 54 (1968), 179.

27. Compare *Ankhsheshonq* 21/20.

28. The word *bw3* (*bw*), one of the key terms in P. Insinger, appears to be used mainly in the sense of "dislike, resentment, blame," and to a lesser extent in the sense of "fault, wrong." The definitions given in *Glossar*, p. 114, "crime, wrong, punishment," require modification.

29. *Ḥrš*, "heavy," here in the sense of "patient, persevering," as also in 19/14 and 21/3.

30. The principal meanings of *btw*, another key term, are "crime," "harm," and "punishment." See also p. 181, n. 17.

31. A word was omitted by the scribe. Volten (*Weisheitsbuch* II,180) restored "father," but other restorations are possible.

32. The refrain sometimes has "sends" and sometimes "determines." Cf. Volten, *Weisheitsbuch* II,108.

33. Emending *wn* to *mn*, as done by Volten, *Weisheitsbuch* II,24–25.

34. So, if one deletes the *f* of *ḫ3t.f.*

35. Emending *š3y* to *šbt*, as done by Volten, *Weisheitsbuch* II,14.

36. *P3 ddy* is not only "the enemy" but also "enmity, hostility," and in 26/4 we have *ir ddy*, "make hostile."

37. The variant in the Berlin papyrus fragment has the better version: "Do not be forgetful when questioned about a report"; see K.-T. Zauzich, *Enchoria*, 5 (1975), 119−120.

38. So, if one accepts the emendations proposed by Volten, *Weisheitsbuch* II,55−56.

39. Emending *nḫt.t* to *nḫt.t*, as done by Volten, *Weisheitsbuch* II,48.

40. Emending *w·* to *rmt*, as done by Volten, *Weisheitsbuch* II,35.

41. I follow Volten, *Weisheitsbuch* II,111−113, in deleting the second negation. M. Gilula's proposal to explain the double negation (*JAOS*, 92 [1972], 460−465) is not convincing because the construction would be unique as well as very awkward, and because it would eliminate the paradoxical meaning which the context requires.

42. Emending *dnt* to *dnf*, as done by Volten, *Weisheitsbuch* II,10, in accordance with the variant of P. Carlsberg II,9.10.

43. *Glossar*, p. 398, suggests that *ḫtb*, "kill," may mean "thrash" and refers to *ZÄS*, 65 (1930), 55. The passage so rendered there is, however, not conclusive. On *3nt*, "draw away, restrain," see *Ankhsheshonq* 21/13 and 24/10.

44. Adopting the emendations of *3my.t* to *tmy* and *r-tb3* to *iw mn*, made by Volten, *Weisheitsbuch* II,25 and 53; cf. P. Carlsberg II,9.22.

45. Again emending *r-tb3* to *iw mn*.

46. Lit., "Do not let pass a crime for him who sets his hand (to it)."

47. Adopting the emendations proposed by Volten, *Weisheitsbuch* II, 43, in accordance with the variant of P. Carlsberg II,10.2.

48. Or emend *3my.t*, "character" to *tmy*, "town," as proposed by Volten, *Weisheitsbuch* II,53−54.

49. I.e., the execution of the thief.

50. Read *pr-ḫt* here and in 17/1.4.10, and see n. 22.

51. Read *tn?*

52. Emending *·f·* to *šft.t*, as done by Volten, *Weisheitsbuch* II,35.

53. This sentence provides the best proof that *t3 wr.t* means "wealth, riches," as also in 18/7, 18/18, and 19/2.

54. On *šrl/šllwl* see *Glossar*, pp. 263 and 520, and Černý, *Copt. Dic.*, p. 240.

55. I believe that Lexa was right in suggesting that the word after "approaches" is *ḥry*, "above, upper," and hence "the peak," and not the numeral 100. The "two-thirds" that are "lost" are the first forty years of life which are described in the next four lines; hence the "peak" of life is at age 60. The *iw* before *wn* is noteworthy.

56. It looks as if *r pḥw* here means "up to," as was suggested by Williams, *Morphology*, p. 74; but in 20/19 the meaning seems to be "after."

57. The ideal life thus comes to one hundred years.

58. The meaning of lines 18/7−11 is that he who acquires wealth by crime will be punished in the hereafter. Hence *ḥm.t*, "hot" either means "aggravating," or should be emended to *ḥm.t*, "small."

59. Reading this word which has not been understood as *ḫn*, "inflammation," cf. *Wb.* 3,367.11 and 384.2.

60. In *Acta Orientalia,* 25 (1960), 38 Volten rendered, "you cannot be blamed on her account." But this requires emending and does not improve the sense.

61. See n. 29.

62. *Rhy,* "evening," is written but *rh/lh,* "worry, anxiety," must be meant.

63. Does *n phw* mean only "at the end"? One expects something else in this context. See also *Ankhsheshonq* 11/22.

64. So, if one accepts Lexa's suggestion that *d3d3,* "head," is a spelling of *ddy,* "course."

65. On *r phw* see n. 56.

66. *Hmy/hmy,* "steering," in the sense of being rightly guided recurs in 21/10, 30/13, and 30/20.

67. On *ddhm/dhm,* "defile," see Černý, *Copt. Dic.,* p. 323.

68. Note the phrase *3my.t nb* which suggests that the basic meaning of *3my.t* was "shape, form," which by extension became "character" and "behavior;" see p. 181, n. 22.

69. For *hn ip* compare 12/16.

70. The derivation and meaning of *pk-h3.t* are problematic, see *Glossar,* p. 141, and Černý, *Copt. Dic.,* pp. 125.2 and 133.1. In *P. Krall* 12/20 *pky n h3.t* is "rashness."

71. Since *in,* "brings," makes little sense Volten, *Weisheitsbuch* II,198, emended to *šn,* "asks."

72. Emending *wn* to *mn,* as proposed by Volten, *Weisheitsbuch* II, 24–25.

73. Apparently a wordplay on *g'/g3,* "chapel," and *g'/gr,* "be silent."

74. Lit., "Harm of killing."

75. Compare Volten's translation of lines 24/1–12 in *Acta Orientalia,* 25 (1960), 39–40.

76. Dwarfs were held in awe.

77. Although *hrš* is not *krš* the meaning "break" is called for. Westendorf, *Kopt. Hw.,* p. 560, adopted "compress," which does not suit.

78. Lexa guessed "ant"; *Glossar,* p. 526, left it untranslated.

79. Compare *Ankhsheshonq* 11/11, 18/13, and 21/25.

80. Lexa and Volten guessed that "make face" means "make grimaces." I think it more probable that it means "show oneself, be conspicuous."

81. Or, "because he undertakes something"? Cf. 27/10.

82. On *syht/sht* see *Ankhsheshonq* 11/5 with n. 39.

83. *'In ht r mst* is "borrow"; *ty ht r mst* is "lend"; see *Ankhsheshonq* 16/9–12 and 16/21.

84. I.e., "except when you have said something you should not have said."

85. This is not the scribe's usual way of writing *hn.*

86. Lit., "picked up," or "brought away."

87. Emending *h.t* to *kty,* as proposed by Volten, *Weisheitsbuch* II,54.

88. On *h'='hm* see *Glossar,* pp. 70 and 351.

89. On *gn=kn* see *Glossar,* p. 581.

90. Lit., "the good work of incense, its portion is in it."

91. *Hm* for *hm-h3.t* as also in 21/18.

92. Compare 21/10.

93. Compare *Ankhsheshonq* 5/6 where the angry god makes "value"

scarce. The two instances show that *šʿr* means something more than "price, valuation," and the rendering "value" is probably not quite exact.

94. *Wr-(n)-ms* is "wellborn," *ʿy/ʿw-(n)-ms* is "old."

95. Lit., "He lets the food of him who brings it be different from that which one brings it to him." The preposition *n3y-tr.t*, which occurred in 4/21 and 29/18, here seems to mean "of" in the sense of "belonging to" or "owing to."

96. Lit., "brother in the crowd" or "brother among the people."

97. The contrasted terms are *sp* and *sp nfr*. In *Miscellanea Gregoriana*, p. 377, Volten gave a rather different rendering of lines 32/22−33/4.

98. In lines 33/3−4 and 10−11, retaliation is a divine force sent by the god, comparable with fate and fortune. But in most of chapter 25 retaliation is the vengeance that people seek and it is condemned as an evil.

99. Emending *r-tb3* to *p3 nty*.

100. Taking the word to be *s.t tb3* in the literal sense, rather than being the writing of *stb*, "damage, misfortune."

Indexes

Indexes

I. DIVINITIES

II. KINGS AND QUEENS

III. PERSONAL NAMES

IV. GEOGRAPHICAL AND ETHNICAL TERMS

V. EGYPTIAN TERMS USED IN THE TRANSLATIONS

VI. EGYPTIAN WORDS DISCUSSED IN THE NOTES